MONOGRAPHS ON GREENLAND
MEDDELELSER OM GRØNLAND
Vol. 141, no. 1

FACSIMILE
EDITION

Erik Holtved

Archaeological Investigations in the Thule District

Analytical Part

MUSEUM TUSCULANUM PRESS
UNIVERSITY OF COPENHAGEN
2010

Erik Holtved
Archaeological Investigations in the Thule District
Analytical Part

© Museum Tusculanum Press, 2010
Cover design: Erling Lynder
ISBN 978 87 635 1636 5 (Facsimile Edition)

Original print edition, Copenhagen, 1944

Monographs on Greenland | Meddelelser om Grønland
Vol. 141, no. 1
ISSN 0025 6676

www.mtp.dk/MoG

Published with financial support from
The Commission for Scientific Research in Greenland.

Museum Tusculanum Press
University of Copenhagen
126 Njalsgade, DK-2300 Copenhagen S
DENMARK
www.mtp.dk

MEDDELELSER OM GRØNLAND
UDGIVNE AF
KOMMISSIONEN FOR VIDENSKABELIGE UNDERSØGELSER I GRØNLAND
BD. 141 · NR. 2

ARCHAEOLOGICAL INVESTIGATIONS IN THE THULE DISTRICT

BY

ERIK HOLTVED

II
ANALYTICAL PART

KØBENHAVN
C. A. REITZELS FORLAG
BIANCO LUNOS BOGTRYKKERI A/S
1944

CONTENTS

	Page
I. Analysis of the excavated material	5—39
Inglefield Land — Thule	6
The mutual relationship of the middens at Thule	16
Mutual ages of house ruins	26
Chronological group-distribution	39
II. Culture developments in the Thule District	40—88
List of chronological occurrence of implement types	42—59
Dorset culture	59
The Thule culture of Inglefield Land	64
The early transitional period	66
The Ruin Island group	70
The Inugsuk period	73
The later transitional period	78
Recent time	82
House types of the various periods	85
III. Thule in relation to the rest of Greenland	89—120
Inugsuk	89
House forms in West and South Greenland	95
East Greenland	105
Northeast Greenland	106
Implement culture	109
IV. Relations with the Dorset and Thule cultures in Canada	121—138
The Dorset culture	121
Mitimatalik	125
Qilalukan	126
Naujan	130
Kuk, Southampton Island	135
V. Relation between the Thule cultures of Inglefield Land and Canada	139
VI. Position of the Ruin Island people in the Eskimo culture	149
VII. Clothing	157
VIII. Contribution of the Thule District towards elucidating the development of the Eskimo culture	161
Summary	177
List of quoted literature	181

I. ANALYSIS OF THE EXCAVATED MATERIAL

In Part 1 the material from the excavations in the Thule District in the years 1935—37 is presented, but with no attempt at classifying it under special points of view beyond the purely typological. It now remains to see what conclusions can be drawn from it, and first and foremost what will contribute towards throwing light upon the chronological conditions in the Thule District.

A glance at the material makes it immediately obvious that it must originate from very different periods; but it is not equally clear in all cases what is earliest and what is latest. Seemingly the thing to do would be to make a direct comparison with the material already treated, both from other parts of Greenland and from America; and of course this will be borne in mind throughout; but it would be fundamentally wrong to make direct conclusions from one to the other, as there is no a priori guarantee that developments were the same at all these places. The Thule District as we know is the broad gateway through which the Eskimos streamed into Greenland, and the road may have been closed now to one side now to the other, with due consequences on developments. It is not thought that Greenland was populated once and for all; the assumption must be that additions to the population came from the west from time to time; and if we are to throw the utmost light on this aspect of the question, it will be necessary first to build up a chronology for the region of the Polar Eskimos as independently as possible, i. e. solely on the basis of what the excavated material in itself has to relate. Only if this fails will it be justifiable to have resort to the surrounding world—and of course one must be prepared for it to fail now and then, as it represents only a part of the culture remains in the Thule District.

As far as Inglefield Land is concerned, conditions made it possible to excavate practically every identified house ruin within a wide area, viz. from Cape Ingersoll to Cape Kent, i. e. a stretch of the coast more than 100 kilometres long. For the entire south district, however, the investigations were confined to a single though large settlement, Ũmánaq

(Thule); on the other hand it is from there that we have the extensive midden finds, which naturally as far as they go are of vital importance to the chronology. It is a question, however, if we can set up a continuous series of periods, stretching from the time of the first settlement up to the present. To do so would require the constant overlapping of the various find-groups, a requirement that may involve considerable difficulty when it is a question of house ruins, and especially when they lie in different localities.

The situation of the houses does not always provide clear indications, for the Eskimos are a wandering people, and in the Thule District it has been their habit up to the present time to live at one place in the district one year, and at another the next; the result is that recent and ancient sites lie intermingled at many places, indeed the houses are often built on top of one another, leaving no clear margin to show how great is the time difference between them. It is possible therefore that even within very limited localities there may be ruins of widely different ages, and there is always the chance that recent and old relics have been mixed together when earlier sites have been cleared.

In the Thule District the height above sea level is another doubtful indicator af age, as both old and new houses lie close to the shore and also well inland. To people to whom ice-hunting and sledge-driving is of greater vital importance than kayak hunting, the nearness or remoteness of the house from the beach is not of much matter.

As far as Thule is concerned Comer's Midden with its layers up to 1.5 metres thick must be the principal time-determining factor, and conditions in the various layers will be the standard by which the finds in the excavated houses must above all be measured. This midden, however, does not contain all the types of implements that were found, and it covers only a part of the periods which it is possible to set up; consequently it will be necessary to choose other routes than that of direct stratigraphy if we are to bring order into the rather variegated collection of types represented in the rest of the material.

Inglefield Land — Thule.

Even a rough examination of the tables in Part I (I. p. 88ff and p. 150 ff.) of the occurrences of the various types found, shows that there is relatively close agreement between Comer's Midden and the rest of the material from Thule itself, whereas on many characteristic points it differs on the whole from what was found in Inglefield Land. This suggests that these two geographically separate regions also signify—roughly speaking—two separate phases of culture. As it would greatly facilitate our further investigation if from the very first it should prove possible to reckon with two separate main periods, this is a matter that will be put to the test first of all, attention mainly being directed towards forms which occur in quantities so large that the element of chance is precluded as far as possible, and which in virtue of their equivalent purpose actually can be seen to have replaced one another. Consideration of these diverging forms will at the same help towards understanding the separate culture picture as a whole within the respective regions.

Barbed harpoon heads[1]) (*Thule 2 type*). All barbed harpoon heads found have an open socket, which shows that the Thule District as a whole did not share in the development of the characteristic forms of harpoons with barbs and closed sockets that characterize West Greenland and have been traced so far back in time as to the ancient midden at Inugsuk[2]).

The total number of barbed heads found is 48, of which 29 are from Inglefield Land and 19 from Thule. As the aggregate number of harpoon heads from the regions in question is 82 and 202 respectively (apart from the small leister or arrow-harpoon heads), the percentage is 35 for Inglefield Land as compared with only 9 for Thule. Judging by the general tendency of development such as we know it outside of the Thule District, this means directly that the culture in Inglefield Land gives the impression of being earlier. However, the difference between the two regions becomes still more obvious if we divide the harpoon heads according to whether they have slots or holes for the lashing around the socket. Such a division is as follows:

	Inglefield Land	Thule
Slotted	24	4
Holed	5	15
Percentage of slotted	83	21

This means that 83 per cent. of Inglefield Land's barbed harpoon heads have slots, compared with 21 per cent. for Thule, which again signifies that it is particularly barbed and slotted harpoon heads that characterize Inglefield Land as against Thule. Of the four slotted specimens from Thule not one is from Comer's Midden, whereas four of the 15 with holes are from the middle part of that midden (layers 5—7). Three of these again are of two types found solely at Thule, viz. with "the blade parallel to the line hole and two unilateral spurs" and the

---

[1]) For simplicity's sake this term is used here in contradistinction to toggle harpoon heads, by which is here meant all unbarbed harpoons. In principle of course the Thule 2 type is also a toggle harpoon head.

[2]) Mathiassen 1930 (a) pp. 168 and 273.

more common form with "oblique spur and the blade at right-angles to the line hole". The latter form is familar to us from the Inugsuk culture and may be regarded as one of the latest forms of the thin Thule 2 harpoon heads[1]).

Thin toggle harpoon heads. Of forms with an *open socket* we found 98, 7 of them in Inglefield Land and 91 at Thule, or $8^1/_2$ and 45 per cent. respectively of the total number of harpoon heads at these places. Furthermore, of the 10 sub-types into which these harpoon heads are grouped only two are represented in Inglefield Land. As far as Thule is concerned Comer's Midden yielded the greater part, 56 specimens distributed as follows:

	I	II	III	IV
Layer	(1—2)	(3—4)	(5—8)	(9—12)
	13	24	17	2
in percentage	65	67	59	25

these percentages being calculated on the total number of harpoon heads in the respective groups. Accordingly it is clear that Thule, particularly Comer's Midden, represents a period when to a great extent the thin barbed harpoon heads had been superseded by open-socketed toggle harpoon heads.

On dividing them as before according to slots or holes we obtain the following figures:

	Inglefield Land	Thule
Slotted	6	5
Holed	1	86
Percentage of slotted	ca. 86	$5^1/_2$

Thus we see a still stronger tendency at Thule than before to replace the slots with holes.

The only holed specimen found in Inglefield Land is a form with "blade parallel with the line hole, sharp cut oblique spur and the bottom of the socket sharp cut" (of the main type Thule 3). This form does not occur at all in Comer's Midden, where on the other hand there are 7 specimens of the related type with the bottom of the socket rounded, distributed as follows:

	I	II	III	IV
	1	2	4	0
percentage	5	$5^1/_2$	14	0

---

[1]) The terms Thule 1, 2 and 3 are those employed by Mathiassen. — Mathiassen 1927 II p. 13.

Of the similar type, only differing in having the spur in continuation of the oblique butt end, Comer's Midden produced 17 with the following distribution:

	I	II	III	IV
	2	8	6	1
Percentage .... ca.	10	22	21	12

Accordingly it is plain that in a period corresponding approximately to Co. A III[1]) there was a strong tendency to replace the sharply cut forms of harpoon head with new ones on which the socket is more rounded and undercut, and on which the spur continues the line of the butt end, the lashing slots at the same time—or rather already earlier—having been replaced by drilled holes. Therefore there is reason to assume that the aforesaid harpoon head from Inglefield Land belongs to a period prior to Co. A III at any rate.

Of the other forms of thin open-socketed toggle harpoon heads, none of which occur in Inglefield Land either, it is worth while to notice the one *without separate blade* (Thule 1 type). Of the 22 specimens found, all with lashing holes, 18 are from Comer's Midden:

	I	II	III	IV (layer 9)
	4	8	5	1
Percentage .... ca.	20	22	17	$12^1/_2$

This then is a relatively late form in the Thule District, and it occurs with increasing frequency up towards recent times.

The latest seems to be the form with the anterior part widened out parallel with the blade slit; there are 17 specimens of it, 14 of them from Comer's Midden:

	I	II	III	IV
	6	6	2	0
Percentage .... ca.	30	17	7	0

Not until very recent times was this superseded by a similar form but with a closed socket, of which only three specimens were found, all in Co. A I, but which to day is the form most commonly used by the Polar Eskimos.

The thin toggle harpoon heads with a *closed socket*, which include the Inugsuk head, seem to have had a course of development differing from those discussed above. The total number found is 89, of which 19 in Inglefield Land and 70 at Thule, or about 23 and $34^1/_2$ per cent. respectively. Of the 34 specimens of the true Inugsuk form (with a deeply-

---

[1]) Comer's Midden is designated Co. A, in contradistinction to the adjacent smaller midden Co. B.

cleft spur or two dorsal spurs), only three come from Inglefield Land, however, as compared with 31 from Thule, i. e. about 3.7 and 15 per cent. respectively of the total number of harpoon heads, which shows that in the development of this type Inglefield Land took only a relatively small share. Comer's Midden produced 14 Inugsuk harpoon heads:

	I	II	III	IV
	0	8	3	3
Percentage .... ca.	0	22	10	$37^1/_2$

These are fairly high percentages, and they are an indication that the Inugsuk culture was already exerting strong influence in Co. A IV, at any rate as regards one of of its most characteristic forms.

Flat toggle harpoon heads. Of these Inglefield Land produced no more than 1 (1.2 per cent.) as against Thule's 18 (9 per cent.). The former has an open socket, whereas Thule has 8 open and 10 closed sockets. The open sockets all have lashing holes. In Comer's Midden the distribution is quite curious:

	I	II	III	IV
open	0	2	0	2
closed	2	1	2	1

It is true that the material is so small that conclusions too far-reaching cannot be drawn from it; but it would seem that neither of the two principles was able really to predominate until recent times.

Dorset harpoon heads. For these the proportions are still more striking, except that here the preponderance is on the side of Inglefield Land. Of 30 specimens only four are from Thule, and none of these four is from Comer's Midden. Thus the percentages are 32 for Inglefield Land against only 2 for Thule. Moreover, 22 of the small harpoon arrow heads were found in Inglefield Land as compared with none at all at Thule.

This preliminary survey of the occurrence of the principal types of harpoon heads in the Thule District shows very clearly that Inglefield Land and Thule, each region regarded as a separate entity, represent two different phases of culture, of which Inglefield Land's must be the earlier; but by how much the two phases are apart in time, and how the transition from the one to the other proceeded, it is impossible to say at present. It must also be left to the following investigation to outline the contours more clearly and perhaps separate find groups from one region which rightly belong to the other. So far it is possible to establish the fact that broadly speaking the harpoon heads evolved from forms with a sharp-cut spur, a mostly open, sharply cut socket and slots for the lashing, to forms on which the spur continues the line of the butt end of the head, a rounded socket with a tendency to closure, and the lashing slots replaced by holes; furthermore, from thin barbed harpoon heads and Dorsed forms to thin toggle heads, as it is only in most recent times that flat forms succeeded in making much impression on the culture picture.

On the whole there is nothing surprising in this course of development when conditions outside are taken into consideration; but it has not earlier been demonstrated systematically for the Thule District. With regard to Alaska, Jenness has already drawn attention to the fact that slotted harpoon heads were earlier than those with holes[1]), an assertion that was confirmed by Collins' excavations on St. Lawrence Island[2]). Thus in this respect there is agreement with the Thule District, and the same holds good of the development of the shape of the socket.

We shall now see to what extent the occurrence of other forms of implements supports these first conclusions, drawn solely on the basis of the harpoon heads—and conversely, whether conditions in general can tell us anything about the relative age of certain forms of implements.

Flint technique. In all we found 15 *harpoon blades* of flint, all in Inglefield Land. Nine of them have a distinctly concave butt edge, whereas five are merely fragments. Flint blades with a concave butt edge are closely associated with the Dorset culture,[3]) which the find combinations in Inglefield Land in fact confirm, they being found mainly in Midden B. II at Inuarfigssuaq together with many other Dorset objects.

Of *flint knife blades* with a tang or opposed lashing notches at the butt we found 18, of which 15 were in Inglefield Land. Some of those included among this total may, however, have been used as arrow heads, as in some instances the identification cannot be said to be quite certain. Thirty-two *scraper blades* have a convex edge; only one of them is from Thule. Of 11 *scrapers with side edge* only two came from Thule;—and finally, we found 79 atypical scrapers and flint flakes, all in Inglefield Land like the only three *adze blades* of flint. In addition there is an overwhelming quantity of flint chips, to which Thule contributed only 8 small pieces. Accordingly there is no doubt that flint implements and flint technique were mainly associated with Inglefield Land.

Sledge shoes. Of a total of 510 pieces 322 can be seen to have been fastened on with pegs, whereas 188 show that they were lashed on to

---
[1]) Jenness 1928 (b) p. 76.
[2]) Collins 1937 p. 309.
[3]) Jenness 1925 p. 431 f.

the runner—with or without the simultaneous use of pegs. Of these sledge shoes 65 were found in Inglefield Land, 445 at Thule, and they are distributed as follows:

	Inglefield Land	Thule
pegged	54	268
lashed	11	177
pegged, percentage	ca. 83	60
lashed, percentage	ca. 17	40

The figures show that at Thule it was much more common to lash sledge shoes on than in Inglefield Land. For the purpose of deriving an idea of the course of this development we again take recourse to Comer's Midden, which reveals the following figures:

	I		II		III				IV			
Layer	1	2	3	4	5	6	7	8	9	10	11	12
Pegged	5	11	25	20	12	19	11	6	6	5	3	0
Lashed	48	43	28	16	11	2	1	2	1	0	0	0
Lashed, percentage	ca. 91	80	53	44	48	$9^1/_2$	8	25	14	0	0	0

In the lower layers the numbers are so small that one would not venture to attach much weight to the proportions; nevertheless there seems to have been a temporary increase for lashed sledge shoes round about layers 8—9—a development which for some reason was interrupted for a time. In the upper half of the midden, however, the figures display rapid development from pegged to lashed, while at the same time there is a displacement in the use of the various materials, as will be shown later. Thus there cannot be much doubt as to the main direction of this development; still, there seems to have been a long time when the lashing of sledge shoes was known without the method having been in general use—and perhaps merely as a kind of emergency measure.

Umiaq and kayak. The number of umiaq parts found is 10, all from Thule, but no definite conclusion can be drawn. In Inglefield Land we found at any rate a toy umiaq. Parts of kayaks were found at both places; but on considering the accessories: harpoon rest, legs for the rack and bone studs for the deck thong, we find that of 20 specimens only one is from Inglefield Land, and that is a harpoon rest with a tenon, unique in this collection (Pl. 18.22). This would suggest that the people of Inglefield Land did not take much part in the later, higher development of the technique of kayak hunting. It is possible, however, that geographical factors played some part in this connection.

Knives. Within the group *knives with end blade* it will be seen that whereas knives of the characteristic type with the fore end slightly widened (Pl. 19.10-16)[1]) and *with a suspension hole* have a distribution of 10 in Inglefield Land and 12 at Thule, corresponding to 18 and 4 per cent. respectively of the total number of knives or knife-fragments within these regions, the corresponding form, but *without a suspension hole*, occurs only at Thule, where the total found was again 12. Of ordinary *whittling knives* of simple type 17 came from Inglefield Land (30 per cent.) and 26 from Thule (9 per cent.); but of similar knives with a unilateral *end knob* there is only 1 from Inglefield Land (ca. 2 per cent.) as against 25 from Thule (ca. 9 per cent.). At the latter place the proportions between the two variants are equal, whereas in Inglefield Land they are 1:17. As regards the old form of knife it is evident that the suspension hole was abandoned in the course of time, perhaps because it was replaced by other forms of flensing knives, and a tendency appears to form knife handles as a whole with end knobs. The latter, however, are often provided with a suspension hole.

For the group *knives with side blade* the position is unusually clear. Disregarding the special Dorset type, we found in all 89 in addition to 22 less certain fragments, all at Thule, where they represent no less than 40 per cent. of the total number of knives found. Fifty-four of them are from Comer's Midden, and the overwhelming majority from the upper half of the midden. It thus seems that the knife with a side blade forms part of a rather late development within the Thule District— actually a striking phenomenon, having regard to the fact that knives with a side blade were known as far back as in the Old Bering Sea culture[2]).

The special *baleen shave* is represented by twelve specimens, all from Thule, whereas *knives made of two halves* were found only in Inglefield Land (5 specimens).

Ulo. Here the difference appears clearly only in respect of the compound ulos, 18 handles and blade-pieces being all from Thule. It is curious that the simple, thick and low ulo handle is represented in Inglefield Land by only two specimens, both of wood, compared with 19 at Thule. Furthermore, the mostly trapeziform ulo handle that thins off abruptly to form the blade part was not found in Inglefield at all, whereas Thule produced 11. As only eight ulo handles in all were found in Inglefield Land, it would not do to draw too many conclusions from this, however.

---

[1]) Where nothing else is indicated, the references are to Part 1 of the present work.

[2]) Collins 1937 p. 333.

Two-handed scraper. As regards this tool, it is significant that the seven specimens from caribou metacarpus are all from Inglefield Land, whereas 22 of bear, bearded seal and walrus bones were all found at Thule. The immediate impression one gains is that in Inglefield Land the people were caribou hunters to a very great extent, whereas the Thule dwellers mostly hunted aquatic animals; or, in other words, in their implement culture the former have reminiscences of a more pronounced inland aspect.

Stone maul with baleen handle. None from Inglefield Land, ten from Thule.

Lamp. The material is not so large as might have been desired. In Inglefield Land we found only nine whole or identifiable fragments, and of these two are small oval sandstone lamps. Of the rest five are of the deep, triangular-oval type with no ledge and rather small, whereas two have knobs.

A comparison with Thule gives the following:

	Inglefield Land	Thule
Deep triang.-oval, big	0 (0 per cent.)	11 (26 per cent.)
— — small	5 (56 —)	2 (5 —)
With knobs	2 (22 —)	14 (33 —)
With ledge	0 (0 —)	12 (28 —)

As far as Thule is concerned the three main types are fairly equally distributed; but having regard to the proportions in Inglefield Land it seems justifiable to assume that the deep, triangular-oval lamp without a ledge is the earliest form; and even though the lamp material must be treated cautiously, one has the impression that in Inglefield Land the lamps were often rather small too.

Lamps having no wick-ledge are familiar from the Canadian Thule culture, Mathiassen having found remains of crude, oval soap-stone lamps, the result, it is supposed, of a lack of good soap-stone[1]). Now, however, it looks as if this particular type is connected with an early tradition, whereas the forms with knobs and a ledge are due to a subsequent development.

Tub staves. A total of 70 of these were found, but only one in Inglefield Land. In Comer's Midden they are to be found right down to the bottom. The knowledge of coopering must necessarily be due to communications southwards via Melville Bay, and in this we have one of the most clear proofs of the spread of the Inugsuk culture to the Thule

---

[1]) Mathiassen 1927 II p. 99.

district. And yet it only just touched Inglefield Land. On this reckoning Comer's Midden cannot date farther back than to the Inugsuk period, which means that the earliest layers at the very outside may be estimated at 13th—14th century, whereas the culture represented by Inglefield Land must be earlier; how much earlier it is impossible to say as yet. Judging from the material known at the time Mathiassen thought it possible that the latest part of Comer's Midden was contemporary with Inugsuk, wherefore the lower part would be somewhat earlier[1]). This supposition, however, was partly based on the assumption that tub staves found previously came from the later part of the midden[2]), whereas it was not taken into account that these staves might also occur deeper. There is no doubt, however, that the explanation is connected with the special circumstances of Comer's Midden, the result of which was that former excavations presumably failed to get down to the earliest layers[3]).

There are still other forms that may be instanced as drawing a distinct line between these two regions. Of the fragments of *bone rims with a row of holes*, probably the frames of skin vessels, one was found in Inglefield Land compared with 34 at Thule, mainly in the upper half of Comer's Midden. Bone rims with grooves, undoubtedly *drum frames*, have similar proportions: none of them came from Inglefield Land, and the 19 fragments found were almost exclusively in the upper layers of Comer's Midden.

Edge mountings of bone were found to a number of 56, but only two of them in Inglefield Land. These mountings undoubtedly are associated with the making of tubs. Four *ladles of musk-ox horn* are all from Inglefield Land, whereas 7 *spoons* of antler are all from Thule. The 37 pieces of *baleen platform mats* are all from Thule too. Mention may also be made of five special forms of baleen snow-beaters which were found exclusively at Thule, i. e. with a unilateral end knob (22), with an unsymmetrical curved butt (23), with a symmetrically widened butt and a hole (16), the narrow stick with a unilateral knob (5), and that with a notched handle (6)—in all 72 specimens. Of long baleen sticks with a hole (and cord) 12 were found at Thule, all in Comer's Midden.

As a preliminary result it may at this stage be said that in the Thule District there were at least two distinctly separated culture periods, of which the earlier, predominant in Inglefield Land, bears most resemblance to the Thule Culture defined by Th. Mathiassen,

---

[1]) Mathiassen 1930 (a) p. 275.
[2]) Mathiassen 1930 (a) p. 296.
[3]) I p. 149.

whereas the later one with its rich employment of baleen, knives with side blades, tub staves and presumably a more advanced kayak technique, etc. displays greater conformity with the Inugsuk Culture.

The Mutual Relationship of the Middens at Thule.

Before we can proceed further with the analyses it is necessary first to place the three large middens in their proper relationship, because by so doing we obtain the largest possible material to aid in determining the age of the various house ruins. First and foremost this calls for a comparison between Co. A and the midden in front of House 21. W and E (Ø), in which of course it will be natural to include the finds in the houses themselves. For the sake of simplicity the entire complex of House 21. W, E, and the midden will be designated "C".

Midden C comprises 30 excavated squares, as shown in fig. 78, where the number of layers is also shown for each square; five of the squares, however, extend into the house site itself. The greatest thickness of the midden is 50—60 cm, and the contents of the layers are so homogeneous that one cannot differentiate between separate periods; it is also impossible to say what came from House W and what from House E. Therefore the whole will be dealt with together, though it must be borne in mind that the site revealed traces of earlier habitation. It is also shown in Part I that House 21. W must be somewhat earlier than House 21. E.

Commencing with a comparison of the harpoon heads, the *barbed heads* suggest at once that C comes closest to Co. A III, as none were found in other parts of Comer's Midden. Of slotted forms there is only one; it is from C and moreover has a hatched field anterior to the line hole (Pl. 3.10). All the other nine from C and Co. A III have lashing holes, and of these the type with the blade at right angles to the line hole preponderates at both places. The only one without a separate blade from Co. A III has vestigial barbs besides the two powerful barbs (L 3: 10966), a feature which otherwise has been found only on slotted barbed harpoon heads (Ruin Island and Inf. House 2)[1]; it looks as if a foreign intrusion had occurred in surroundings where it was the custom to use harpoon heads with lashing holes.—Of more specific similarities there is the type with the blade parallel to the line hole and two unilateral spurs (Pl. 3.19), which was found only at these two places in the Thule District.

Of the *thin toggle harpoon heads* with an open socket and *slots* only one was found (L 3: 11093) in Co. A, and, curiously enough, right up in Layer 3, where it has the effect of a stray bird; its occurrence there,

---
[1] Inf. is an abbreviation for Inuarfigssuaq.

of course, may be due to a clearance from an earlier house; in C we found none. The forms with the open socket and *holes* are decidedly the most numerous at both places, and of these the type with the spur continuing the curved end of the butt and the undercut socket is the more common at both places. Of two forms each of which was found at only one of these places the hexagonal type with a sharply cut socket (Pl. 4.5) is from C, whereas the later form with deep-cut line grooves was found only in Co. A. This harpoon group does not tell us much about the mutual positions of the middens.

Among the thin toggle harpoon heads with a *closed socket*, however, we find another type which unites C with Co. A III, viz. the one with the blade parallel with the line hole and an *oblique spur*—a form that has been somewhat ignored side by side with the Inugsuk harpoon heads and seems to form a transition between the latter and the earlier forms with an oblique spur. The *Inugsuk harpoon head* is relatively frequent both in Co. A and in C; but at the latter locality it is exceeded in number by the closely related type with only one dorsal spur. Eight of these were found in C, and five of these eight came from House 21. W. Co. A produced only two of the type with one spur, which on the whole gives the impression of belonging to an earlier stage than the Inugsuk harpoon with its two spurs. The foregoing suggests at least that C comes closest to the lower part of Co. A. Something of the same kind is indicated by the characteristic type with the blade at right angles to the line hole and a *lateral keel* (Pl. 4.9-11). Of this definitely old type five were found on Inglefield Land and eight at Thule, four of them in House 21. W and E. Not one is from Comer's Midden; but the finding of a fragment earlier[1]) shows that it was not unknown.

Of *flat toggle harpoon heads* C contained four with a closed socket and two dorsal spurs, viz. in House 21. E and the two upper layers of the midden. In Co. A there were 5, two of them in III and one in each of the other groups. Finally, two of Dorset type were found in C, but none in Co. A.

It is evident that the harpoon heads cannot say clearly how C is to be placed in relation to Co. A; but they tell us this much, that C belongs at any rate to the period represented by Co. A, and if anything to its early or earliest part. On the other hand it is not certain that C coincides exactly with a phase in Comer's Midden; it may even be more probable that the two settlements in fact were not inhabited simultaneously; indeed there are signs suggesting that C dates from a time when the harpoon heads with a lateral keel were more common than can be seen in any phase of Comer's Midden.

---

[1]) Mathiassen 1927 II p. 27.

As for Co. B, the harpoon-head material is so slender that one cannot build much upon it. The Inugsuk type is most numerous (three specimens), and the thin toggle type with a closed socket and oblique spur occurs there as in Co. A III; but a specimen of the form with an open socket and the fore end widened parallel with the blade slit points more in the direction of the upper half of Co. A.

Then let us see whether a little more light on the subject cannot be obtained from some of the other implement types. First and foremost it is worth noting that of the 70 *tub staves* found, no fewer than 45 are from C, whereas only 19 were unearthed in the whole of Comer's Midden. Of these 19, however, 7 are from IV, that is to say the lowest layers; III contained no more than four, and it is only when we come to II that we find 7 again. Accordingly, in Co. A tub staves seem to have been relatively common even in the earliest period, so that there can hardly be any doubt that C more correctly belongs somewhere in the vicinity of Co. A IV. The inordinate number of tub staves in C is also an indication that we are now in the high time of the Inugsuk culture— the new culture element has become fashionable. From C and Co. A III we have also the only spoons of antler with a slender, carved handle, and of Norse origin there is a chess-man from House 21. W and the side of a box with chip carving from Co. A III (layers 6—8).

If we take *the knives*, and examine the proportions between those with an end blade and those with side blades, we arrive at the following figures:

	C.	Co. A: I	II	III	IV
end blade	37	4	17	15	7
side blade	43	9	28	16	1
side blade %	ca. 54	69	62	51	$12^1/_2$

The figures for Co. A IV are so small that we cannot venture to read too much from them; but the others again show that C lies nearest to Co. A III.

For the *snow knives* the picture is not absolutely clear; but of the three specimens found with only one shoulder and a continuous back one is from C (House 21. E) and one from Co. A III (layer 5). In C we have eleven specimens of compound snow knives, which in Co. A are represented only by two blade fragments in II. Naturally it may be accidental that none were found in Co. A III; but it is also possible that this is one more element, besides the keeled harpoon head, that separates C from Co. A.

On considering the proportion of fixed to movable *harpoon foreshafts* we find the following figures:

	C	Co. A: I	II	III	IV
fixed	22	6	18	22	5
movable	9	2	3	5	2
movable, %	ca. 30	25	14	19	29

Even if in this case too we must reckon with a large margin for Co. A IV, the course of the percentages suggests that it is this group that comes closest to C. What is more, we receive the impression that kayak hunting was pursued in relatively lively fashion in the period, for the movable foreshaft is chiefly associated with the kayak harpoon, whereas the fixed foreshaft belongs to the ice-hunting harpoon. However, it seems slowly to recede again—how far cannot be seen from these figures; but there is a minimum between Co. A II and I. In Co. A I the percentage has risen again for the movable foreshaft, signifying that kayak hunting once more has acquired greater importance. Now as we know from historical sources that among the Polar Eskimos the kayak was quite forgotten until the latter part of the 19th century, it is natural to assume that there is a certain agreement between this fact and the above figures.

In this connection it may be mentioned that *harpoon-line tension pieces* occur only in C and Co. A II and III, whereas the *harpoon-line stopper*, which belongs to ice-hunting, was not found in any of these middens (though nine specimens were recovered from other places).

Cylindrical *socket pieces* of the relatively short type (Pl. 6.9) occur both in C and in Co. A II, III and IV, whereas the heavy socket piece with the scarf face occurs only in C. Of the specimens found there, two are from House 21. W, where on the other hand there are no cylindrical specimens, a circumstance which conforms very well to the fact that House 21.W belongs to the earliest part of the complex C. Accordingly, C seems to lie at the transition from the earlier, heavy type to the cylindrical, and it is also possible to conclude that the oldfashioned socket piece must still have been known at any rate in the period Co. A IV, and presumably somewhat later too.

Of *ice picks* there are two types, one with a scarf face and one with an almost triangular-pyramidal butt. Both are fairly equally represented both in C and in Co. A III; but the triangular form does not occur in either Co. A II or IV. In proportion to the number of finds the total of ice picks in the lowest part of Comer's Midden is surprisingly low; this, however, may possibly be understood in conjunction with the more highly-developed kayak-hunting technique.

Sealing-stool seats of wood connect C with Co. A III and the upper layer of IV, and the same applies to the special slender, biconical type of leg for these (Pl. 8.5).

The side prong for bird darts with inside barbs occurs in both middens. In C, however, there were also two specimens with both inside and outside barbs, so that it would seem that for this type too we have to do with a transitional period—while at the same time it helps to give

C a certain special character vis-à-vis Comer's Midden, as was mentioned above.

Fragments of *bows and arrows* are numerous both in C and in Co. A, especially in III. More curious, however, is the very small number in Co. A layers 2 and 3—where by the way the sole specimen of an arrow head with a screw (fragment) was found. This indicates that we are now close to the period when the bow suffered the same fate as the kayak.

Implements found solely in C and Co. A III are *the barb for a salmon spear, with holes and projecting neck* (Pl. 13.14), *the cornet-shaped baleen scoop* (Pl. 48.3) and the special form of *gull hook*, on which the barb consists of a thin bone inserted through a hole in the shank (Pl. 14.2). To this it may be added that *fish hooks* were found only in C.

Sledge shoes. It was shown in the foregoing that in the course of time there was a change in the proportions between pegged and lashed sledge shoes, a demonstration that was based upon the rich material in Comer's Midden. In C the proportions were in all 61 pegged and 13 lashed, which gives about 18 per cent. lashed. In order to obtain a more varied picture of the change in Co. A we shall try taking four layers together:

	Layers 4—7	5—8 III	6—9
pegged	62	48	42
lashed	30	16	6
lashed, per cent.	ca. 33	25	$12^{1}/_{2}$

According to this C corresponds most nearly to the lower part of Co. A III, which agrees with the fact that certain objects in the foregoing already pointed in the direction of IV.

However, let us look at the use of the various materials employed for sledge shoes:

	C	Co. A: I	II	III	IV
walrus ivory	0	12	4	1	0
narwhal ivory	2	28	17	7	3
bone	65	63	67	53	10
baleen	4	1	1	3	2
walrus ivory %	0	$11^{1}/_{2}$	4	$1^{1}/_{2}$	0
narwhal ivory -	$2^{1}/_{2}$	27	20	11	20
bone -	$91^{1}/_{2}$	$60^{1}/_{2}$	75	83	67
baleen -	6	1	1	$4^{1}/_{2}$	13

In Co. A there is an increase for walrus ivory and a decrease for baleen. For narwhal ivory the figures point towards a relative minimum between III and IV—and, conversely, that bone has a maximum at the same place. On turning to C we find that the percentages just fill up this gap between III and IV in Co. A, thus confirming in full the conclusions drawn by other means in the foregoing. Besides this, however, we learn that C coincides with a turning point; it must be a period when new impulses are exerting strong influence on the course of developments within the culture.

What has been said here regarding the materials as a matter of fact also strengthens the probability that the disproportionately high percentages for lashed sledge shoes in Co. A. layers 8—9 are not quite accidental (p. 12). The obvious thought of course is the influence of the Inugsuk culture from the south; but other contributory factors are also imaginable, and they will be examined in the following.

Before proceeding, we must again glance at the relation between Co. B and Co. A. After all, the number of finds from the former is so relatively small that the degree of certainty in a statistical investigation cannot be very great. The harpoon heads gave no entirely clear result, but the occurrence of the thin toggle harpoon head with its open socket and widened fore end suggests the upper half of Co. A. Bows of antler seem to point in a similar direction, as a fragment was found only in Co. A I and Co. B. This is only a very slender material, it is true; but it must be viewed in the light of the fact that the antler bow otherwise was not found at all, the other bow fragments being either of wood or baleen, apart from a few braces of antler, which, however, date from a much earlier period. It would thus seem that for a long time the antler bow was not in general use in the Thule District, until it was reintroduced last century. This particular specimen, however, was found in the uppermost layer of Co. B, so that it is not necessarily indicative of the midden as a whole.

Of sledge shoes 21 were pegged and 4 lashed; this gives about 16 per cent. lashed, a fact which points a little farther back in time. We are perhaps told a little more by a leg for a kayak rack, also found in Co. A II, but not deeper, and drum frames of bone with a single groove (fig. 102.8), which were found mainly in Co. A I and II. However, these few things cannot be said to weigh much against the fact that most of the finds made in Co. B correspond most nearly to the contents of Co. A III, so that it will be reasonable to reckon that Co. B belongs to a period very close to Co. A III.

To conclude this examination of the relative ages of the middens it would be well to have another look at the use of the various materials in order to see whether anything more of interest can be derived from it, or at least anything to support what has been assumed in the foregoing. In the two tables below, A and B, I have first shown the actual numbers found in the various layers, and next given a list of the percentages of some of the find-categories, including only those which by virtue of their numerically large volume can really mean anything in this connection, and yet which, taken all together, give an almost exhaustive picture of the extent of the use of these materials. "Bone etc." includes objects of bone, ivory and antler and also the remaining objects that are not included in the totals of stone, wood and baleen. It may thus be regarded almost as a collective group, although the great majority of its contents are just bone objects and the like. The "unidentified objects", which weigh heavily numerically, are all objects that have been worked, for which reason it seems reasonable to include them here, where the question is one of the use of the materials.

Table A. Comers's Midden.

Layer	1	2	3	4	5	6	7	8	9	10	11	12
found in all	240	233	465	482	339	278	222	191	122	110	69	40
soapstone	13	14	26	15	11	8	17	11	7	2	6	4
whetstones & hammerstones	7	6	11	7	6	7	5	4	2	2	1	0
stone scrapers	5	8	12	3	6	4	2	4	1	2	0	0
stone in all	25	28	49	25	23	19	24	19	10	6	7	4
wood shafts	5	3	7	4	3	10	1	3	0	1	0	0
arrow shafts	1	0	5	7	3	6	3	4	0	1	2	2
lamp trimmers	11	14	39	42	30	24	24	13	11	9	10	4
meat trays	0	5	6	20	11	10	4	1	3	2	1	0
tub staves	0	1	3	4	3	1	0	0	2	2	2	1
Unident. wood	64	29	68	109	70	54	48	44	25	26	13	4
wood in all	81	52	128	186	120	105	80	65	41	41	28	11
baleen in all	7	12	31	51	39	30	33	29	24	12	15	11

Percentage of occurrences.

Layer	1	2	3	4	5	6	7	8	9	10	11	12
soapstone	5	6	$5^1/_2$	3	$3^1/_4$	3	$7^1/_2$	6	6	2	$8^1/_2$	10
whetstones & hammer stones	3	$2^1/_2$	$2^1/_2$	$1^1/_2$	$1^3/_4$	$2^1/_2$	$2^1/_2$	2	$1^3/_4$	$1^3/_4$	$1^1/_2$	0
stone scrapers	2	$3^1/_2$	$2^1/_2$	$1/_2$	$1^3/_4$	$1^1/_2$	1	2	$1^1/_4$	$1^3/_4$	0	0
stone in all	10	12	$10^1/_2$	5	$6^3/_4$	7	11	10	9	$5^1/_2$	10	10
wood in all	34	22	$27^1/_2$	$38^1/_2$	35	37	36	34	34	37	$40^1/_2$	$27^1/_2$
baleen in all	3	5	7	$10^1/_2$	$11^1/_2$	11	15	15	20	11	22	$27^1/_2$
bone etc.	53	61	55	46	$46^3/_4$	45	38	41	37	$46^1/_2$	$27^1/_2$	35

Table B. C (House 21. W, E and Midden) and Co. B.

	W	E	Layer							Co. B
			1	2	3	4	5	6	7	
found in all......	357	534	317	473	350	369	213	92	20	262
soapstone........	17	27	15	23	11	17	17	5	0	9
whetstones & .... hammerstones ..	17	25	5	4	2	6	4	1	0	3
stone scrapers	3	13	2	3	3	1	1	1	1	2
stone in all	37	65	22	30	16	24	22	7	1	14
wood shafts	3	7	3	18	8	4	5	1	0	5
arrow shafts	10	8	5	5	4	2	0	3	1	5
lamp trimmers ...	28	41	38	73	48	46	31	14	2	10
meat trays.......	4	3	10	17	8	10	6	0	0	5
tub staves........	1	2	6	17	10	6	3	0	0	0
unident. wood	62	103	92	104	112	108	59	29	5	56
wood in all	108	164	154	234	190	176	104	47	8	81
baleen in all	75	63	15	26	27	21	9	5	1	44

Percentage of occurrences

	W	E	Layer							1—7 and W-E	Co. B
			1	2	3	4	5	6	7	1—7		
soapstone........	5	5	5	5	3	$4^1/_2$	8	$5^1/_2$	0	5	5	$3^1/_2$
whetstone & hammerstones ..	5	5	$1^1/_2$	1	$^1/_2$	$1^1/_2$	2	1	0	1	$2^1/_2$	1
stone scrapers	1	$2^1/_2$	$^1/_2$	$^1/_2$	1	$^1/_4$	$^1/_2$	1	5	$^3/_4$	$1^1/_2$	$^3/_4$
stone in all	10	10	7	6	$4^1/_2$	$6^1/_2$	10	$7^1/_2$	5	7	8	$5^1/_4$
wood in all	30	50	$48^1/_2$	50	54	$47^1/_2$	49	51	40	50	$43^1/_2$	31
baleen in all	21	12	5	$5^1/_2$	8	6	4	5	5	6	9	17
bone etc.	39	48	$39^1/_2$	$38^1/_2$	$33^1/_2$	40	37	$36^1/_2$	50	37	$39^1/_2$	$46^3/_4$

If we take Table B first, it becomes evident that in Midden C there are relatively constant proportions between the various materials through all the layers, expressed roughly by the ratios of 7:50:6:37. This homogeneity is most clearly manifest in the largest numerical group. i. e. wood, where accident has the least margin. The fluctuations in the other materials at any rate are not so great that one would venture to ascribe them to changes in the culture. All in all it confirms the picture provided also by the implement types, that as a whole the midden was fairly homogeneous in its composition and must mainly date from a period of very limited duration. If houses W and E are included in the comparison the picture is changed somewhat; but as it is desired to make direct comparisons with the other middens, it will doubtless be more correct to leave the houses out of consideration for the moment, as their contents undoubtedly are more subject to accidental circumstances.

Matters are somewhat different for Comer's Midden, as in some cases the variations between the layers are of such a character that they cannot be ascribed solely to chance. This is particularly evident as regards baleen, as the quantity of this material decreases steadily throughout the midden, except for a rather sudden but merely temporary fall in Layer 10, which coincides with a corresponding decrease in the quantity of stone objects and is offset by a larger number of bone objects, whereas those of wood seem not to be affected. This decrease of baleen cannot have anything to do with weathering, as this would also be expected to affect wood, and this is not the case—at any rate to nothing like the same extent. Whereas the percentage of baleen falls to less than one-fifth, the percentage of wood drops only to a little more than half, and at the same time it increases for bone, ivory etc. to more than double. This must be a reflection of something really connected with changed conditions.

Furthermore, wood and baleen do not decrease at the same rate; from a minimum in Layers 8—9 wood displays a tendency to increase in Layer 4 to a height approximating the maximum in Layer 11, whereafter there is an abrupt fall in Layers 2 and 3. It is not until we reach Layer 1 that we find a new increase for wood. It looks as if the figures here reflect the period of wood scarcity when the kayak fell into disuse and the woodwork of the houses had to be replaced by stone constructions— a period which would coincide with Layers 2 and 3 and which must have extended into the 19th century. The final increase for wood must undoubtedly be placed in connection with the white whalers and the many expeditions in that century. If we work downwards we find that the percentage of wood falls only little from Layer 7 to Layers 8—9, whereafter it rises again to Layer 11, where we explain the high figure by the strong influence from the south, the effects of the Inugsuk culture.

During the whole of this period from Layer 4 to (10)—11 the course of developments otherwise in the midden seems to have been so continuous that there could scarcely have been any great leap forward, and thus the changes in the relative proportions of the materials used provide further evidence that as a whole Comer's midden represents the development right from early Inugsuk times to close up to modern times. It will be shown later that another period of more recent times—presumably not a short one—is missing; all the same, this does not seem to distort the picture of the course of developments.

If now we try to find where the conditions at C best fit in with the table for Comer's Midden, we shall see that there are two possibilities, viz. in Layers 3—4 and in Layers 10—11. The former, however, is contradicted by the implement types, whereas the latter corresponds more closely to what we have arrived at by other means; this indicates that C's place is within the lower part of Co. A. In the same manner Co. B seems to come closest to Co. A Layers 9—10—i. e. a little farther back than previously estimated.

Of course it is a question how much weight may be attached to calculations of this kind; to some extent it must depend upon whether the result agrees with what has been arrived at along other channels; but by means of mutual correction it should be possible to arrive at the most certain result possible. Another thing is that despite an apparent continuity in the course of the midden layers and the types they contain, one cannot ignore the possibility that long periods may have elapsed when the midden received no contribution to its growth—when so to say it was not inhabited; but there is nothing to show this, because developments in themselves have followed an even line. This latter seems to have been the case through the greater part of Comer's Midden, and it should be permissible from this to conclude at any rate that no impulses—at any rate no revolutionary impulses—reached the Thule District in the time between the Inugsuk influence, presumably in the 13th—14th century, and the new immigration from the west in the 19th century.

There is another question, however: when was the connection with the south severed? We know that it must have happened a considerable time before the colonization of Upernavik District. The first step towards this colonization was taken in 1769, so the assumption is that the connection petered out at the latest in the first part of the 18th century, but possibly before. That it happened fairly early is also supported by the fact that in the Thule District practically nothing has been found that can be attributed to the whalers in the 17th—18th centuries, neither directly nor indirectly. I was successful in finding nothing more than half of a blue bead, picked up on the beach near Comer's Midden, but nothing during the actual excavations.

It has not proved possible to arrive at any unequivocal placing of the middens in relation to one another; but there cannot be any doubt as to the mutual relationship as a whole. Undoubtedly we come very close to reality by setting up the following chronology: Co. A I,

II, III, Co. B, the complex C—Co. A IV, with the reservation that C's relation to Co. A III and IV is not quite certain, but is assumed to be nearer IV.

Mutual Ages of House Ruins.

The next problem is to find out to what periods the excavated houses belong. But as there is no stratification here to help us, and as it always is more or less accidental what one finds inside a house, this problem is one of greater difficulty than the former one, and to some extent the investigation must assume the character of guesswork. Here again it will be best to begin on a broad basis, and the first step will be to ascertain what houses produced artefacts showing dependence on the Inugsuk culture and the ancient Norsemen. It having been found in the foregoing that this is one of the things that particularly separate Thule from Inglefield Land, we may thus expect at the same time to get the differential lines drawn more distinctly.

The objects of most importance in this connection are, according to Mathiassen[1] original Norse objects, tub staves, spoons of antler with a long handle, ornamental bodkins, knives with side blades (with a thin blade part), baleen saws, and possibly the baleen dagger with a narrow handle and a wide blade.

Of these there were:

Norse objects in Ruin Island Houses 4,5 and 6; Inf. Houses 3,13 and 30; Thule Houses 10, 16, 21. W and Co. A Layers 6—8.

Tub staves in Inf. House 11; Thule Houses 1, 6, 12, 17, 21. E, Co. A Layers 2—12.

Ornamental bodkins in C. Russell House 1; Thule Houses 4, 12, 21. E, Co. A Layer 4.

Knife with side blade in Thule Houses 1, 3, 8, 17, 20, 21. E, 22, and Co. A Layers 1—8.

Baleen saw in Thule House 21. E and Co. A Layers 4—10.

Baleen knife in Ruin Island House 6; Thule Houses 11, 16, 21. E and Midden, and Co. A Layer 3.

Of the baleen knives, however, only those from House 11, the midden in front of House 21. E and Co. A are of a type with a broad lancet-shaped blade; the others are shaped more like a sheath-knife (Pl. 49.12 and 15) and resemble the small knives (amulets ?) Pl. 39.10 and 11 that were found in Inf. Houses 3 and 6 as well as at Thule.

About these houses we may say with great certainty that they cannot be earlier than the 13th—14th century at any rate. This however

---

[1] Mathiassen 1930 (a) p. 295 ff.

leaves a very broad margin, and therefore we must see whether by means of other implement types we cannot build up a more detailed grouping, which would also include the remaining houses. Here again I shall make use of the division of Comer's Midden into I (Layers 1—2), II (Layers 3—4), III (Layers 5—8) and IV (Layers 9—12).

Thule.

The group "knives with side blade" suggests that these houses can hardly be much earlier than Co. A III, as these knives only become common in the course of that period. However, House 1 has a number of types that prove that it is earlier than the others, viz. Dorset harpoon heads and Dorset knife, Thule-2 harpoon head with slots, thin toggle harpoon head with slots and oblique spur, and thin toggle harpoon head with holes and sharply-cut socket. House 1 has these last two types in common with Inf. House 5, and the last type also with Thule Houses 8, 24 and 21. E-midden.

In the keeled harpoon head with the blade at right angles to the line hole we have another type that connects House 1 with House 21. W and E and House 24, but at the same time with House 19, Inf. Houses 2, 4 and 30, and Ruin Island Houses 2 and 3. A. Dorset harpoon heads and Dorset knife were also found in House 21. E and midden, so there can scarcely be any doubt but that Thule House 1 also has its rightful place in the vicinity of Co. A IV.

On considering the other houses in Thule we find that slotted harpoon heads occur only in Houses 16 and 19, whereas the toggle harpoon head with a sharply-cut, oblique spur and an open, sharply cut socket occurs in Houses 1, 8, 21. E-midden and House 24, and the closed-socket type with the oblique spur (Pl. 4.13) in Houses 4, 8, 10, 19, 21. E and W, Co. A III and Co. B. This suggests a grouping:

4, 8, 10, 24 and 1, 16, 19, 21. E—W.

In these houses the ordinary Inugsuk harpoon head occurs only in 10 and 21. E; whereas it was found in Houses 3, 5. S, 7, 10, 17, 21 .E, 22, Co. A II, III, IV and Co. B. In Houses 5. S however there was a Thule-2 harpoon head (with holes, the blade parallel to the line hole, and an oblique spur) as in House 4, so that it will be reasonable to move House 5. S to this group, whereas in Houses 3, 7, 17 and 22 there is nothing to show that they are not later. Thus we can now experimentally set up the following groups:

a) Houses 3, 7, 17, 22   b) Houses 4, 5. S, 8, 10, 24
   (Co. A II, III)   (Co. A III, Co. B)
              c) Houses 1, 16, 19, 21. E—W
                  (Co. A IV)

In *House 5. N* only one harpoon head was found, a Thule-2 with holes and no separate blade, the same as in Houses 8, 24 and Co. A III, so that without hesitation it may be placed in group b).

House 6 contained no harpoon heads at all, but a small harpoon-arrow head (Pl. 4.32), a type which was found only in one other place,— House 21. E-midden. There are no knives with a side blade, but an ulo handle of wood which, in addition to Thule House 8 and 21. E-midden was found at two places in Inglefield Land. House 6 also has a tub stave and a piece of a foursided cooking pot. All in all this suggests that the house comes nearest to group c), and the almost obliterated character of the site also indicates that it is one of the earliest houses at Thule.

Of harpoon heads *House 11* has only a toggle head of the Inugsuk type with a single spur; however, it also has a thick foreshaft for a whale harpoon (Pl. 6.21), an arrow head with a scarf face (Pl. 11.27), a bola, oblong ferrule, baleen knife, whittling knife with unilateral end knob, baleen shave, adze with transversal holes and adze with a curved hole in the underside; further, a heavy, deep, triangular-oval lamp without ledge, which apart from this house was found in Houses 1, 5. N, 10, 16, 21. E—W and midden, but not in Co. A; and finally ornamented comb, doll with arms, and toy lance of baleen, otherwise found only in 21. E-midden. On the whole House 11 comes near to group b), but the more special points of similarity to House 21. E make it possible that like House 6 it comes nearest to group c).

House 12 resembles House 11 in its bad state of preservation. The only harpoon head found in it is of the Thule-1 type, i. e. thin with an open socket and holes, but no separate blade. Harpoon blades of baleen bring House 12 close to House 21. E, whereas salmon spear barb with holes has its parallel only at Inf. Midden A (in front of House 16). It also contained a kayak-harpoon rest with a broad foot, the blade part of a compound ulo, a two-handed scraper of bearded-seal tibia, ornamental bodkin, two tub staves, doll with kamiks and feet, toy sling handle of wood, and a foursided toy cooking pot. Although some of these things seem to point backwards in time, most of them are of such a character that House 12 should if anywhere be placed in Group b).

House 18, which turned out to be an annex to House 17, does not differ perceptibly from it as regards the finds.

House 20 has a Thule-2 harpoon head with holes and the blade at right angles to the line hole, which places it nearest to Co. A III; the same applies to two Thule-3 harpoon heads with the spur in continuation of the butt end, whereas a bone "bolt" (like Pl. 9.23) is more indicative of earlier times (House 21. E-midden and Co. A Layer 12), and a trapeziform trace buckle points towards House 1 and Inglefield Land. In addition, however, there are a leg for a kayak rack (Pl. 17.13), three knives with side blade, an ulo with an abruptly narrowed-in blade part, a stone maul with a baleen handle, a lamp with knobs and an ajagaq of seal radius—all things which with great distinctness point towards group b).

House 25 proved to be almost sterile, a fact which in itself justifies the attribution of high age. The same is indicated by the unique carrying or quiver handle with longitudinal grooves Pl. 12.11, whereas a fragmentary snow knife with a knob on the back is more incomprehensible. Without doubt, however, this house belongs to Group c).

House 26 contains very little, but a sling handle of wood points towards Houses 1 and 21. E and W (as well as Inglefield Land). An amber bead was also found there. This, in conjunction with the state of preservation, suggests that the house must be placed in the vicinity of House 6 and 11, i. e. nearest group c).

This subjective valuation of the find material—for it cannot be called more than that—has thus led to the following sequence:

    a) Houses 3, 7, 17, 18, 22 (Co. A II, III)
    b) Houses 4, 5. N, 5. S, 8, 10, 12, 20, 24 (Co. A III)
    c) Houses 6, 11, 26, and 1, 16, 19, 21. E, 21. W, 25 (Co. A IV).

There is one thing, however, which we have not yet taken into consideration in this connection, and that is *the shape of the houses*. How does this agree with our grouping?

Houses 1, 19, 21. E and W, and 25 are all buildings with a separate and carefully built-out *kitchen*; the great mutual resemblance excludes all doubt of their relationship. House 16 had no kitchen, but as it must be regarded as a qagsse, there is nothing contradictory in its being in the same group. On the other hand separate kitchens were also found in Houses 8 and 20, so it is probable that they too belong to the vicinity of group c).

Houses 6, 11, 26 and 12 were in such poor condition that it is difficult to say anything about them. On the other hand there was nothing to show that they had had a separate kitchen. House 12 has a room at the side of the passage, but no ashes or slag could be found in it.

Houses 3, 10 and 24 are alike in respect of the peculiar off-shoots only faintly delimited and evidently with a large opening in towards the room; in this respect they are so peculiar that it would be incredible if they were not close together in time. Houses 5. N and 5. S should presumably be placed with them.

There remain Houses 4, 7, 17—18 and 22. These are roomy, but on the whole not very solidly built houses of a more or less regular clover-leaf shape. In House 7 there are fireplaces at the front wall on both sides of the passage, which runs in almost to the middle of the house. In the others there was no deposit of slag, but conditions at the front wall with the low gravel bench were of the same character as in House 7, and this feature was not an outstanding one in the other groups. Judging from their whole character and state of preservation these houses are, however, close to the series 3, 10, 24, 5. N, 5. S, as indeed their mutual situations would suggest, and it is presumable that the unexcavated houses 9, 13, 15 and 23 belong to the same category. All these houses just referred to are so prominent in both size and number that they presumably belong to a time when there was a relatively numerous population. In this connection one should also remember the relatively great density of the finds in some of the fields of Co. A II (Layers 3—4).

Adjustment on the basis of the house types has now given the following chronological grouping:

		Co. A. I, (II)
A)	Houses 4, 7, 17, 18, 22	
		Co. A II, III
B)	Houses 3, 5. N, 5. S, 10, 24	Co. B
C. 1)	Houses 8, 20, and 6, 11, 12, 26,	
C. 2)	Houses 1, 16, 19, 21. E, 21. W, 25	Co. A IV.

Now there may be some doubt as to whether the last series really represents the earliest houses at Thule. It is hardly probable that they do, but we are unable to produce any that are definitely older and consequently would correspond to the very lowest layers of Comer's Midden or the time before that. South of Co. B, in the direction of the Thule mountain, lie remains of houses that are almost washed away, but we know nothing of how they were; to judge from their position they might correspond to House 1. If there are other sites in the vicinity they have at any rate been thoroughly obliterated. On the other hand there is also the possibility that at least some of the houses shown under C. 1 are earlier than those with a properly built-out kitchen; the ultimate examination of this question must however be left until we have examined conditions on Inglefield Land.

Cape Kent.

House 1 contained only an unfinished flat harpoon head with open socket, a separate blade and two dorsal spurs, similar to those found at Thule in House 19 and Co. A II and IV. A side prong for a salmon spear, with two holes, forms a bridge with House 21. E-midden. Thus these two artefacts point to Co. A IV.

In *House 2* there was a Thule-2 harpoon head without blade and with slots, but also one with a blade, unfinished, but apparently intended to have holes. There was also a toggle harpoon head, thin with a closed socket, a blade and an oblique spur (type pl. 4.13). The latter reaches up into Co. A III, but the former drags the time back towards IV or even further, and a small socket piece with a triangular butt (Pl. 6.6), also found in Cape Kent House 4, connects it with the Dorset midden Inf. B. II. It is true that there are also a bird-dart side prong with only inside barbs and an ajagaq of seal humerus (Thule House 1 and 5. N), but these types may well date farther back than to Co. A IV. Dolls with a hood and coat (old type) seem to have their upper boundary in Thule House 21. E-midden, and toy lamps with knobs as well as oval cooking pots also point in that direction. The only knife is of old type with an end blade and suspension hole. Actually there is nothing to place this house in any of the periods represented at Thule, and conditions on the whole argue that it is older.

The other houses at Cape Kent produced no harpoon heads at all (an Inugsuk specimen was found in the terrain in front of them). In *House 4* there was a quiver handle with holes from side to side (Pl. 12.17), a feature otherwise found only in Thule Houses 19 and 21. E; and in *House 5* was a harpoon rest with tenon (Pl. 18.22). As already stated, Inglefield Land contained no knives with side blade. *House 4* has moreover a flint scraper (atypical) that does not occur at Thule at all, and *Houses 4 and 5* alone have bone mauls (Pl. 28.1-2). At Thule the only house with a pointed radius is House 21. E, whereas musk-ox horn ladles like that found in House 4 do not go beyond Inglefield Land. "Winged buckles" (Pl. 38.15) were found at Thule in Houses 20 and 24, but of a rather different form.

The material on the whole from Cape Kent is not large, but the especially characteristic things capable of being used for comparison show at the very outside an association with the earliest habitation at Thule. On the other hand, as there is nothing to indicate Inugsuk influence, it is probable that all the artefacts from Cape Kent are from an earlier period. The mutual resemblance of the houses, especially with regard to the small offshoots in the front wall or the corners, shows moreover that they must belong to the same period (perhaps with the exception of House 8), and therefore it is justifiable to take Cape Kent as an expression of a phase of the history of the Thule District lying prior to the Inugsuk period. The forms singled out above, however, suggest that the phase is very close to the Inugsuk time.

Cape Russell.

The material from the two houses here is very sparing, but a few things give us a hint. In *House 2* we found a whittling knife with a unilateral end knob, a type otherwise occurring only at Thule, and the same applies to the cutting board with a "head" from *House 1* (Pl. 31.7). This house also produced the handsome ornamental bodkin (Pl. 36.18) and a small anchor-shaped thimble holder (Pl. 36.22), as well as an ajagaq of seal radius, which also belongs to Thule (House 20 and Co. A I—II III). All in all it is presumable that Cape Russell corresponds most nearly to the period Co. A IV. In construction the houses are reminiscent of those at Cape Kent, and the probability is that they are not far removed in time.

Inuarfigssuaq.

Group I. Relatively few harpoon heads were found in this group. Houses 18 and 21 each produced a Thule-2 without blade and with slots—in House 18 together with an Inugsuk harpoon head, which also occurs in House 20, and in House 21 together with the similar type but with a single spur. The latter was also found in House 16. Houses 18, 20 and 21 and Houses 14 and 19 are the most obliterated sites in the group and undoubtedly the earliest.

In House 11 we have two Thule-2 harpoon heads with holes and the blade parallel to the line hole; this indicates at once that this house is later. Thus there seem to be at least two periods in group I. We know already that House 11 must be within the Inugsuk period, for a tub stave was found in it, and the same applies to House 13, where there was a cooking-pot leg of brass (Pl. 44.4). The question now is whether any of the other houses resemble these two so much that they must be placed to the same period, even if the circumstantial evidence is not so strong.

From Houses 12 and 20 we have a harpoon-line stopper with holes (Pl. 5.11) which was not found elsewhere, and from Houses 11 and 20 an oblong bladder-mouthpiece (Pl. 5.17,18), a type also found at Cape Kent and Thule House 1 (as well as Co. A II). Houses 12 and 14 contained the cylindrical harpoon socket-piece, whereas in House 11 there was a heavy socket-piece with a scarf face. Altogether, however, this seems to say merely that we are here at the beginning of the use of the cylindrical socket-piece.

The ice-pick with a scarf face was found in Houses 11, 16 and 17; in House 11, however, there were also two with a triangular butt and in House 21 a piece of a wooden shaft for one of these. If we cast a side glance over to group II, where the triangular butts occur in the houses but not in the Dorset middens, we get an inkling that ice-picks with a triangular butt belong to a relatively late period.

House 14 contained an arrow head with opposite barbs, which points towards Thule House 21. E, and in the midden in front of House 16 we found a salmon-spear barb with holes, a type otherwise found only in Thule House 12; accordingly, both these finds point upwards in time, and the same seems to apply to the bola (Houses 14 and 17), found here only in group I, but relatively common at Thule.

A total of 17 sledge shoes had pegs, and only a single piece from House 17 has lashing holes. Two snow knives from Houses 12 and 17 have a bent back and a sloping shoulder as in Co. A II—III, and in House 12 there was also a handle for a compound snow knife. Two adze heads with a curved canal on the underside, from House 16, also point upwards, as does the hand pick with teeth (Pl. 30.16) from House 17, this form recurring at Cape Russell. Furthermore, dolls with a toupé and feet connect House 16 with Thule Houses 1 and 21. E-midden, and House 17 has a toy lamp with a ledge.

Altogether this gives the impression that group I is not so far removed from the period Co. A IV, and actually there is no gap between Houses 11—13 and the others; it looks almost as if the tub stave and the cooking-pot leg were foreign elements in these two houses. As yet it is not a question of a real intrusion by the Inugsuk culture, but on the other hand these two elements bear witness that it is on its way, and they provide some information as to the approximate age of the houses— at any rate the later houses. This applies to Houses 11 and 13, to which come Houses 12, 16, 17 and presumably 14, whereas Houses 18, 19, 20 and 21 are earlier; what we do not know is how much earlier they are. The last three are small "round" houses; but in reality they do not differ much from the others, remembering only that some of the latter are double. If the Inugsuk period is placed at the 13th—14th century, there will scarcely be much wrong in placing Inf. group I to the 12th—13th century.

Group II. Here things look even more varied than in group I; but here again we have something to work upon, the chess-man that was found in House 3. The Thule-2 harpoon head with slots was found in Houses 1, 2, 3, 4, 6, 7 and 9, and the toggle harpoon head with slots in Houses 2, 5 and 10. In Houses 4 and 7, however, we also found Thule-2 with holes, and in House 5 a toggle harpoon head with holes, but with a sharply cut socket, so that at any rate Houses 4, 5 and 7 must come very close to Thule. The toggle harpoon heads with a closed socket and an oblique, or single dorsal spur do not tell us much that is positive; but it is curious that the Inugsuk harpoon head with the cleft spur was not found in group II at all. Houses 2 and 4, on the other hand, contained the keeled harpoon head with the blade at right angles to the line hole.

Dorset harpoon heads were found in Houses 1, 2, 6 and 7, but conditions there make it possible that they were associated with earlier houses built over by the present ones. Most of the Dorset artefacts were found in the middens, which in the whole are of a different character to the houses above them. But it is impossible to say off hand how great the time difference may be.

Among other elements it may be recalled that the wooden stiletto handle (Pl. 7.10-11) was found in Houses 5 and 16 (group I). The ice-pick with scarf face was found only in the midden B. II and in House 22, three specimens in all, whereas the triangular butt occurs in all the other houses except 8 and 9, in all 9 specimens and two shaft ends; (for House 4 the find refers to the upper layer of the midden). In these circumstances we have perhaps a hint that Houses 8, 9 and 22 are somewhat earlier than the other houses of the group, an idea that is strongly supported by their state of preservation. In House 8 we found something that recalls the Dorset culture, a fragment presumably of a foreshaft with an elongated, cut hole at one edge (L 3: 1221), and in House 22 a knife of Dorset type. However, Dorset objects were also found at Thule, and these two specimens need not indicate any close connection with the Dorset people. The same may be said of two Dorset "spatulas" from Houses 2 and 4. Furthermore, we also found a lump of copper (L 3: 1220) in House 8; similar fragments from Houses 5 and 3, however, when analyzed proved to be native copper[1]), so that these finds say nothing definite about age—if anything that the houses in question are relatively old.

The arrow head with a blade lashed on to one side (Pl. 11.22-24) occurred in Houses 3, 4 and 6 (and in House 26 in group III and in Thule House 16). Similarly, the compound snow knife was found in Houses 4 and 5 and in the midden B. I, where presumably it came from House 6. In Houses 1 and 8 we found pieces of the small, deep, triangular-oval lamp, and also in B. I and B. II; on the other hand the lamp with knobs came from Houses 3 and 5.

The chess-man in House 3 (Pl. 44.9) places this house in line with Houses 11 and 13 in group I. But what was said of most of the other houses in group I may also be said of group II: even if there is necessarily some time difference between them, it is impossible to draw any definite line, and in this respect the three Houses 8, 9 and 22 occupy a position corresponding to that of Houses 19, 20 and 21 in group I; they are evidently older than the others, but how much it is impossible to say. Nevertheless we get the impression that there is a difference between the two groups. Disregarding the three houses mentioned above, group II is richer than group I; though of course this may have something to do with its having been inhabited longer, as in fact is indicated by the midden layers and the more complicated conditions inside the houses.

---

[1]) P. Bergsøe 1941 p. 111; I p. 303 f.

Here too occurs the clover-leaf shaped house, i. e. three houses built together, each with its own main platform, whereas two is the highest in group I.

Group III. Here again we perceive that there was an early and a somewhat later period. The few harpoon heads would almost seem to suggest that House 24 is earlier, whereas Houses 26 and 30 are later. The same thing is indicated by a stiletto handle and a two-pronged leister in House 30, as well as a barbed arrow head with a lashed-on blade in House 26. House 30 contained a tub bottom with circles, of Norse origin, which brings matters quite in line with the other two groups. House 29 was almost totally obliterated, and is doubtless the oldest in the group.

Aunartoq.

Group A. The finds here are not very informative, but the houses and their state of preservation suggest that they must be classed among the early Inuarfigssuaq houses.

Group B. Here the houses seem to be of rather recent date; they have a stone roof and, as regards Houses 9 and 10, are well preserved. House 11 must be somewhat older, but its construction places it together with the other two. Presumably they belong to the period Co. A I or II.

Aunartoq koroq.

The almost obliterated houses here are of a character similar to the worst preserved at Aunartoq A, and there is nothing to show that *they are not from* the same period.

Keeping to the settlements on the mainland for the time being, we have seen that the difference in the state of preservation of the houses argues that the earlier habitation extended over a period of considerable dimensions, and we know for certain that it extended up into the Norse period, but that the Inugsuk culture has not yet asserted itself.

On the other hand I have been unable to ascertain the presence of different culture phases on Inglefield Land (if we disregard the touch of Dorset culture in Inf. group II), and the implements show that the community up there lived under the Thule culture. Then in addition there are the few later houses at Cape Russell and Aunartoq B.

It is most probable that *the Dorset middens* are earlier than the houses at Inuarfigssuaq. The relation to Cape Kent is more problematic, because this isolated settlement cannot be placed directly in relation to Inuarfigssuaq, and the houses at Cape Kent have such a character of their own that they may be presumed to occupy a separate position, although it cannot be seen that the finds in them differ much from the others. However, a quantity of baleen was found in the houses at Inuarfigssuaq and at Cape Kent, in which respect they both differ from the Dorset middens, which so to say are innocent of baleen. This certainly indicates that the houses at both places are later than the middens. For if there had been a baleen culture with an intermediate period of Dorset culture, it is improbable that the use of baleen would disappear without leaving any trace. On the other hand, if the Dorset people used baleen, it would be remarkable if some of it did not find its way to the middens; if it did, it must have disintegrated, which also means that the middens are older than the houses, where the baleen objects to a great extent are particularly well preserved. Thus conditions in every case suggest that the Dorset people were the first Eskimos to come into Inglefield Land—and presumably into Greenland as a whole.

Ruin Island.

This locality has been kept till last, as in many respects it has the effect of being a stranger among the others; and its seven houses conform so well mutually that it is justifiable to treat them together, though it is beyond doubt that they were not inhabited at the same time.

Here the harpoon heads are of two main forms: Thule-2 with slots and the keeled harpoon head with the blade at right angles to the line hole. On the Thule-2 heads, however, there are some curious special features, occurring either solely on Ruin Island or outside it, having only a very limited distribution within the Thule District. For example, the form with *vestigial barbs* (Pl. 3.7-8) was found in House 4 and Inf. House 2, and even then the style is somewhat different. (Vestigial barbs also occur on a Thule-2 harpoon head with holes from Co. A Layer 5; L 3: 10966). Two heads have a *vestigial spur* (Pl. 3.5-6), a feature that recurs in Thule House 19 (L 3: 4681). Vestigial spurs in combination with a toggle harpoon head occur in Thule Houses 16 and 19 (Pl. 3.14 and 13), the latter also having vestigial grooves for side blades. Furthermore, two of the Thule-2 harpoons have a very narrow, forward curving line hole like Pl. 3.8, and two others have a triangular line hole, a feature also present on one from Inf. House 24.

Outside of Ruin Island we find the keeled harpoon head at Inf. Houses 2, 4 and 30 and Thule Houses 1, 19, 21. W, E and 24. If we consider all the harpoon heads, we find that there is a distinct similarity, especially to Thule Houses 16 and 19. The house shapes, with the *separate kitchen*, also connect Ruin Island particularly with the houses of the period Co. A. IV, and it does not seem to be quite fortuitous that both Ruin Island Houses 6 and Thule House 16 must be regarded as qagsse's.

Two harpoon-line stoppers are of the type without holes (Pl. 5.12-13); the form with a lashing both above and below the spike was found only on Ruin Island in House 6 and in Thule Houses 16, whereas the one with the spike at the end occurs also in Inf. House 2 and Thule House 24. Large oval bladder mouthpieces (Pl. 5.16) were also found in Inf. House 8 and Thule Houses 1 and 16, but nowhere else, and the oblong mouthpiece with a flat underside (for the bladder dart) (Pl. 5.14) occurs again in Inf. House 2 and in Thule House 21. E and Co. A Layer 7. Ruin Island House 2 has the broad finger rest with curved-in sides (Pl. 5.23) in common with Inf. House 8 and Thule House 21. W, while the lance foreshaft for a lashed-on blade (Pl. 7.1) from Ruin Island House 5 recurs in Inf. House 7 and Thule House 21-midden, below. The quiver handle with holes from side to side (Pl. 12.15-17) occurs only in Ruin Island House 5, Cape Kent House 4 and Thule Houses 19 and 21. E, and the handsome specimens with carved animal figures (Pl. 12.12-13) come from Ruin Island House 3 B and Inf. House 8. On the other hand the carved drag-line handle (Pl. 9.1) is peculiar to Ruin Island House 1.

In connection with the foregoing it is curious that *lashed-on* sledge shoes of baleen were found only in Ruin Island House 6 and Thule Houses 16 and 21. E, and the trapeziform trace buckle in Ruin Island House 1, Inf. House 2 and Thule Houses 1 and 20. The knives of Ruin Island all have the blade at the end: three of the old type with the suspension hole, two whittling knives of wood, and two pieces of knives made of two halves. There are two knife blades of flint, but also three of iron. Flint technique on the whole is common, and the culture of Ruin Island altogether is old in character. Of *Dorset types* found there were two "spatulas" in House 4, and it is possible that a small oval lamp of sandstone from House 1 and a carved disc of walrus ivory with facial features (Pl. 1.26) have some connection with that culture. And finally there are a number of *Norse objects*: a piece of chain mail, a spear blade, a comb and a draughts-piece, all shown on Pl. 44, and a piece of thick cloth (fig. 110). On the other hand there is nothing on Ruin Island to suggest dependence on the Inugsuk culture. In parallel with this a Norse object occurs in Thule House 16 too, the spoon-shaped box Pl. 44.13.

Ruin Island's association with the period Co. A IV is unmistakable; but the absence of Inugsuk culture elements nevertheless places it quite outside; and, as we have seen, several forms of implements point towards a closer connection with the Inuarfigssuaq houses, though the Norse objects draw a certain time limit downwards. It would be most reasonable to compare with Houses 3, 13 and 30, in which Norse objects were also found, but no Inugsuk culture; the other more specific points of resemblance to houses that presumably are earlier may be explained by a partially common origin from an earlier foundation.

Ruin Island is separated from Inuarfigssuaq, however, on a very important point, viz. that the houses have a separate kitchen, a feature never observed in the excavated region of the mainland. It is just this same point that specially connects Ruin Island with Thule, from which on the other hand it is separated by other factors. For example, it can hardly be imagined that the houses on Ruin Island received their well-built kitchens through influences from Thule, for in that case some of the forms of the Inugsuk culture would undoubtedly have accompanied them. On the contrary, it must have been the Ruin Island people that carried the knowledge of a separate kitchen to Thule; they are new people coming in from America, and at the very time when Norse objects occur. This, however, is not saying that these particular "Ruin Island people" necessarily were the first to bring this new culture feature to Thule; but they represent what was undoubtedly a relatively short immigration phase. At Thule Houses 16 and 19 bear witness of that time. However, the most alien features seem to disappear early—they are ground down under the influence of the culture prevailing on the spot, and the peculiarities of the new people become absorbed into the Inugsuk culture.

What is the fate of the kitchens at Thule? They too disappear again. We find a few large houses with peculiar offshoots, like Houses 3, 10 and 24; but they shrink in too, and then we have the large houses 4, 7 and 22 with a slight bulge in the front wall. Down in West Greenland, however, houses with a kitchen become common, as Mathiassen's excavations in Disko Bay and the Julianehaab District have shown; the wave has moved onwards and Thule has settled down again, continuing to build upon its ancient traditions.

Now it would also seem as if the houses in Thule which we grouped under Co. A IV, but which had no kitchen, must represent the direct line from Inglefield Land, so that in the period of Co. A IV we have two threads that converge, one being the old culture of the place, the other the new one from the west. The latter is a rich whaler culture, evidently with great powers of expansion, and possibly we have it to thank in part for the rich development of the baleen technique of which the subsequent period (Co. A III) still bears witness, but which thereafter dies away.

But if we consider the distribution list of the finds (I pp. 88 ff and 150 ff), we observe at once what little agreement there is strictly speaking between Ruin Island and Co. A IV, whereas the resemblance to 21.W—E especially is great. In the chronology it will therefore be natural to place Ruin Island plus Thule Houses 16 and 19 nearest to House 21. W and E, while Co. A IV receives a place in the transitional period which we set up between Thule and Inugsuk cultures and where Cape Russell and Cape Kent also seem to belong. Similarly it will be practical to insert a transitional period between Inugsuk and recent times. As the result of the foregoing investigation it is now possible to draw up a list in which the various find localities are placed in their chronological order, and which consequently can provide a basis for a more detailed account of the culture developments in the Thule District.

Chronological group-distribution.

Recent time:
    Co. A I

Late transitional period:
    Co. A II,
    Thule Houses 4, 7, 17, 18, 22 .... (Thule a)

Inugsuk period:
    Thule Houses 3, 5. N, 5. S, 10, 24 .... (Thule b)
    Co. A III,
    Co. B
    Thule Houses 8, 20 .... (Thule c)
    Thule Houses 1, 21. E, 21. W, 25 .... (Thule d)
    Thule Houses 16, 19 .... (Thule e)
    Ruin Island

Early transitional period:
    Co. A IV
    Thule Houses 6, 11, 12, 26 .... (Thule f)
    Cape Russell
    Cape Kent
    Inuarfigssuaq Houses 3, 11, 13, 30 .... (Inf. a)

Thule culture:
    Inuarfigssuaq House 4 and midden, upper layer,
       —   Houses 5, 6 7 .... (Inf. b)
       —   Houses 1, 2, 10, 12, 14, 16,
       —   Midden A, Houses 17, 26 .... (Inf. c)
       —   Houses 8, 9, 22, 18, 19, 20, 21, 24, 29... (Inf. d)

Dorset culture:
    Inuarfigssuaq midden B. I, B. II,
       —   midden before House 4, lower part.

II. CULTURE DEVELOPMENTS IN THE THULE DISTRICT

The foregoing analysis, which was based first and foremost on direct stratigraphy, and secondly on direct comparisons with the observable strata—and, where this possibility is lacking, on a more general estimate, enables us now to combine the whole of the find material into one single summary, from which it is possible directly to read the occurrence of the various culture elements or implement types in time and space within the Thule District. I have found it possible to establish a line: Dorset—Thule—Inugsuk—late local Polar Eskimo culture to which at a certain juncture came an intrusion of a more foreign phase of Thule culture.

In establishing the chronology the Norse relics have been of vital importance, and within a fairly large sector of the line it is very probable that the dating is correct to less than a century. This sector covers the period from the 13th century upwards, with some reservation for the 17th—18th centuries which are only poorly represented, if at all. For the time prior to the 13th century we have actually no definite criteria beyond the account in the saga that when the Norsemen came to the country they saw signs of human beings. This means that possibly there were Eskimos in Greenland in the 10th century.

In the following survey the dates are appended, though of course their placing is open to well-founded criticism. In this connection I mean especially the difficulty of dating the various types of Norse objects. Dr. P. Nørlund, with whom I have discussed the subject, informs me that none of those found in the Thule District are capable of being placed definitely to any particular century, and therefore the initial point of the chronology is closely connected with Th. Mathiassen's remarks on the subject of the Inugsuk find in the Upernavik District[1]).

The type distribution employed is the same as in the Descriptive Part. For simplicity's sake the objects are totalled within the various

---

[1]) Mathiassen 1930 (a) p. 294.

groups, their distribution over the various find localities being visible from the specified lists of finds (I, pp. 88 ff and 150 ff). The excavated houses, which are comprised under the terms Thule a—e and Inf. a—d, etc., will be seen on the list p. 39. In some cases the list of finds includes fragments (e. g. of knives, snow knives, adze heads etc.) and a few subordinate features (triangular line hole and the like); such details are not included in the following statistical considerations. In a few instances—for example fragments of cooking pots, certain types of snow beaters, etc.—there may be some uncertainty of classification, as a limit had to be drawn for how detailed the grouping could be. In no case, however, are these matters that are likely to exercise much influence on the conclusions drawn. (See the tables pp. 42—59).

It is clear that the bulk of the material comes within the period of time that is dominated by the Inugsuk culture, Norse relics occurring all the way from the late Inuarfigssuaq houses to the next-youngest of the excavated houses at Thule, including Co. A III and IV, that is to say Layers 5—12. The tub stave and ornamental bodkin continue still farther up in time, in Co. A II and the latest of the excavated houses; in this period, however, the culture begins to acquire its own stamp, characterized especially by the dominating part played by the thin toggle harpoon heads with the open socket (Thule 1 and 3), in addition to the disappearance of a number of types of the previous period, the Inugsuk period, which possesses almost a luxurious wealth of forms. Co. A I (Layers 1—2) alone remains to represent the later and most recent times at Thule.

Inglefield Land represents the old Thule culture, i. e. the culture as it was before the influence of the Norsemen was able to assert itself. Accordingly it is a question of to what extent the Inugsuk culture in the Thule District is indebted to the Upernavik and more southerly districts in Greenland. Some forms must necessarily have been evolved in the south, especially the tub staves; but at any rate theoretically there is no reason why the purely Eskimo side of the culture could not have begun a development, for example with a more advanced kayak technique, in the Thule District itself, especially if climatic conditions in the early Middle Ages occasioned longer periods of open water. The question of a deterioration of the climate towards the close of the Middle Ages has been discussed by P. Nørlund, who advances several arguments in support of the theory[1]), and the geologist Johs. Iversen has since demonstrated that at any rate the climate has become drier[2]). The fact that there was also a change in that direction in the Thule District is proved by conditions at Cape Kent, where remains of peat were found

---

[1]) P. Nørlund 1924 p. 228 ff.
[2]) Johs. Iversen 1934 p. 352.

Table.

		Plate[1]	19	16			15					14	13				12				10
			Co.A I	II	Thule a	b	Co.A III	Co.B	Thule c	d	e	Ruin Isl.	Co.A IV	Thule f	C.Russell	C.Kent	Inf.a	b	c	d	Dorset
Barbed harpoon heads thin	socket	**Harpoon heads.**																			
		A. Slotted:																			
		I. No blade:																			
		a) common type....... 3.1-4									2		2		1	1	3		4		1
		b) vestigial barbs...... 3.7-8											1				1				
		c) — spur....... 3.6										1	1								
		d) vest. spur, more than two barbs.......... 3.5											1								
		II. Blade ≠ linehole...... 3.9															1				
	Fragments					1							2					1	1		3
	open	B. Holed:																			
		I. No blade 3.15-16				2			1								3				
		— — vest. barbs....				1															
		II. Blade ≠ linehole:																			
		a) oblique spur........ 3.17-18		1	1					1					?	2					
		b) two unilateral spurs .. 3.19				1				1											
		III. Blade ∟ linehole....... 3.20				2			1	3											
		Y-ornament								1							3	1			1
		Triangular linehole											2					1			
		Curved, narrow linehole									1										
Toggle harpoon heads thin	open	A. Slotted, blade ≠ linehole:																			
		1) obl. spur 3.11-12		1						1							1	5			
		2) — — and vest. spur 3.14										2									
		3) — — — — — and vest. grooves for sideblades 3.13								1											
		B. Holed:																			
		I. No blade (Thule 1)..... 4.1-3	4	8			5			3			1	1							
		II. Blad ≠ linehole:																			
		a. 1) obl. spur, sharp-cut socket (hexag. type) 4.4-6				1		1	3							1					
		2) obl. spur, rounded socket	1	2		1	4			2											
		b) evenly slanting spur, arched socket 4.7	2	8		1	6		2	10			1								
		c. 1) like b, but extended fore-end 4.14	5	6	1		1	1		1											
		2) — — — — and well-formed line grooves	1				1														
		III. Blade ∟ linehole....... 4.15							1												

[1]) Plate numbers refer to Part I.

II Archaeological Investigations in the Thule District. 43

Table (continued).

		Plate	Cent. 19	16		15				14			13				12				10
			Co. A I	II	Thule a	b	Co. A III	Co. B	Thule c	d	e	Ruin Isl.	Co. A IV	Thule f	C. Russell	C. Kent	Inf. a	b	c	d	Dorset
Toggle harpoon heads	thin closed	A. Rounded type:																			
		I. No blade 4.8	1	..	..	..	..	..	..	..	..	..	..	..	..	..	..	..	..	..	..
		II. Blade ≠ linehole:																			
		a) oblique spur 4.16	..	..	1	2	2	1	1	2	1	..	..	..	..	..	1	1	2	1	..
		oblique spur and vest. side grooves 4.12	..	..	..	..	..	..	..	..	..	..	..	..	..	..	..	1	..	..	..
		b) single dorsal spur 4.17-18	1	..	2	..	1	..	1	..	9	..	..	..	1	..	..	2	1	1	..
		c) two dorsal spurs (Inugsuk) 4.19-21	..	8	4	3	3	3	..	7	..	..	..	3	..	..	..	..	..	2	..
		d) single spur, modern type 4.22	3	..	..	..	..	..	..	..	..	..	..	..	..	..	..	..	..	..	..
		B. Lateral keels:																			
		I. Blade ≠ linehole 4.11	..	..	..	1	..	..	..	..	..	..	..	..	..	..	..	1	..	..	..
		II. Blade ⊥ linehole 4.9-10	..	..	..	2	..	..	..	..	5	1	2	..	..	..	1	1	1	..	..
		C. Whaling harpoon head	..	..	..	..	..	..	..	..	..	1	..	..	..	..	..	..	..	..	..
	flat open	A. Horizontal linehole, blade... 4.28	..	..	..	..	..	..	..	1	..	..	..	..	..	..	..	..	..	..	..
		B. Two converging lineholes, dorsal opening:																			
		I. No blade 4.27	..	..	1	..	..	..	..	..	..	..	..	..	..	..	..	..	..	..	..
		II. Blade ≠ spur plane, 2 (cleft) dorsal spurs 4.29	..	2	..	..	..	..	..	..	1	..	1	..	1	..	..	..	..	..	..
		Blade ≠ spur plane, 3 dorsal spurs 4.31	..	..	..	..	..	..	..	..	..	..	..	1	..	..	..	..	..	..	..
		C. Two vertical lineholes 4.30	..	..	..	..	..	..	..	..	1	..	..	..	..	..	..	..	..	..	..
	closed	Curved linehole, blade:																			
		a) single dorsal spur	1	..	..	..	..	..	..	..	..	..	..	..	..	..	..	..	..	..	..
		b) two dorsal spurs 4.23-24	..	1	..	..	2	..	..	4	..	..	1	..	..	..	..	..	..	..	..
		c) two bilateral spurs 4.25	1	..	..	..	..	..	..	..	..	..	..	..	..	..	..	..	..	..	..
	Dorset	Open socket, no blade, one linehole 1.1-2	..	..	..	..	..	..	..	..	..	..	..	..	..	..	..	2	..	..	1
		Closed socket:																			
		I. No blade, two lineholes, cleft butt 1.3	..	..	..	..	..	..	..	..	..	..	..	..	..	..	1	1	..	..	4
		II. Blade:																			
		a) one linehole, plain butt... 1.4	..	..	..	..	..	..	..	..	..	..	..	..	..	..	..	..	..	..	3
		b) two lineholes, cleft butt... 1.5-6	..	..	..	..	..	..	..	..	1	..	..	..	..	..	..	2	..	..	6
		c) heavy type 1.7	..	..	..	..	..	..	..	..	3	..	..	..	..	..	1	3	..	..	2
		Leister harpoon 1.8-9	..	..	..	..	..	..	..	..	..	..	..	..	..	..	1	2	..	..	19
		— — (?) two bilateral barbs 4.32	..	..	..	..	..	..	..	..	1	..	..	1	..	..	..	..	..	..	..

44 ERIK HOLTVED. II

Table (continued).

Plate	Cent....	19	16	15					14	13				12				10
		Co. A I	II — Thule a	— b	Co. A III	Co. B	Thule c	— d	— e	Ruin Isl.	Co. A IV	Thule f	C. Russell	C. Kent	Inf. a	— b	— c	— d	Dorset

	Plate	Co. A I	II Thule a	— b	Co. A III	Co. B	Thule c	— d	— e	Ruin Isl.	Co. A IV	Thule f	C. Russell	C. Kent	Inf. a	— b	— c	— d	Dorset
Other parts of the harpoon.																			
Harpoon blade, flint	2.1-4	..	..	..	..	..	..	..	..	2	..	..	..	..	..	1	1	..	11
— slate	5.1	..	..	..	..	..	..	1	..	..	..	..	..	..	..	..	..	..	..
— iron	5.4	..	..	..	1	..	1	1	1	..	1	..	1	..	..	..	1	..	..
— bone	5.2-3	..	1	..	1	..	..	..	1	..	..	1	..	..	..	..	..	..	..
— baleen	5.5	..	..	..	..	..	..	..	1	..	..	..	1	..	..	..	..	..	..
Tension piece for harpoon line	5.6-7	..	3	..	..	..	2	..	..	1	..	..	..	..	..	..	..	..	..
Swivel, barrel-shaped		..	..	..	..	..	..	..	..	..	..	1	..	..	..	1	..	..	..
— — open rear-end	5.8	..	..	..	..	..	..	..	2	..	..	..	..	..	..	..	..	..	..
— spindle	5.9	..	..	1	..	..	..	..	..	..	..	..	1	..	..	..	..	..	..
Stopper, spike at one end	5.13	..	..	..	1	..	..	..	..	1	1	..	..	..	..	1	..	..	..
— spike in the middle	5.12	..	..	..	..	..	..	..	..	2	1	..	..	..	..	..	..	..	..
— with lashing holes	5.11	..	..	..	..	..	..	..	..	..	..	..	..	..	..	1	1	..	..
Mouthpiece for bladder, flat	5.16	..	..	..	..	..	..	..	1	1	4	..	..	..	..	..	1	..	..
— — oblong	5.17-18	..	1	..	..	..	..	..	1	..	..	..	2	1	..	..	1	..	..
Plug for mouthpiece	5.20	..	..	2	2	2	..	..	3	..	..	..	..	..	1	2	..	..	1
Heavy toggle for bladder	5.33	..	..	..	1	..	..	1	1	..	..	..	..	1	..	1	..	..	..
Fastening peg for bladder (?) wood	5.34	..	1	..	..	1	..	..	..	..	..	..	..	1	..	..	..	..	..
— — (?) baleen	48.14	..	1	..	..	..	..	..	..	..	..	..	..	..	..	..	1	..	..
Mending disc, wood, no groove		..	..	..	..	1	..	..	..	..	..	..	..	..	..	..	..	..	..
— ivory, small	5.21-22	..	..	..	..	..	..	..	..	..	..	..	..	..	..	1	2	..	..
— wood	5.31-32	..	1	..	..	..	..	..	7	1	..	..	..	..	..	..	..	..	..
— baleen	49.2-3	..	1	..	1	1	..	..	..	..	..	1	..	..	..	..	..	..	..
Foreshaft for ice-hunting harpoon	6.11-14, 16-17	6	18	4	2	22	..	5	22	2	1	5	6	1	1	2	..	..	2	..
— whaling harpoon	6.21	..	..	..	..	..	..	..	..	..	..	1	..	..	..	..	..	..	..
— ituartit —	6.15	..	1	..	..	..	..	..	..	..	..	..	..	..	..	..	..	..	..
— C. Dorset —	1.10-11	..	..	..	..	..	..	..	..	..	..	..	..	..	..	1	..	1	4
Movable foresh., conical butt, one hole	6.18-20	..	3	..	2	3	..	..	5	..	..	1	1	..	..	1	1	1	..
Movable foreshaft, two holes	6.10	..	..	..	1	1	..	..	..	..	..	..	..	..	..	1	..	..	..
— three holes		..	..	..	..	..	..	..	1	..	..	..	..	..	..	..	..	..	..
— fragment		1	..	1	1	1	..	..	3	1	..	1	..	..	..	1	..	2	..
— extra butt-piece	fig. 105.9	1	..	..	..	..	..	..	..	..	..	..	..	..	..	..	..	..	..
Socket piece, heavy with scarf	6.1-4	..	..	2	2	..	..	..	5	1	..	..	2	..	..	3	3	1	..	2
— cleft butt, heavy		..	..	..	..	..	..	..	..	..	..	..	..	..	..	1	..	..	..
— — small	6.7	..	..	..	..	..	..	..	1	..	..	..	..	..	..	..	..	..	..
— triang. butt, heavy	6.5	..	..	..	..	..	..	..	1	..	..	..	..	..	..	..	..	..	..
— — small	6.6	..	..	..	..	..	..	..	..	..	..	..	2	..	..	..	..	..	1
— conical butt, small		..	..	..	..	..	..	..	1	..	..	..	..	..	..	..	..	..	..
— cylindrical, oblong	6.8	..	..	..	..	..	..	..	..	..	..	..	..	..	..	2	..	..	..
— — short	6.9	..	1	..	..	..	..	..	3	..	..	1	..	..	..	..	..	..	..
— — late type		..	..	..	..	1	..	..	..	..	..	..	..	..	..	..	..	..	..
Wooden shaft for cyl. socket piece	7.9	..	2	..	1	1	..	..	2	1	..	..	..	..	..	..	..	..	..
Finger rest, slender	5.24-30	..	1	..	..	1	1	..	4	1	1	2	..	..	1	..	..	..	..

Table (continued).

Plate	Cent....	19	16		15					14	13				12				10
		Co. A I	II	Thule a	b	Co. A III	Co. B	Thule c	d	e	Ruin Isl.	Co. A IV	Thule f	C. Russell	C. Kent	Inf. a	b	c	d	Dorset
Finger rest, curved-in sides 5.23		..	..	..	..	..	..	1	..	1	..	..	..	..	..	..	..	1	..
Ice pick, with scarf 7.7-8		4	..	2	1	3	2	1	8	..	..	2	4	1	3	3	..	4	1	2
— triangular butt 7.5-6		..	..	3	6	1	..	1	4	1	..	..	1	..	..	4	6	3	..	..
Wooden shaft for triang. butt		1	..	2	..	1	..	..	3	2	..	..	..	..	..	..	1	1	1	..
Ice pick fragment		1	4	..	..	5	2	..	11	1	..	..	..	..	..	..	..	..	..	..
Lance.																				
Lance head, no separate blade fig. 105.2		..	..	..	..	..	..	..	1	..	..	..	..	..	..	..	..	..	..	..
— scarf, blade slit 7.3-4		..	..	1	..	1	1	..	..	..	..	..	..	..	..	..	..	..	..	..
— movable, face for blade 7.1-2		..	..	..	..	..	..	..	1	..	2	..	..	..	..	..	1	..	?	..
— fore end, face for blade		..	..	..	..	..	..	..	..	..	..	..	..	..	..	..	..	..	..	3
Lance (or knife-) fore end, blade slit. 7.12-13		1	..	..	..	1	..	1	1	..	..	..	1	..	..	..	..	..	..	..
Lance blade, stone 25.1-2		..	1	..	..	2	..	..	1	..	..	..	..	..	..	..	..	..	..	..
Reserve lance head, (closed socket) 7.14-15		..	..	..	..	1	1	..	..	..	..	..	..	..	..	..	..	..	..	..
Stiletto handle, wood 7.10-11		..	..	..	..	..	..	..	..	..	..	..	..	..	..	..	1	1	1	..
Accessories for kayak- and ice-hunting.																				
Harpoon rest, baleen 45.16-17		..	..	..	..	..	..	..	4	..	..	..	..	..	..	..	..	..	..	..
Harpoon sledge runner 8.11		1	..	..	..	..	..	..	1	..	..	..	..	..	..	..	..	..	..	..
Wound pin, bone 9.3-5		..	1	2	1	2	..	2	13	1	1	1	1	1	..	2	1	2	3	1
— baleen 9.6		..	..	..	..	..	..	..	1	1	..	..	..	..	..	..	..	..	..	..
Wound plug, wood 9.7		..	..	..	..	..	..	..	1	..	..	..	..	..	..	..	1	..	..	..
Sealing stool, seat, bone 8.1		..	..	..	..	..	..	..	1	..	..	..	..	..	..	..	..	..	..	..
— — antler (one-legged?) 8.14		..	..	..	..	..	..	..	..	..	..	..	..	..	..	..	1	..	..	..
— — wood 8.2,15		..	..	1	2	..	..	2	..	..	1	..	..	..	..	1	..	..	..
— leg, bone 8.3-4		..	..	..	..	..	1	..	1	..	..	..	1	..	..	..	..	..	..	..
— — wood 8.6		2	6	..	1	6	1	..	4	..	..	..	..	..	..	..	1	..	..	..
— — — slender 8.5		..	..	..	..	4	..	..	6	..	..	1	1	..	3	..	..	1	..	..
Seal scratcher 8.7		..	..	..	..	1	..	..	..	..	..	..	..	..	..	..	..	..	..	..
Toggle, bone 16.11,13		..	..	..	..	..	..	..	2	1	..	1	..	..	1	..	..	..	..	..
— bear tooth 16.14		..	1	..	..	..	..	..	..	..	2	..	..	..	..	..	..	..	..	..
— small with oblong hole 16.8		1	1	..	..	..	..	..	4	..	..	..	1	..	..	..	..	..	..	..
— 2 or 3 holes (for towing line). 16.3-7		1	2	..	1	1	..	..	5	..	..	1	..	..	..	..	..	..	..	..
Drag line handle, wood 8.12-13,16-17		..	2	..	..	..	1	1	4	..	3	..	..	..	..	1	2	..	..	..
— with groove 8.8		..	2	1	..	..	..	..	..	..	..	2	..	..	..	..	..	..	..	..
— curved hole 8.9		..	..	..	..	..	..	..	1	..	..	..	..	..	..	..	..	..	..	..
— W-shaped 9.2		..	..	..	..	..	..	..	..	..	..	..	..	..	..	1	..	..	..	..
— with carved figures 9.1		..	..	..	..	..	..	..	..	..	..	1	..	..	..	..	..	..	..	..
— carved bear head 38.5		..	..	..	..	..	..	..	..	..	..	1	..	..	..	..	..	..	..	..
Other hunting implements.																				
Bladder dart head 9.8-10		..	2	..	..	..	..	..	2	..	..	..	..	..	..	..	..	..	..	..
Mouthpiece for bladder dart bladder 5.14,15,19		..	..	..	..	1	..	..	1	..	1	..	..	..	..	..	1	..	..	..

Table (continued).

Plate	Cent.	19 Co. A I	16 II	15 Thule a	b	Co. A III	Co. B	Thule c	d	e	14 Ruin Isl.	13 Co. A IV	Thule f	C. Russell	C. Kent	12 Inf. a	b	c	d	10 Dorset
Foot for bladder (?)	p. 208																1			
Bird dart head (butt with knobs)	9.11-12		1		1		1		1					1						
— sideprong, barbs on both sides	10.1-5				3			1	3	1							1			
— — inside barbs	10.6-10	2	1		1	1			5			1	1		1		1		1	
— — no barbs	10.11		1																	
— — fragment		1							1	1		2								
Throwing board	fig. 84		1	1		1			2				1			1		1		
Bow, wood	10.17-19		2	1	1	2		1	7	2	2	4			6				3	
— antler	10.20	1					1													
— baleen	47.6-8	2	1	2	6	5	3		9	1		1	4		2	1	2	1	2	
Bow brace, wood	10.22								2								1			
— antler	10.21,23	1							1				1			1	1		1	1
Sinew twister, wood	10.12								1											
Arrow heads, conical tang with knobs:																				
Round, blunt	11.2,4,6		1	1		1			1				1	1						1
— pointed	11.3						1		2											1
Egg-shaped fore end, blade slit	11.16,18-21			2		1	1	1					2	1	1					
Lanceolate, unsymmetr., no blade	11.7-9					1		6	4			1	2		2		3	1		
— symmetr., no blade	11.10-11		1	1	3	7	1	2	7				1		5	4		3	2	1
One barb no blade	11.5,17,25,12.3-5			3	1	1		2	5											
Two unilat. barbs, no blade	12.1-2																1			1
Two bilat. barbs, no blade	11.28		1						1								1			
— slender barbs	11.29									1										
Seating for blade, no barbs	11.22								1		1					2				
— one barb	11.23-24															1	1			
Fragments of butts with knobs		1		2	2	3			5	2	1				2	3	3		1	
— — screw	11.30		1																	
Arrow head with scarf	11.26-27							1				1		1	1					
Arrow shaft	12.6-7,9-10	1	12	11	7	16		6	41	6	11	5	16		14	16	15	20	4	2
Arrow (or lance-) blade, flint with tang	2.6								1								1			
Quiver handle, vertical holes	12.14,18,21		1	1			1		1		2		1				1			
— holes at right angle	12.19					1														
— horizontal holes	12.15-17,20								1	1			1							
— with carved heads	12.12-13									1									1	
— with grooves	fig. 105.7-8		1		1											1				
Handle with longitudinal grooves	12.11								1											
Sling handle, wood	14.17-21	1				1			6		4	1	1		3	2	2	1	1	
— — (?) Dorset	14.16																			1
— baleen	45.19-20					1			3							1			1	
Bola ball	10.15-16			1			1	4		2		1					2			
Salmon spear, centre prong	13.5-6	1	1						1		1				2					
— side prong, with scarf	13.1,4								1								1	1		

II Archaeological Investigations in the Thule District. 47

Table (continued).

Plate	Cent.	19	16	15					14	13				12				10
		Co. A I	Thule a — II	Thule a	b	Co. A III	Co. B	Thule c	d	e	Ruin Isl.	Co. A IV	Thule f	C. Russell	C. Kent	Inf. a	b	c	d	Dorset

	Plate																		
Salmon spear, side prong V-groove	13.3	..	..	..	..	..	..	..	..	..	..	..	..	1	..	..	..	..
— two holes	13.2	..	..	..	..	..	1	..	..	..	..	1	..	..	..	..	..	..
— barb, with scarf	13.7,9-13	3	..	1	2	1	..	..	4	3	1	..	1	..	6	4	2	1	3	..
— round or keel	13.22-23	..	..	..	1	..	..	..	..	..	..	..	2	..	..	1	..	..
— with holes	13.15-17	..	..	..	..	..	..	..	..	..	1	..	..	..	..	1	..	..
— holes and neck	13.14	..	..	..	..	1	..	1	..	..	..	..	..	..	..	..	..	..
Leister prong	13.18-21,28-35	2	1	2	2	3	2	1	11	..	1	..	..	..	1	3	..	..
— baleen	fig. 108.1	..	..	..	..	..	2	..	..	..	..	..	..	..	..	..	..	..
Two-pronged leister	13.24,27	..	..	..	..	..	1	..	..	..	..	..	1	1	..	..
Fisk hook, bone	14.13	..	..	..	..	..	2	..	..	..	..	..	..	..	..	..
— baleen	fig. 108.9	..	1	..	1	..	..	..	..	..	..	..	..	..	..	..
Stone sinker	14.14-15	..	..	..	1	..	..	5	..	..	..	..	..	..	..
Bone sinker		..	..	..	..	..	1	..	..	..	..	..	..	..	..
Fish decoy, fish figure	14.10-11	..	..	..	..	1	..	..	..	..	..	1	4	3	..	1	..
— bear tooth	14.12	..	..	..	..	..	..	..	..	1	..	..	..	..	..
Trout needle	14.3-6	..	2	..	1	..	1	..	2	1	..	1	..	..	..	1	1
— baleen	49.4	..	..	1	..	..	..	..	..	1	..	..	..	..	..
Baleen ice scoop, cone-shaped	48.3	..	..	..	1	..	..	1	..	..	..	..	..	..	..
— racket-shaped	47.2	..	..	..	1	..	..	..	..	..	..	..	..	..
Gull hook, oblique groove	14.1,7	2	3	..	4	6	1	1	31	..	..	1	1	1	2	7	..	2	..	..
— inserted barb	14.2	..	..	..	..	2	..	..	2	..	..	..	..	..	..
— barb		..	1	..	1	..	..	..	5	..	..	2	..	..	..	..	..	1	..
Gorge	14.8-9	..	..	1	1	..	..	..	2	..	..	..	..	..	..
Ferrule, conical or cylindrical	9.15-19	..	1	1	1	2	..	..	..	..	..	2	..	..	1	..	1	..
— egg-shaped (for snow probe)	9.21-22	..	..	..	1	..	..	..	..	..	..	..	..	2	..
— with end groove (for bird dart)	9.20	..	..	..	..	..	..	..	..	..	..	..	..	1	..	..
— tube-shaped	9.18	..	..	..	..	..	..	..	..	1	..	..	1	..	..	..	1	..
— flat heart-shaped (for paddle?)	9.13-14	..	..	..	..	..	2	..	..	..	1	..	..	..	..
Bone "bolt"	9.23	..	..	..	..	1	3	..	..	1	..	..	..	..
Nail of bone, with head	12.24,26	..	..	..	..	..	2	..	..	..	..	..	1	..	1	..
Means of communication.																			
Sledge runner, bone	15.1,4	1	..	1	..	..	2	..	..	..	..	..	..	..	1	3	..	..
— — compound	15.8,11	10	1	..	1	1	..	..	2	..	..	..	..	..	..	..	..	..
— — wood	15.5	..	..	..	..	1	..	..	1	..	1	1	..	1	..	2	1	..
— — walrus ivory		..	..	..	..	..	..	..	2	..	..	..	..	..	..
— shoe, walrus ivory		12	4	..	..	..	..	2	..	..	..	..	..	..	?	..	..
— — narwhale ivory	15.7	28	17	..	..	7	2	1	2	..	3	1	..	..	2	1	..
— — bone	15.6	63	67	17	4	53	23	3	70	7	..	10	5	..	1	4	6	9	5	2
— — antler	15.9	3	..	..	..	..	..	..	3	..	..	..	..	1	..	..	..
— — baleen	fig. 86	1	1	2	2	3	..	9	4	11	14	2	..	..	6	6	4	3	..
— cross slat, bone	15.2,10	2	4	..	2	4	..	..	6	..	1	..	2	..	..	3	1	4	3	..

Table (continued).

	Plate	Cent.... 19	16			15					14		13			12				10
		Co. A I	II	Thule a	b	Co. A III	Co. B	Thule c	d	e	Ruin Isl.	Co. A IV	Thule f	C. Russell	C. Kent	Inf. a	b	c	d	Dorset
Sledge, cross slat, wood		..	..	..	..	1	..	..	1	1	..	1	..	..	..	..	..	..	..	..
— angle brace	15.3	..	..	..	..	..	..	..	..	..	1	..	..	1	..	..	..	..	..	..
— upstander, bone	15.12	..	..	..	..	..	..	..	..	2	..	..	..	..	..	..	..	..	..	..
— — antler	fig. 103.10	..	..	..	..	..	..	..	..	..	..	..	..	..	..	..	1	..	..	..
Toggle for draught line, wood	16.15-16	..	1	..	1	..	1	..	1	..	..	1	..	..	..	..	1	..	..	..
Trace buckle, ovoid	16.26-30	3	3	6	2	8	4	2	10	1	1	4	..	..	1	..	1	1	1	1
— — baleen	46.13	..	..	1	..	1	..	..	..	..	..	1	..	..	..	..	..	..	..	..
— trapeziform	16.22-23	..	..	..	..	..	..	1	1	..	1	..	..	..	..	..	1	..	..	..
— holes at right angles	16.25	..	..	1	1	..	..	..	1	..	..	..	..	1	1	..	..	..	..	1
— oblique hole	16.24	..	..	..	..	..	..	..	..	..	..	1	..	..	..	..	..	..	1	..
Swivel, baleen, heavy	46.20	..	..	..	..	..	..	..	..	1	..	..	..	..	..	..	..	..	..	..
Dog harness		..	..	..	..	..	..	..	..	1	..	..	..	..	..	..	..	..	..	..
Dog boots	fig. 88	..	..	2	..	..	..	..	..	..	..	..	..	..	..	..	..	..	..	..
Whip shank, bone	16.20-21	..	..	..	..	..	..	..	2	1	..	..	..	..	..	..	..	..	..	..
— wood	16.17-19	..	2	1	..	1	..	..	4	..	..	1	..	..	..	..	..	..	..	..
— baleen	46.15,17-18	1	..	1	..	1	..	1	1	..	..	1	..	..	..	..	..	..	..	..
Umiaq rib, bone	17.1	..	..	1	..	..	..	..	..	..	..	..	..	..	..	..	..	..	..	..
— wood	17.2	..	..	..	..	..	..	..	1	7	..	..	..	..	..	..	..	..	..	..
Umiaq oar blade (?) scapula	17.7	..	..	..	..	..	..	..	..	?	..	..	..	..	..	..	..	..	..	..
Kayak stem	17.4-5	..	..	..	..	1	..	..	..	3	..	..	..	..	..	..	..	1	..	..
— gunwale	17.3,6	..	..	..	..	1	..	..	..	2	..	..	..	..	..	..	..	3	..	..
— rib	17.9-11	..	2	2	1	1	1	..	..	5	..	..	..	..	..	..	..	2	1	..
— deck rib, bone	fig. 103.12-13	..	..	..	1	..	..	..	..	1	..	4	..	..	..	..	..	..	..	..
— — wood		..	..	..	1	..	..	..	..	1	..	..	..	..	..	?	..	..	?	..
— paddle	17.14	..	..	..	..	..	..	..	..	..	..	..	1	..	..	..	..	..	..	..
End mounting for kayak paddle	16.31-32	..	1	..	..	..	1	..	..	..	..	..	..	..	..	..	..	..	..	..
Harpoon rest, low, bone	18.17-19,24	..	1	..	..	1	..	..	..	2	..	..	..	..	..	..	..	..	..	..
— — wood	18.14-16	..	..	..	..	1	..	..	..	1	..	..	..	..	..	..	..	..	..	..
— — baleen	48.4	..	..	..	..	1	..	..	..	..	..	..	..	..	..	..	..	..	..	..
— with foot, bone	18.20-21	1	3	..	..	..	..	..	..	2	..	..	1	..	..	..	..	..	..	..
— with tenon, bone	18.22	..	..	..	..	..	..	..	..	..	..	..	..	1	..	..	..	..	..	..
— with foot, wood		..	..	..	..	..	..	..	..	1	..	..	..	..	..	..	..	..	..	..
— for kayak rack (?)	fig. 106.6	..	..	..	..	1	..	..	..	..	..	..	..	..	..	..	..	..	..	..
Stud for kayak thong	18.23	..	..	..	..	1	..	..	..	..	..	..	..	..	..	..	..	..	..	..
Leg for kayak rack	17.12-13	..	1	..	..	..	..	1	1	..	..	..	..	..	..	..	..	..	..	..
Tools.																				
Snow knife, two shoulders	18.4	..	4	..	..	3	1	..	..	..	..	..	..	..	..	..	2	..	..	..
— abruptly bent back	18.3	..	..	..	..	1	1	..	..	..	..	..	1	..	..	..	..	..	..	..
— knop at back	18.6	1	..	..	..	..	1	..	2	..	..	..	..	..	..	..	..	..	..	..
— one shoulder	18.5,7	..	..	..	1	..	1	..	..	1	..	..	..	..	..	..	..	..	..	..
— with hole-handle	18.2	..	..	..	..	..	..	..	..	..	..	..	..	..	..	..	1	..	..	..
— separate handle	18.8,10-13	..	..	..	1	..	..	1	4	..	..	..	..	..	..	..	2	1	..	1

II   Archaeological Investigations in the Thule District.   49

Table (continued).

Plate	Cent....	19	16		15					14	13				12				10
		Co. A I	II	Thule a	b	Co. A III	Co. B	Thule c	d	e	Ruin Isl.	Co. A IV	Thule f	C. Russell	C. Kent	Inf. a	b	c	d	Dorset
Snow knife, separate blade 18.9		..	2	..	3	..	..	1	8	..	1	..	..	..	..	3	..	..	..	1
— fragments		2	5	3	2	8	3	..	9	1	..	2	2	1	..	1	1	1	2	..
Snow shovel, bone................ 17.8		..	..	..	..	..	..	..	1	..	..	..	..	1	..	..	..	..	..	..
Snow probe, bone 17.15-19		..	..	4	2	4	4	..	9	1	..	..	1	..	1	3	2	2	..	..
— baleen		..	..	..	..	..	..	..	1	..	1	..	..	..	..	..	..	..	..	..
Bone knife, sharp 19.4-6		..	3	..	..	2	..	..	2	..	..	1	..	..	..	1	..	..	..	..
— blunt................. 19.1-3		1	2	..	..	..	1	..	..	..	..	..	..	..	..	1	..	..	..	..
Slate knife..................... 21.22		..	1	..	..	..	..	..	..	..	..	..	..	..	..	..	..	..	..	..
Baleen knife 49.10-15		..	1	..	..	..	..	..	5	1	1	..	1	..	..	..	..	..	..	..
Knife with end-blade:																				
Old type, no suspension hole ... 19.10,15		..	1	2	1	1	..	1	3	2	..	1	..	..	..	..	..	..	..	..
— suspension hole 19.11-14,16		..	1	1	2	..	1	..	3	4	3	..	..	..	1	1	2	3	..	..
— ornamental nails 19.7-8		..	..	..	1	..	..	..	1	..	..	..	..	..	..	..	..	..	..	..
— fragments		..	2	1	..	3	..	..	2	1	..	..	..	..	..	..	..	1	..	..
Unilateral end-knob............ 19.18-26		1	2	1	3	2	2	..	8	..	..	3	3	1	..	..	..	..	..	..
Whittling knife, simple......... 20.5-9,17-20		..	..	2	4	4	3	2	7	1	2	1	2	..	3	..	4	5	2	..
Handle of two halves 21.6-7		..	..	..	..	..	..	..	..	..	2	..	..	..	..	1	..	..	..	2
With blade-slit, bone 20.1-4,11		1	1	..	..	1	1	1	2	..	..	..	..	..	1	1	1	..	..	..
— wood 20.13-14		..	..	..	..	..	..	..	..	..	..	1	..	..	..	..	1	..	..	..
— (?) fragments...		?	5	1	1	3	..	..	8	..	..	?	..	..	..	..	..	..	..	..
Face for blade, wood 20.15		..	..	..	..	..	..	..	1	..	..	..	..	..	..	1	..	..	..	1
Lateral face for blade, wood (Dorset?) 20.16		..	..	..	..	..	..	..	..	..	..	..	..	..	..	1	..	..	..	..
Side-groove at fore end, bone... 20.21-23,29		1	..	1	..	1	..	..	2	..	..	..	..	..	..	..	..	..	..	..
— — wood ... 20.24		..	..	..	..	..	..	..	..	..	..	..	..	..	..	..	1	..	1	..
Knife with sideblade:																				
On one side................. 20.25-28,30-31		4	11	2	2	6	..	1	19	..	..	..	..	..	..	..	..	..	..	..
On two sides................. 21.2		2	6	1	..	1	..	2	2	..	..	..	..	..	..	..	..	..	..	..
Row of sideblades 20.32		1	1	..	1	..	..	1	..	..	..	..	..	..	..	..	..	..	..	..
On one side and end-blade 21.4		..	4	1	1	4	..	..	9	..	..	..	..	..	..	..	..	..	..	..
On two sides and end-blade 21.1		..	1	..	..	..	..	..	1	..	..	..	..	..	..	..	..	..	..	..
Row of side-blades and end-blade		..	..	..	..	1	..	..	1	..	..	..	..	..	..	..	..	..	..	..
Butt part with scarf........... 21.8-9		2	..	..	..	..	..	..	3	..	..	..	..	..	..	..	..	..	..	..
Fragments		..	5	..	..	4	..	..	7	..	..	1	..	..	..	..	..	..	..	..
Dorset type, one blade......... 1.12		..	..	..	..	..	..	..	1	..	..	..	..	..	..	1	..	1	3	
— two blades........ 1.13-14		..	..	..	..	..	..	..	1	..	..	..	..	..	..	1	..	..	3	
Broad blade part, narrow handle (ulo?) 21.10-16		..	2	..	1	..	..	..	6	..	..	1	..	..	..	..	..	1	..	..
Baleen shave................... 21.18-21		..	2	..	..	2	1	..	5	..	..	1	1	..	..	..	..	..	..	..
Knife blade, flint............... 2.5-13		..	..	2	..	..	..	..	1	..	2	..	..	..	1	1	2	2	7	
— slate, one edge 21.25-26		..	..	..	..	..	..	..	1	..	..	..	..	..	..	..	1	..	..	..
— — two edges..... 21.23-24,27		..	1	..	..	..	..	..	..	..	..	1	..	..	1	..	..	..	..	1
— iron................		..	2	1	..	..	..	1	6	..	3	..	..	..	..	2	2	1	1	

Table (continued).

	Plate	Cent....	19 Co. A I	16 II	16 Thule a	15 b	15 Co. A III	15 Co. B	15 Thule c	15 d	15 e	14 Ruin Isl.	14 Co. A IV	13 Thule f	13 C. Russell	13 C. Kent	12 Inf. a	12 b	12 c	12 d	10 Dorset
Hand drill, bone	24.3-5,17		1	1	..	1	..	1	..	5	..	..	..	..	..	..	..	2	..	1	1	2
— wood	24.15		..	..	..	..	1	..	..	..	..	..	..	1	..	..	1	..	..	..
Drill bow	24.6-8		..	..	..	1	..	..	..	..	..	1	..	..	..	1	..	..	..	..	..
— shank, bone	24.9-11,18-20		1	6	1	..	1	..	..	9	1	..	1	..	..	..	..	..	..	..	..
— — wood	24.12-14		1	1	1	..	..	1	..	..	..	..	1	..	..	..	..	..	3	1	..
— — ivory, with four points	fig. 106.11		..	..	..	..	..	..	..	..	..	1	..	..	..	..	..	..	..	..	..
— foreshaft	24.22-23		..	..	1	..	2	..	..	..	..	..	1	1	..	..	..	1	..	1	..
— mouthpiece, reindeer astragalus	24.24-25		2	1	5	1	..	..	..	..	..	..	..	..	..	..	..	..	1	2	..
— — bone	24.26		..	..	1	..	..	..	1	..	..	..	1	..	..	..	..	..	..	..	..
Drill bit, flint	24.27-30		..	..	..	..	..	..	..	..	..	1	..	..	..	..	1	..	..	1	4
Baleen saw	49.5-9		..	1	..	..	2	..	..	3	..	..	1	..	..	..	..	..	..	..	..
Whetstone	29.29		11	16	18	8	18	2	6	57	11	4	5	10	..	1	4	4	7	4	1
— asbestos	29.28		..	..	1	..	..	..	..	..	..	..	..	..	..	1	..	..	..	..	..
— with grooves	29.30-31		..	..	..	..	..	..	..	..	..	..	1	..	..	2	..	..	..	..	..
Hammerstone	29.26-27		2	2	7	2	4	1	2	13	..	3	..	3	..	1	6	6	16	6	3
Stone maul with baleen shaft	28.5		..	..	1	1	..	..	1	2	1	..	..	..	..	..	..	..	..	..	..
— head			..	..	..	..	..	..	..	3	1	..	..	..	..	2	..	..	..	..	..
Bone maul	28.1-2		..	..	..	..	..	..	..	..	..	..	..	..	..	2	..	..	..	..	..
Adze head, no blade	28.3		..	..	..	..	..	..	..	1	1	..	..	..	..	..	..	..	..	..	..
— no holes	28.6-9		..	2	..	..	2	..	..	2	..	1	..	..	..	..	..	..	..	..	..
— — Dorset type	1.19-20		..	..	..	..	..	..	..	..	..	..	..	..	..	..	..	..	..	..	3
— vertical holes	28.10-12		..	1	2	..	..	..	..	..	1	..	..	..	..	..	..	..	..	..	..
— horizontal holes	28.13,17		..	..	..	..	..	..	..	2	1	..	..	1	..	..	2	..	..	..	..
— — and curved hole	28.14-16		..	..	..	1	1	..	..	..	..	..	1	..	..	..	..	2	..	..	..
— fragments			..	..	..	..	1	..	3	..	..	..	..	..	..	..	..	..	..	..	..
Adze handle, one hole	28.20		..	..	..	..	..	1	1	..	..	..	..	..	..	1	..	..	..	..	..
— 3 or 4 holes	28.19,21		..	..	1	..	..	1	1	..	..	..	..	..	..	..	..	..	..	..	..
Adze blade, flint	28.18		..	..	..	..	..	..	..	..	..	1	..	..	..	1	..	..	..	..	1
— iron			..	..	..	..	..	..	..	..	..	1	..	..	..	..	..	..	..	..	..
Hand pick, rib	30.8,13-14		..	1	2	1	1	..	..	2	..	..	..	2	..	..	..	1	1	..	..
— antler	30.7		..	..	..	..	..	..	..	..	..	..	..	..	..	2	..	..	..	..	..
— — with teeth	30.16		..	..	..	..	..	..	..	..	..	..	..	..	1	..	..	1	..	..	..
— — transverse handle	30.12		..	..	..	..	..	..	..	..	..	..	..	..	..	..	..	1	..	..	..
Moss spade	30.9		..	..	..	1	..	..	..	..	..	..	..	..	..	..	..	1	..	..	..
Hatchet head, ivory	30.6		..	..	..	..	..	..	..	..	..	..	..	..	..	..	..	..	..	..	1
Mattock head, with hole	30.3		..	..	..	..	..	..	..	..	..	1	..	..	..	..	..	..	1	1	..
— — groove	30.2		..	..	..	..	..	..	..	..	..	..	..	..	..	..	..	1	..	..	..
— seating for handle	30.1,4-5		..	1	..	1	1	..	..	2	2	2	1	1	..	..	1	..	..	..	1
— fragment			..	1	1	..	1	..	1	..	1	2	..	..	..	..	..	..	..	..	1
Pick axe head	30.10		..	..	..	..	..	..	..	..	..	1	..	..	..	..	..	..	..	..	..
Mattock handle	30.11		..	..	..	..	..	..	..	..	..	..	..	..	..	..	..	..	..	1	..
Flint flaker, walrus penis bone	27.11		..	..	..	..	..	..	..	1	1	..	..	..	..	..	1	4	..	..	..

II Archaeological Investigations in the Thule District.

Table (continued).

Plate	Cent.	19	16			15					14	13				12				10
		Co. A I	II	Thule a	b	Co. A III	Co. B	Thule c	d	e	Ruin Isl.	Co. A IV	Thule f	C. Russell	C. Kent	Inf. a	b	c	d	Dorset
Flint flaker, walrus rib	27.12	..	..	..	1	..	..	1	..	..	..	..	..	..	..	..	..	..	..	..
— antler	27.13	..	..	..	..	..	..	..	1	..	1	..	..	..	1	..	3	1	1	..
— ivory	27.10,14	..	..	..	..	..	..	..	1	..	..	..	..	..	..	..	..	1	..	..
— — with curved handle	27.9	..	..	..	..	..	..	..	1	..	..	..	..	..	..	..	..	..	..	..
Wedge	29.19-25	9	21	6	3	9	2	1	47	4	1	6	3	..	..	3	8	5	6	3
Marline spike, flat	29.9,12	..	1	1	..	1	..	..	2	..	..	1	..	2	..	..	..	..	1	..
— — with hole	29.13	..	..	..	..	..	..	..	2	1	..	1	..	..	..	1	..	..	..	..
— — narrow fore end	29.14-16	..	..	1	..	..	..	..	2	..	..	..	..	..	..	1	..	1	1	..
— round, pointed	29.3-8,18	2	6	..	1	3	..	..	8	..	..	1	..	..	..	1	1	..	..	1
Pointed fibula, seal	29.10	..	..	..	1	..	..	..	..	..	..	1	..	..	..	..	..	..	..	1
— bear	29.1	..	..	..	..	..	..	..	2	..	..	..	..	1	..	1	..	..	..	..
Pointed ulna, reindeer	29.2	..	1	..	..	..	..	..	1	..	..	..	..	..	..	..	..	..	..	..
Cutting board, bone	27.18	..	..	..	..	..	..	..	1	..	..	..	..	1	..	..	2	1	..	..
— wood	27.7, 31.3-5	..	2	4	..	..	..	1	6	..	..	..	..	..	..	..	1	..	..	..
— — with "head"	31.6-7	..	..	..	1	..	..	..	1	..	..	..	1	..	..	..	..	..	..	..
— baleen		..	..	..	..	..	..	..	..	..	..	..	1	..	..	..	..	..	..	..
Arrow straightener	27.16	..	..	..	..	..	..	..	1	..	..	..	..	..	..	..	1	..	..	..
Box, boat-form	fig. 90	..	..	..	..	..	..	..	1	..	..	..	..	..	..	..	..	..	..	..
— small, gouged	34.17-18	..	?	..	..	..	..	..	2	..	..	..	..	..	..	1	..	..	..	..
— foursided	34.20	..	..	..	1	..	..	..	..	..	..	..	..	..	..	..	..	..	..	..
atyp. stone knife, ground edge	25.5-6	1	..	..	1	1	..	..	4	..	..	..	..	..	..	..	..	..	..	..
— — not ground		..	2	..	..	1	..	..	8	..	..	..	..	..	..	..	..	..	..	..
Ulo of slate	22.1-2	..	..	..	..	..	..	1	2	..	..	..	..	..	..	..	..	..	..	..
— baleen	49.1	..	..	..	..	..	..	..	1	..	..	..	..	..	..	..	..	..	..	..
Ulo handle, low and wide, bone	22.5,8-9,11	1	..	2	3	2	..	..	7	..	..	..	..	..	..	..	..	..	..	..
— — wood	22.6-7	..	..	..	..	..	..	1	2	..	1	..	1	..	..	..	1	..	..	..
— even trans. to broad back, bone	22.13-14,16,20	..	..	..	..	1	1	..	2	..	..	1	..	..	..	..	..	..	1	1
— even trans. to broad back, wood	22.12	..	..	..	..	1	..	..	..	..	..	..	..	..	..	..	..	..	..	..
— even trans. to broad back, hole	23.6,11	..	..	1	..	..	..	1	..	1	..	..	..	..	..	2	..	..	..	..
— thin blade part	22.19,21-22,24	..	2	1	..	1	..	1	5	1	..	..	..	..	..	..	..	..	..	..
— — hole	23.2-3	..	1	..	..	..	1	..	1	..	..	1	..	..	2	..	..	..	..	..
— projections at blade side	22.10	..	..	..	..	..	..	..	1	..	..	..	..	..	..	..	1	..	..	..
Compound ulo, handle of bone	23.4	..	..	..	..	..	..	..	2	..	..	..	..	..	..	..	..	..	..	..
— — wood	23.7-8	..	1	..	..	..	..	..	..	..	..	..	..	..	..	..	..	..	..	..
— blade part	23.9-10	2	4	..	..	1	..	..	6	..	..	1	1	..	..	..	..	..	..	..
Ulo blade, slate		..	..	..	..	..	..	..	1	..	..	..	..	..	1	..	..	..	..	..
— iron		..	..	..	..	1	..	..	2	..	..	..	..	..	..	..	..	..	..	1
End scraper, convex, flint	2.25-33	..	..	..	..	..	..	..	1	..	3	..	..	..	3	1	7	2	15	
— — other stone	25.9	..	..	..	..	..	..	..	..	..	..	..	..	..	..	..	1	..	1	..

Table (continued).

	Plate	19 Co. A I	16 II	15 Thule a	15 b	15 Co. A III	15 Co. B	15 Thule c	15 d	15 e	14 Ruin Isl.	14 Co. A IV	13 Thule f	13 C. Russell	13 C. Kent	12 Inf. a	12 b	12 c	12 d	10 Dorset
Side scraper, convex, flint	2.16-19																1	2		3
— concave, flint	2.20									2										3
— — other stone	25.10,12						1	1												
atyp. flint scraper										2					1	5	13	8	3	28
Flint flake	2.22-24									10				1	2				1	5
Handle for flint scraper	23.14			1				1												
Stone scraper, blunt	25.11,13-15,17-18	3	7		1	10	1	1	20	1	1				2		2	1	1	
— — Dolomite	25.16,19	10	8	4		6	1		8	1		3								
End scraper, narrow, bone	26.11-12,14,17,18-19			6		3	3	1	13	1	1		1		1		1	1		
— — wood	26.15-16									6										
— broad, bone	26.6,8-10		1		3	1	3		5				1					2	1	
— — scapula	26.7									1						1				
— antler, projecting handle	26.1-5		1							2					1			1	1	
— hoop-shaped handle	26.13										1									
Scraper handle, trapeziform	23.12-13										1					1	1			
Scraper, iron blade, modern type	23.17	1																		
Side scraper, open at the end	27.15																	1		
Two-handed scraper, ivory with human head	fig. 92										1									
Two-handed scraper, reindeer metacarpus	27.6														2		5			
Two-handed scraper, reinder tibia (one edge)										1										
Two-handed scraper, muskox (?) tibia							1													
Two-handed scraper, bearded seal tibia	27.2		2	1		3	1		4	1			1							
Two-handed scraper, walrus rib										1										
Two-handed scraper, walrus penis-bone	27.1									2										
Two-handed scraper, bear femur										1										
— — ulna	27.3-4									2										
— — radius	27.5									2										
Cup-shaped scraper, ivory	24.2			1							1					1				
— walrus palatal bone	24.1			1																
Sewing needle, bone	36.1-2												1			1		1		
Bodkin	36.3-6			1		2			2					1						
— ornamental	36.10-13		1	1						3			1	1						
— — "human"	36.7-9	1	1	1		1														
Winged needle-case	36.18-19									1								1		
Thimble	36.20																	1		
Thimble holder, hook-shaped	36.29																	1		
— two unilat. hooks	36.26														1					

Archaeological Investigations in the Thule District.

Table (continued).

	Cent.	19	16	15					14	13				12			10
Plate		Co. A I	II / Thule a	b	Co. A III	Co. B	Thule c	d	e / Ruin Isl.	Co. A IV	Thule f	C. Russell	C. Kent	Inf. a	b	c	d / Dorset
Thimble holder, anchor-shaped	36.21-25	..	1	..	2	1	..	..	2	..	..	..	1	..	..	..	..
Boot creaser	36.15-17	..	2	..	1	..	..	..	2	..	1	..	1	..	..	1	..
Spatula-shaped implement, heavy	1.15	..	..	..	..	..	..	1	..	..	..	..	..	1	..	..	..
— — Dorset	1.21-25	..	..	..	..	..	..	..	..	2	..	..	..	..	2	1	.. 4
Household utensils.																	
Pyrites	31.18	..	..	2	1	1	..	2	6	..	..	1	..	1	..	1	.. ..
— with handle	31.20	..	..	..	..	..	..	..	..	..	..	..	1	..	..	..	..
Fire drill	31.17	..	..	..	..	..	..	..	..	..	..	1	..	..	..	..	..
— top-piece, wood	31.8	..	..	..	..	..	..	..	..	..	..	1	..	..	..	..	..
Fire drilling hearth	31.16,21	..	..	..	..	1	..	1	..	1	..	..	..	..	..	..	..
Wick moss	31.19	..	..	..	..	..	..	..	1	..	..	1	..	1	..	..	..
Lamp, unworked stone	32.11	..	..	..	..	..	..	..	..	..	..	3	..	..	..	..	..
— sandstone, small oval	2.34-35	..	..	..	..	..	..	1	..	1	..	..	..	..	..	..	1
— deep triang.-oval, no ledge, heavy	fig. 94	..	..	1	2	..	..	..	6	2	..	..	1	..	..	..	..
— deep triang.-oval, no ledge, small	32.4	..	..	..	..	..	..	..	..	1	..	..	..	..	1	1	2
— with knobs	32.1,3,8	..	2	1	1	..	..	1	1	2	..	..	1	..	..	..	..
— — open ledge	32.2,6,7	..	..	..	1	..	1	..	4	..	..	..	1	..	..	..	..
— — ledge		..	..	..	1	1	..	..	3	1	..	2	..	..	..	..	..
— — vestigial ledge	32.9	..	1	1	..	..	..	..	1	..	..	1	..	..	..	..	..
— of clay-like substance	32.10	..	..	..	..	..	..	..	1	2	..	..	..	..	..	..	..
(see further toy lamps)																	
Lamp stool		..	..	..	..	..	..	..	..	..	..	1	..	..	..	..	..
— trimmer, stone		..	..	2	..	..	..	..	1	..	..	..	..	..	..	..	..
— — asbestos		..	..	..	..	..	..	..	2	..	..	..	..	..	..	..	..
— — wood		+	+	+	+	+	+	+	+	+	+	+	+	+	+	+	+
— — — with groove	31.23-25	4	15	1	1	4	..	..	18	2	..	1	2	..	..	..	..
Shaft for lamp trimmer	31.22	..	..	..	..	..	..	..	..	1	..	..	..	..	..	..	..
Cooking pot, oval, transverse holes	33.1	1	2	..	1	..	..	..	5	..	..	1	..	..	..	..	..
— — inside holes	33.2,5,7	1	2	3	1	5	..	..	5	..	..	1	2	..	..	1	..
— — inside rim	33.6,8	..	..	..	..	..	..	..	1	2	..	..	..	..	..	..	..
— — outside line	33.10	..	..	..	..	..	..	..	1	..	..	..	..	..	..	..	..
— rounded-foursided, outside rim	33.11-12	..	..	..	..	..	..	..	8	..	..	..	..	..	..	..	..
— foursided, rounded corners	33.15-16	4	3	..	1	2	..	1	16	1	..	1	..	..	2	..	..
— inside handle	33.4	..	..	..	..	..	..	..	1	..	..	..	..	..	..	..	..
Drying rack, baleen	47.1	..	1	1	..	..	..	..	2	2	2	..	..	..	..	..	..
— wood, foursided	fig. 107.2	..	..	..	..	..	..	..	7	?	..	..	..	..	..	..	..
Soapstone bowl	33.14	1	..	..	1	..	..	..	1	2	..	..	..	..	3	1	.. ..
Meat tray, wood	fig. 95	5	26	5	6	26	5	7	63	..	2	6	6	..	2	4	5 3 .. 1

54 ERIK HOLTVED. II

Table (continued).

Cent.	Plate	19	16	15						14	13			12				10
		Co. A I	II	Thule a	b	Co. A III	Co. B	Thule c	d	e	Ruin Isl.	Co. A IV	Thule f	C. Russell	C. Kent	Inf. a	b	c	d	Dorset
Bowl, side of baleen		1	..	1	..	..	..	1	1	1	1	..	2	..	..	..	1	..	..	..	..
— bottom, oval bone	34.2	..	1	..	1	..	1	..	2	..	..	..	..	..	..	..	..	1	..	..	..
— — wood	34.1	..	3	1	2	7	2	1	21	2	1	2	2	..	1	1	1	..	1	..
— — baleen	46.14	..	1	2	..	..	..	..	..	..	..	..	..	..	..	1	..	..	..	..	..
Cup side, baleen	48.1-2	..	..	..	..	..	..	1	1	..	..	..	..	..	..	..	..	..	..	..
— bottom, wood,	34.3-4	..	2	3	1	1	..	..	2	..	..	1	1	..	..	..	1	2	..	..	..
— — baleen		1	..	..	..	4	..	..	..	..	1	..	..	..	..	..	..	2	..	..	..
Tub stave	34.21-23	1	7	1	..	4	..	..	..	46	..	..	5	3	..	..	..	1	..	..	..
— groove at both ends	34.24-25	..	..	..	..	..	..	..	..	..	..	..	2	..	..	..	..	..	..	..	..
Coiled basket	34.19	..	..	..	..	..	..	..	..	..	..	..	..	..	..	..	..	1	..	..	..
Ladle, hollow stone		..	..	..	..	..	..	..	..	..	..	..	..	..	2	?	..	..	..	..
— muskox horn	34.7-8	..	..	..	..	..	..	..	..	..	2	..	..	..	1	..	..	1	..	..	..
— wood	34.5-6,11,14	..	1	2	2	..	..	..	3	..	2	..	1	..	..	..	..	..	..	..	..
— — small	34.12-13	..	..	..	1	..	1	..	2	..	..	..	..	..	..	..	..	..	..	..
— soapstone	34.9-10	..	..	..	..	..	..	..	1	..	..	..	1	..	..	..	..	..	..	..
Spoon, ivory	35.26	..	..	..	..	..	..	..	..	..	..	..	..	..	..	..	..	1	..	..	..
— antler	35.16	..	..	..	..	2	..	..	..	..	1	..	1	..	..	..	..	..	..	..
— — small	35.17	..	..	..	..	..	..	..	..	..	1	..	..	..	..	..	..	..	..	..
— — slender handle	35.20,25	..	..	..	..	1	..	..	..	..	1	..	..	..	..	..	..	..	..	..
Marrow extractor (?)	35.18-19	..	..	..	..	..	..	..	..	..	1	3	..	..	..	..	..	..	..	..
Sucking tube	34.16	..	..	..	..	..	..	..	..	..	1	..	..	..	..	..	..	..	..	..
Meat stick, rib	31.9,11,13	3	6	1	2	5	1	2	14	..	..	1	..	..	..	1	1	1	1	..
— antler	31.10,12	..	..	..	..	..	..	..	5	..	..	..	..	3	..	3	3	1	1
Blubber fork, barbed, bone	31.26	..	..	..	..	..	..	..	1	..	..	..	..	1	..	..	..	..	..	..
— — wood	31.14-15	..	..	..	..	1	1	..	3	..	..	..	..	..	..	..	..	..	..	..
— baleen	47.9-10	..	2	1	..	..	..	..	2	1	..	..	..	..	..	..	..	..	..	..
Hook, antler	30.18-21	1	..	..	..	..	..	..	4	1	..	..	..	..	1	..	..	1	..	..
— bone	30.17	..	..	..	..	..	..	..	..	..	..	..	..	..	1	..	..	..	..	..
Carrying stick (?) baleen	46.24,48.13,15,16	..	1	1	1	1	4	..	1	..	..	2	..	..	..	..	..	..	..	..
— (?) wood		..	..	..	..	1	..	..	3	..	..	3	..	..	..	..	1	..	..	..
Wooden handle (?)		..	..	..	..	..	..	..	2	..	..	..	..	..	..	..	..	..	..	..
Baleen handle		..	1	..	..	..	..	..	1	..	..	..	..	..	..	..	2	..	..	..
Bone rim with row of holes (for vessel)	35.5	19	10	..	..	4	..	..	1	..	..	..	..	..	..	..	1	..	..	..
Rib for skin vessel (?) bone	35.21,23	..	2	..	..	1	..	..	1	..	..	..	..	2	..	..	..	..	..	..
— (?) wood	35.22,24	3	..	2	..	2	..	..	5	..	2	..	1	..	..	..	..	1	..	..
Edge mounting	35.1,4	..	2	2	1	3	1	..	12	..	..	..	3	..	..	..	..	..	..	..
Bone mountings	35.6,11-15	4	7	1	1	6	1	..	8	1	1	..	1	..	..	..	..	1	..	..
Gut-skin pane (?)		..	..	1	1	..	..	..	1	..	2	..	..	..	..	1	..	1	..	..
Baleen platform mat	fig. 96	..	6	3	7	8	..	..	3	2	..	8	..	..	..	..	..	..	..	..
Clothing and ornaments																				
Bird-skin jacket		..	..	..	..	..	..	..	..	..	1	..	..	..	..	..	..	..	..	..
Boot		..	..	..	..	1	..	..	..	..	2	..	1	..	1	..	1	..	..	..	..

Archaeological Investigations in the Thule District.

Table (continued).

Cent.	Plate	19 Co. A I	16 II	Thule a	b	15 Co. A III	Co. B	Thule c	d	e	14 Ruin Isl.	Co. A IV	13 Thule f	C. Russell	C. Kent	Inf. a	12 b	c	d	10 Dorset
Baleen wool		..	..	1	1	..	..	..	4	..	2	..	1	..	2	1	..	1	..	..
Mitten	fig. 97	..	..	..	..	..	..	..	..	..	..	..	..	..	..	1	1	..	..	..
Bone button	37.24-26	..	..	..	1	..	..	..	..	1	2	..	..	..	..	..	1	..	..	..
— "winged"	37.27	..	..	..	..	..	..	..	..	..	..	..	..	..	..	..	1	..	..	..
Line buckle	38.6-9	1	..	..	..	..	..	..	1	..	..	..	1	..	..	1	..	..	..	..
— with bust	38.10-12	..	1	..	..	..	..	..	1	1	..	..	..	..	..	..	..	..	..	..
Tube-shaped bead with transv. lines	38.13	..	..	..	..	..	..	..	1	..	..	..	..	..	..	..	..	..	..	..
— button	38.14	..	..	..	..	..	..	1	..	..	..	..	..	..	..	..	..	..	..	..
— buckle with "wings"	38.15-18	..	..	..	1	..	..	1	..	..	..	..	1	..	..	..	..	..	..	1
Snow goggles	38.1-2	..	..	1	..	1	..	..	..	..	..	..	..	..	..	..	..	..	..	..
Brow band, antler	38.3	..	..	..	..	..	..	..	1	..	..	..	..	..	..	..	..	..	..	..
— brass	38.4	..	..	..	1	..	..	..	..	..	..	..	..	..	..	..	..	..	..	..
Bead, soapstone	37.21	..	..	..	..	..	..	..	1	..	..	..	..	..	..	..	..	..	..	..
— amber	37.28	..	..	..	..	..	..	..	..	..	..	..	1	..	..	..	..	..	..	..
— fish vertebra	37.20	..	..	..	..	..	..	..	..	..	..	..	..	1	..	..	..	3	..	..
Pendant, stone	37.14-17	..	1	..	..	..	..	..	1	..	..	..	..	..	..	..	1	..	..	..
— bone	37.32-33	..	..	..	..	..	..	..	1	..	..	..	..	..	..	..	2	..	..	..
— — "winged"	37.30-31	..	..	..	..	..	..	..	..	..	2	..	..	..	..	..	..	..	..	..
Tooth pendant	38.19-28	..	..	1	3	2	..	..	1	1	3	1	..	..	..	10	2	3	1	..
— bear tooth	38.29-30	..	1	3	2	1	..	..	4	4	7	..	..	..	1	..	1	..	2	..
Chain ornament	37.18-19	..	..	..	..	..	..	..	..	..	2	..	..	..	..	..	..	..	..	1
Ornamental plate, dot ornam.	37.22	..	1	..	..	..	..	..	..	..	..	..	..	..	..	..	..	..	..	..
— human face	1.26	..	..	..	..	..	..	..	..	..	..	..	1	..	..	..	..	..	..	..
Snow beater, bone	31.1-2	..	..	..	..	2	..	..	1	..	..	..	..	..	..	..	..	..	..	..
Snow beater, baleen:																				
simple	45.14	..	4	..	1	4	..	2	2	..	3	1	..	..	..	..	1	1	..	..
unilateral end-knob	45.1-4	..	7	..	..	8	1	1	2	..	..	2	..	..	..	..	..	..	..	..
asymmetr. curved butt	45.5-10	1	2	3	..	1	1	1	9	1	..	1	3	..	..	..	..	..	..	..
narrow butt with hole	45.13	..	..	..	..	1	..	..	..	..	1	1	..	..	..	..	..	..	..	..
symm. widened butt	45.12	..	2	2	1	4	2	2	4	1	..	..	3	..	..	..	..	1	1	..
— — with hole	46.1-5	..	3	..	1	2	2	..	2	1	..	2	3	..	..	..	..	..	..	..
— concave butt	46.7	..	..	..	..	1	..	1	..	..	..	..	..	..	..	..	1	..	..	..
— — hole	46.6	..	..	..	..	..	..	..	1	1	..	..	..	..	..	..	..	..	..	..
Baleen stick, narrow, unilat. end knob	46.23	..	1	1	..	1	1	..	..	..	..	..	1	..	..	..	..	..	..	..
Baleen stick, narrow, unilat. finger grooves	46.9	..	..	2	..	1	1	..	..	1	..	..	1	..	..	..	..	..	..	..
— long, hole (and line)	46.10-12	..	2	..	..	5	3	..	..	..	..	2	..	..	..	..	..	..	..	..
Comb, narrow handle	37.2-3	..	..	..	..	..	..	..	..	..	..	..	..	1	..	..	1	..	..	..
— rounded rear end	37.4	..	1	..	..	..	..	..	1	..	..	..	..	..	..	..	..	..	..	..
— trapeziform	37.8	..	..	..	1	..	..	..	..	1	..	..	..	..	..	..	..	..	..	..
— hexagonal handle	37.1,5	1	..	..	..	1	..	..	..	..	..	..	..	..	..	..	1	..	..	..

Table (continued).

Plate	Cent.	19	16	15					14	13				12				10
		Co. A I	— II	Thule a	— b	Co. A III	Co. B	Thule c	— d	— e	Ruin Isl.	Co. A IV	Thule f	C. Russell	C. Kent	Inf. a	— b	— c	— d	Dorset

	Plate																		
Comb, concave, or double-convex sides	37.6,10,13	..	1	..	..	..	..	1	1	..	..	1	..	..	..	..	..	..	..
— "human"	37.9	..	..	..	..	..	..	..	..	..	..	..	..	..	..	..	..	1	..
Mica mirror with skin frame	36.27	..	..	..	..	..	..	..	..	..	..	..	..	1	..	..	..	..	..
Mica with cut edges	38.33	..	..	..	..	..	..	..	1	..	..	..	..	4	5	..	1	3	
— unworked		..	..	..	..	..	..	1	1	..	..	..	..	6	3	8	2	7	
Ornamented wooden stick, Dorset	1.17	..	..	..	..	..	..	..	..	..	..	..	..	..	..	..	..	..	1
Ivory with etched figures	36.33	..	..	..	..	..	..	..	1	..	..	..	..	..	..	..	..	..	..
Indeterminable ornam. objects	36.28,31	..	1	..	..	1	..	..	1	..	..	..	..	..	..	1	..	..	..
Games and toys.																			
Ajagaq, seal humerus	39.1-2	..	..	..	1	..	..	..	1	..	..	..	..	1	1	..	..	..	..
— — radius	39.3	1	4	..	..	1	..	1	..	..	..	..	1	..	..	..	..	..	..
— — penis bone	39.4	..	..	1	..	..	..	..	..	..	..	..	..	..	..	..	..	..	..
— stick	39.5-7	..	1	1	..	1	..	1	2	..	..	..	..	2	..	..	..	..	1
Gambling bone	39.22-23	1	4	8	8	4	3	1	26	1	14	8	3	..	3	29	6	5	5
— carved of ivory	39.24-25	..	..	..	2	..	..	..	..	..	..	..	..	..	..	..	..	..	..
String for string-figures		..	..	..	1	..	..	..	..	..	..	..	..	..	..	..	..	..	..
Top disc, bone	42.4	..	..	..	..	..	..	..	1	..	..	..	..	..	..	..	..	..	..
— ivory with "eyes"	42.9	..	..	..	..	..	..	..	..	..	1	..	..	..	..	..	..	..	..
— baleen	48.11	..	3	2	..	..	..	1	2	..	..	2	..	..	2	..	..	..	..
— — indented edge	48.10	..	1	..	..	..	..	..	..	..	..	..	..	..	..	..	..	..	..
— soapstone	42.8	..	..	..	..	..	..	..	..	..	..	..	..	..	..	..	1	..	..
Top pivot	42.5-7	..	..	..	..	4	..	..	2	..	..	1	1	2	..	..	..	..	..
Propeller, baleen	48.12	..	..	1	..	..	..	..	..	..	..	..	..	..	..	..	..	..	..
Carved animal figures:																			
Whale	38.32	..	..	..	1	..	..	..	..	..	..	..	..	..	..	..	..	..	..
Seal	38.36,40-42	..	1	..	1	..	..	..	1	..	..	..	..	..	..	..	..	1	1
— Dorset (wood)	1.18	..	..	..	..	..	..	..	..	..	..	..	..	..	..	..	..	..	1
Bear	38.38	..	..	..	..	..	..	..	..	1	2	..	..	..	..	..	..	..	1
— baleen	49.21	..	..	1	..	..	..	..	..	..	..	..	..	..	..	..	..	..	..
Dog	38.39	..	..	..	..	..	..	..	1	..	1	..	..	..	..	..	..	..	..
Fox	38.37	..	..	..	1	..	..	..	..	..	..	..	..	..	..	..	..	..	..
Bird	38.31	..	..	..	..	..	..	..	1	..	..	..	..	..	..	..	..	..	..
Doll, no feet	40.1-7	1	4	1	5	7	..	1	17	..	..	2	..	..	2	1	2	6	..
— slender type	40.12-14	..	1	..	2	..	..	..	5	..	..	..	..	..	1	..	..	..	..
— with toupé	40.15-16,21-23	..	1	..	..	1	..	..	7	..	..	..	..	..	..	1	1	..	..
— — boots	40.8-10	1	1	1	3	5	..	..	1	..	..	3	1	..	1	..	3	2	1	1
— — hood and jacket	40.18,19,27	1	..	..	..	..	..	..	3	..	..	..	..	..	1	..	..	1	..	1
— — arms	40.17	..	..	..	..	..	..	..	1	..	..	1	..	..	..	..	..	..	..
— naturalistically carved, ivory	40.20	..	..	..	..	..	..	..	..	..	..	..	..	..	..	1	..	..	..
— Norseman	40.26	..	..	..	..	1	..	..	..	..	..	..	..	..	..	..	..	..	..

II   Archaeological Investigations in the Thule District.   57

Table (continued).

Plate	Cent.	19	16	15					14	13				12				10
		Co. A I	II	Thule a	b	Co. A III	Co. B	Thule c	d	e	Ruin Isl.	Co. A IV	Thule f	C. Russell	C. Kent	Inf. a	b	c	d	Dorset

	Plate																		
Doll, soapstone	40.29	..	..	..	..	..	..	..	1	..	..	..	..	..	..	..	..	..	..
— baleen	49.16	..	..	..	..	..	..	..	1	..	..	..	..	..	..	..	..	..	..
Toy harpoon head, Thule 2, wood.		..	..	..	..	..	..	..	..	..	..	..	..	..	1	..	..	..	..
— — foreshaft	41.23	..	1	..	..	..	..	..	1	..	..	..	..	..	..	..	..	..	..
— — with tenon	41.24	..	1	..	..	..	..	..	..	..	..	..	..	..	..	..	..	..	..
— — wood	41.34-35	..	2	..	..	..	..	..	..	..	..	..	..	..	..	..	..	..	..
— — baleen	48.7-9	..	2	..	2	..	..	..	3	..	..	..	2	..	..	..	..	..	..
— bladder dart head, baleen	48.18	..	1	..	..	..	..	1	1	..	..	..	1	..	..	..	..	..	..
— (?) baleen with many barbs	48.19-21	..	1	..	..	..	..	..	..	..	..	3	..	..	..	..	..	..	..
— lance, baleen	48.5-6	..	..	..	..	..	..	..	1	..	..	..	1	..	..	..	..	..	..
— side prong for bird dart, wood		1	..	..	..	..	..	..	..	..	..	..	..	..	..	..	..	..	..
— — — baleen	49.18-19	..	..	..	2	..	..	..	..	..	..	..	1	..	..	..	..	..	..
— bow, wood	41.18-22	..	1	..	1	1	..	..	5	1	..	..	1	..	1	..	..	..	..
— arrow, extended fore end	41.26	..	2	1	1	5	3	2	3	..	..	..	2	..	1	..	..	2	..
— — pointed	41.30-31	..	..	..	..	..	1	..	2	..	..	..	..	..	..	..	..	..	..
— — head	41.36-40	..	3	..	..	5	..	..	2	..	..	..	..	..	..	..	..	1	1
— — shaft	41.27	..	2	..	1	5	..	..	6	..	1	..	2	..	5	..	2	1	3	..
— — baleen		..	..	..	..	..	..	..	..	..	1	..	..	..	..	..	..	..	..
— sling handle, wood	42.11-13,27-29	..	..	1	1	..	..	..	2	..	..	..	1	..	..	..	4	1	1	..
— — baleen		..	..	..	..	..	..	..	1	..	..	..	..	..	..	..	..	..	..
— sledge runner, wood	41.1-3	..	3	1	..	1	..	..	2	..	..	..	1	..	..	..	..	..	..
— — cross slat, bone	41.4,6	..	2	..	..	..	..	..	1	..	..	..	1	..	..	..	1	..	..
— — — wood	41.5,7-10	2	4	2	1	5	1	..	5	..	..	..	2	..	..	..	2	..	..
— — — baleen	49.28	..	..	..	..	1	..	..	..	..	1	..	..	..	..	..	..	..	..
— — upstander, wood	41.11-13	..	..	..	..	1	..	..	2	..	..	..	..	..	..	..	..	..	..
— — — — modern	41.14	1	..	..	..	..	..	..	..	..	..	..	..	..	..	..	..	..	..
— whip handle, wood	41.15-17	..	..	2	..	..	..	..	2	1	1	..	..	..	..	..	..	..	..
— — baleen		?	..	..	..	..	..	..	1	..	..	..	..	..	..	..	..	..	..
— umiaq, wood	42.14	..	..	..	1	..	..	..	..	..	..	..	..	..	1	..	..	..	..
— — baleen	49.22-24	..	..	..	..	..	..	..	3	..	..	..	..	..	..	..	..	..	..
— kayak	42.15-16	..	1	..	..	1	..	..	1	..	1	..	..	..	2	..	..	..	..
— — gouged	42.17-18	..	..	..	1	..	..	..	2	1	..	..	..	..	..	..	..	..	..
— — baleen	49.25	..	..	..	..	..	..	..	1	..	..	..	..	..	..	..	..	..	..
— boat (?)	42.2-3	..	..	1	..	..	..	..	..	..	..	..	..	..	1	..	..	..	..
— kayak paddle	42.22-23,25-26	..	1	1	..	2	1	..	6	..	..	..	1	..	..	..	..	..	..
— — narrow type	42.24	..	..	..	..	..	..	..	1	..	..	..	..	..	2	..	..	..	..
— ulo handle	42.10	..	..	..	..	..	..	..	1	..	..	..	..	..	..	..	..	..	..
— snow beater, wood		..	1	..	..	..	..	..	..	..	..	..	..	..	..	..	..	..	..
— — baleen	49.32	..	1	..	1	1	..	..	..	..	..	..	..	..	..	..	..	..	..
— snow knife, baleen	49.17	..	..	..	1	..	..	..	1	..	..	..	..	..	..	..	..	..	..
— lamp, no ledge	43.2-4	1	..	1	2	2	..	..	7	..	..	..	..	..	..	..	..	..	..
— — knobs	43.7	..	..	..	..	..	..	..	1	..	..	..	..	1	..	..	..	..	..

Table (continued).

Cent.	19	16	15					14	13			12				10
Plate	Co. A I	II / Thule a	b	Co. A III	Co. B	Thule c	d	e / Ruin Isl.	Co. A IV / Thule f	C. Russell	C. Kent	Inf. a	b	c	d	Dorset
Toy, lamp, open ledge 43.8,11	..	..	1	..	..	1	1	..	..	..	..	..	..	..	..	..
— — ledge 43.9-10	..	1	..	1	..	..	3	1	..	..	..	..	..	1	..	..
— — vestigial ledge	..	..	..	..	..	..	..	1	..	..	..	..	..	..	..	..
— — ledge near back 43.12	..	..	..	..	..	..	1	..	..	..	..	..	..	..	..	..
— — no ledge, modern 43.13	1	1	..	..	..	..	..	..	..	..	..	..	..	..	..	..
— — simple 43.1,5	..	1	1	2	..	..	4	..	..	..	..	1	..	..	..	..
— cooking pot, round 43.18	..	1	..	..	..	..	1	..	..	..	..	1	..	..	..	..
— — oval 43.17,20-21	..	1	..	..	..	..	4	..	..	..	..	1	..	..	..	..
— — foursided 43.15-16,19	1	1	1	..	2	..	6	..	..	..	3	..	..	..	..	..
— — simple 43.14	..	..	..	..	..	..	2	..	..	..	1	..	..	..	..	..
Round stone	..	..	..	..	..	1	2	..	..	..	..	2	2	3	2	1
Objects connected with intellectual culture.																
Drum, bone 35.2-3,8-9	4	9	..	..	3	1	..	1	..	..	1	..	..	..	..	..
— baleen 47.5	..	1	..	1	1	..	1	..	2	1	..	..	?	..	..	..
— handle, wood 39.13-14	..	?	..	..	2	..	..	3	..	..	..	..	..	..	..	..
Drum stick, bone 39.12	..	1	..	..	..	..	..	..	..	..	..	..	..	..	..	..
— — baleen 47.3-4	..	..	..	..	3	..	..	..	1	..	..	..	..	..	..	..
Amulet bundle	..	..	..	..	..	..	..	..	1	..	..	..	..	..	..	..
— stone 39.9	..	..	..	..	..	..	..	1	..	..	..	..	..	..	..	..
Miniature baleen knife 39.10-11	..	..	..	..	1	..	..	3	..	1	..	..	1	6	..	..
Split bear mandible 39.8	..	..	..	1	..	..	..	1	..	..	..	..	..	..	..	..
Amulet box 39.18-21	..	2	..	..	1	..	..	1	..	..	..	1	1	..	..	..
— with two compt's 39.17	..	..	..	..	..	..	..	..	..	..	..	..	1	..	..	..
— (?) kayak-shaped 39.16	..	..	..	..	..	..	..	2	..	..	..	..	..	..	..	..
Skin cap (?) .... fig. 98	..	..	..	1	..	..	..	..	..	..	..	..	..	..	..	..
Sundries.																
Baleen, quadrangular plaiting 49.20	..	1	..	..	..	..	..	1	..	1	..	..	..	..	..	..
— line with knots	4	11	51	21	36	10	25	103	20	74	16	19	..	9	24	46	16	4	1
Drilled bone	27	35	..	1	16	..	2	17	..	2	..	..	..	..	..	3	..
Waste flint	..	1	1	..	1	..	4	2	3	7	..	..	2	7	16	14	4	+
— slate	..	1	1	..	..	..	1	2	..	..	..	..	3	1	..	1	2
Amber, unworked	..	..	..	..	..	..	..	1	..	..	..	..	..	..	..	..
Iron (total)	..	2	1	..	3	..	2	10	2	6	1	..	1	..	4	3	1	2
Copper	..	..	..	1	..	..	..	6	1	1	..	..	..	1	2	..	1	..
Ornamental elements:																
Y-ornament	..	..	..	..	..	..	..	1	..	..	..	..	..	3	2	..	1
spur line	..	..	..	1	..	..	..	1	1	1	..	1	..	1	1	2	2	..	..
dot ornament	..	1	..	..	..	..	..	1	..	..	..	..	..	..	..	1	..

Table (continued).

Plate	Cent....	19	16			15					14		13				12			10
		Co. A I	II	Thule a	b	Co. A III	Co. B	Thule c	d	e	Ruin Isl.	Co. A IV	Thule f	C. Russell	C. Kent	Inf. a	b	c	d	Dorset
dot and circle		..	..	..	..	1	..	..	..	..	..	..	..	..	..	..	..	..	..	..
plug ornament		..	..	..	1	..	..	..	1	..	1	..	..	..	..	1	..	..	..	..
line ornament		..	..	..	..	..	..	..	..	..	..	..	..	..	..	..	1	..	..	..
open work		..	1	..	..	..	..	..	..	..	..	1	..	..	..	..	..	..	1	..
seal tail (?)		..	..	..	..	..	..	..	1	..	..	..	..	..	..	..	..	..	..	..
Naturalistic etching		..	1	..	..	..	..	..	1	..	..	..	..	..	..	..	..	..	..	..
Objects of Norse origin	44.1-13	..	..	..	1	1	..	..	..	1	1	5	..	..	..	..	3	..	..	..

in the houses, whereas now there is no peat anywhere in the nearest hinterland, and even the fluvial plain was nothing but a stony waste. Finally, there may have been impulses from the outside, i. a. from the newly immigrated people who are represented by Ruin Island; these were great whalers who apparently were the bearers of traditions from more southerly latitudes in America. For obvious reasons they did not carry a knowledge to the Norse side of the Inugsuk culture, but they may have had their share in the Eskimo side, and it will be of interest to obtain more light on this question. In some respects the culture of these people rather closely resembles the Thule culture of Inglefield Land but, as already stated, it differs on important points, especially as regards the houses. However, it will be best not to deal with the house forms until we have gone through the various culture phases and picked out their characteristics.

Culture Phases of the Thule District.

Dorset culture.

In the three middens at Inuarfigssuaq, B. I, B. II and the lower layers of the midden in front of House 4, we found in all 75 different implement types in accordance with the classification employed in the foregoing. Of these the following were found solely at the said three places:

Dorset harpoon head with closed socket, one line hole, square-cut butt end, inserted blade.
sling handle (butt end Pl. 14.16)
adze head (Pl. 1.19-20)

hatchet head of walrus ivory
ornamented wooden stick
seal figure (Pl. 1.18).

This gives six types, or 8 per cent. of the total number. The following occur solely in the middens and the early Thule culture on Inglefield Land:

Dorset harpoon head with open socket, one line hole, no blade,
Dorset harpoon head with closed socket, two line holes and cleft butt, no blade,
leister harpoon head,
foreshaft of Dorset harpoon,
small socket piece with triangular butt,
arrow head with two unilateral barbs
convex-edged side scraper of flint,
knife handle of wood with side groove towards the end.

These are eight types, or over 10 per cent., that express the special likeness to the Thule culture of Inglefield Land. If we include the whole of the early transitional period and the group consisting of Ruin Island and Thule Houses 16 and 19, we get furthermore:

harpoon blade of flint with concave butt,
knife handle in two halves,
drill bit of flint,
adze blade of flint,
flint scraper with concave edge,
atypical flint scraper,
flint flake,
spatula-shaped implement,
small, deep, triangular-oval lamp without ledge,
worked mica,
bear figure of walrus ivory

or 11 types in all. Together with the foregoing 8 it makes 19, or about 25 per cent. indicating the special agreement with the ancient-looking culture of the Thule District.

However, it will be reasonable to include the relationship with the Inugsuk period, for here we actually find objects distinctly Dorset in character, without being able in every case to decide whether they may have come from a now obliterated Dorset habitation. Thus we have:

Thule-2 harpoon head with slots, no blade,
Dorset harpoon head with closed socket, two line holes, cleft butt, and blade,
Dorset harpoon head of heavy type,
lance head with seating for blade,
arrow head, round, pointed, with knobs,
knife handle of wood with seating for end blade,
Dorset knife with one side blade,
Dorset knife with two side blades,

flint flaker of antler,
marline spike with constricted fore end,
pointed seal fibula,
flat ulo handle (with iron blade—Pl. 22.13),
ulo blade of iron,
flint scraper with convex end edge,
small oval lamp (sandstone)
meat fork of antler,
tubular "winged" buckle,
chain ornament,
Y-ornament,

19 types in all. With the above two groups this gives 38, so that we find that about 50 per cent. of the types in the Dorset middens are apparently associated with the early culture.

The only objects that are solely in common with the Ruin Island group are the concave flint scraper and the bear figure of walrus ivory, which does not suggest any very close connection. We must add, however, that of the small oval lamps the two from Ruin Island and Inf. B. II are of sandstone, whereas a third (from Thule House 21. E) is of soapstone. The round, pointed arrow head and the chain ornament are the only objects solely in common with the Inugsuk period.

There would thus seem to be every reason for assuming that the three Inuarfigssuaq middens, which must be considered to represent the earliest habitation of Inglefield Land, come closest to the ancient Thule culture in respect of culture characteristics. However, it is necessary to take the aforementioned element of uncertainty into consideration when reviewing the relations between these two culture phases, as nearly all the types shown as common (except the arrow head with two barbs and the small socket piece) were found during the excavation of the house ruins above the middens, and under such conditions that it could not be decided whether they belonged to the one or the other, so that there is the possibility that the markedly Dorset types, representing at any rate four out of the eight, also came from the earliest habitation. In that case of course the special character of the Dorset period grows considerably when measured in percentages; and what is more, there is nothing to indicate a closer connection with the Thule culture of Inglefield Land than with any of the other phases, Ruin Island and Inugsuk. The mutual relationship need not be based upon anything else than the mutual dependence of the respective phases on an earlier culture, and to me it seems probable that the Thule culture as found on Inglefield Land came along with an independent immigration,— later and with no close connection with the foregoing Dorset phase. The latter comprised in fact more special forms than appears from the present material; Mathiassen has described for instance a curious carrying handle[1]), harpoon head, pendant and boot creaser (?)[2], the latter being very like the spatula-shaped implements.

For the sake of completeness we may list the remaining 31 types of more general distribution which have also been found in the Dorset middens:

    plug for bladder mouthpiece,
    heavy socket piece with scarf face,
    ice pick with scarf face
    wound needle,
    bow brace of antler,
    blunt, round arrow head,
    symmetrical lanceolate arrow head,
    arrow shaft,
    sledge shoe of bone,
    trace buckle, ovoid form,
    snow knife with separate blade,
    knife blade of flint,
    knife blade of slate, two-edged,
    knife blade of iron,
    hand-drill shank of bone,
    whetstone,
    hammer stone,
    mattock head with seating for handle.
    wedge,
    round, pointed marline spike
    blunt stone scraper
    lamp trimmer of wood,
    meat tray of wood
    ajagaq stick
    gambling bones
    seal figure,
    doll in boots,
    doll in coat and hood,
    toy arrow head,
    baleen line with knots.

It is perhaps an open question if the baleen line really dates from the Dorset period, and the same may apply to one or two of the others; but it is impossible to pick them out with complete certainty. But even if the relationship with the Thule culture is conspicuous, the forms of implements found in the three middens have such a peculiar stamp about them that one would hesitate to call them simply a phase of the Thule culture. That culture seems to have come later, and at the present stage of the investigation it is impossible to say anything about the relationship. It would seem to be quite justifiable to talk of a Dorset

---

[1]) Mathiassen 1927 p. 166, fig. 10.1.
[2]) Mathiassen 1928 (a) p. 214, fig. 10.1-3.

culture here in contrast to the Thule culture. Whether this Dorset culture here is "pure" or not is strictly speaking a subordinate matter. It all depends on what one understands by a pure Dorset culture. Jenness states that in 1936 M. Leechman found a settlement with pure Dorset culture on the island of Nuvuk, a little to the southwest of Cape Wolstenholme (in Labrador where the Hudson Strait opens into Hudson Bay)[1]; but no exhaustive definition of the Dorset culture has yet been given.

However, we are now able to form a picture—if not an exhaustive one at any rate a fairly comprehensive one—of the Dorset culture on Inglefield Land. It has had a number of characteristic forms of harpoon heads, most of which, to judge from the foreshafts, were used for ice hunting. Furthermore, the slender leister-harpoon or harpoon-arrow heads are common; presumably they were used for catching salmon, and no doubt the same applies to the smallest of the harpoon heads.

The only harpoon head found that was not one of the special Dorset forms is of the Thule-2 type with lashing slots. The specimens are rather slender and smaller than is usual for this type.

In most cases the harpoon blades are of flint with a concave butt. The lances had a blade lashed on to a seating; whether the head was fixed or movable cannot be determined from the fragments found, but the former seems the more likely. Bow and arrow were used for hunting both caribou and birds. The bow was of antler with a sinew backing, to judge from the brace found.

Whether or not the kayak was used is hard to say; a plug for a bladder mouthpiece alone suggests a knowledge of the harpoon bladder, though it may have been that of a bladder-dart, to which presumably the small socket piece with the triangular butt belongs; but this too argues the use of a vessel for hunting marine animals. It is beyond question that the Dorset people hunted the walrus, but they may have done so from the ice. They knew the dog sledge, and that was undoubtedly the principal means of conveyance.

Their flint technique was well advanced, but they also knew iron; the analyses have established the fact that it is meteoric iron. The knives have either an end blade (and wood handle) or a side blade, sometimes with one on each side and each near one end. The knife with the handle of two halves was an important implement. Apparently it had a burin-like blade for cutting the narrow grooves when carving in bone or antler. No such blade was found in the Thule District, but to me it is probable that at any rate some of the "drill bits" described by Solberg from West Greenland served this purpose[2]. The ulo found with an iron blade has a handle of narwhal ivory. The flint scrapers had both convex and

---

[1] National Mus. Can. Bull. 89 (1938) p. 7.
[2] Solberg 1907, Tafel 6, 1—16.

concave edges, sometimes both combined in one, and there was a wealth of less typical forms, the most peculiar being the small specimen shown in Pl. 2.15. The flint objects were fashioned by means of a flint flaker of antler. Hand drills were used with a shank of bone or antler, and presumably the bow drill was also known, although the small drill bits of flint may have been for hand drills. Among other implements we know the hammerstone, whetstone, wedge, marline spike and mattock.

The lamps had no wick ledge and presumably they were small. The most remarkable are the oval patterns, ground out of sandstone. Then we have the peculiar ornamentation, which is also applied on some of the harpoon heads (I p. 194). It is possible that chain links and the "winged" buckle are part of the Dorset culture, and presumably the snow knife with the separate blade, although this question is open to some doubt, as in some of the foregoing cases. On the subject of clothing no more can be said than that the women's coat had a rather large hood, possibly the amaut hood. Finally, mention must be made of the curious "polishing stone" of flint, described in I p. 245. It was not found in any of the middens, but in Inf. House 6, which lies just above B. I., so that it may well date from the Dorset period. It is very reminiscent of some that are mentioned by Jenness from Cape Dorset[1]).

All in all the impression gained is of a culture based to a great extent on ice hunting, but otherwise on the hunting of both land and sea animals, salmon fishing being of considerable importance too. In all probability the people lived in permanent winter houses of stone and turf, but they also knew the snow house. As to the form of the houses we can say nothing for certain, nor whether they employed whale bones in the roof construction. Conditions argue, however, that they did not go in for rational whaling at any rate.

In his first description of the objects from Cape Dorset Jenness referred to the unusual patina, indicating that they were very old— though he admits that patina is a criterion that must be used with caution. To this I may say that the Dorset objects from Inglefield Land also have a very characteristic, warm yellowish patina which imparts to them a special and easily recognizable character over against the other finds.

The Thule Culture of Inglefield Land.

This is represented by 243 types, of which the following 28 have not been encountered outside the period:

Thule-2 harpoon head with slots and the blade parallel to the line hole,
thin toggle harpoon head with closed socket, oblique spur, a blade, and vestigial side-blade grooves,

---

[1]) Jenness 1925 p. 432.

stopper for harpoon line, with holes,
small mending disc with groove, of walrus ivory,
oblong, cylindrical socket piece,
sealing-stool seat of antler (for one-legged stool),
foot for bladder-dart bladder,
cylindrical ferrule with socket (for bird dart),
sledge upstander of antler,
snow knife with hole-handle,
knife handle of wood with seating for lateral end-blade,
hand-pick of antler with cross handle,
mattock head with socket for handle,
mattock handle,
convex end-scraper of stone (not flint),
side scraper of antler (Pl. 27.15),
thimble of skin,
hook-shaped thimble holder,
pyrites with handle,
coiled basket,
spoon (?) of walrus ivory,
winged button,
"human" comb,
mica mirror with skin frame,
top-disc of soapstone,
naturalistic human figure of walrus ivory,
toy harpoon head, Thule-2, of wood,
line ornament.

The types that are shared solely with the Dorset middens are shown in the foregoing (page 60), though now we can include only 7 of the 8 features, the small socket piece from Cape Kent having to be omitted in this connection.

Types that are shared exclusively with the subsequent transitional period are the following nine:

barrel-shaped swivel with side opening,
stiletto handle of wood,
arrow head with one barb and seating for blade,
salmon-spear barb with holes (no projection on back),
trace buckle with hole running obliquely to the end,
knife handle of wood with slit for end blade,
hand-pick with teeth,
two-handed scraper of caribou metacarpus,
(mitten),
bead of fish vertebra.

The mitten is omitted, as it cannot be included as a special feature. Only three types are shared exclusively with the Ruin Island group:

Thule-2 harpoon head without blade, with slots and vestigial barbs,
quiver handle with carved figures,
flint flaker of walrus ivory.

For the Thule period we have thus about 11 per cent. of special features, under 4 per cent. are shared exclusively with the subsequent transitional period, about 3 per cent. with the Dorset period, and only a little over 1 per cent. with the Ruin Island period, whereas the remaining 81 per cent. indicate the greater or lesser similarity to all periods or combinations of periods. This strengthens the supposition voiced in the foregoing that there was no close connection with the people of the Dorset period, nor as it seems with Ruin Island. The group of special features and that with transitional features contain a number of special types, of which pyrites with a handle and mica mirror with a frame have not previously been recorded[1]), to my knowledge, whilst sledge upstanders of antler, basket, side scraper of antler, and stiletto handle of wood of this type have not previously been found in Greenland.

Of the 81 per cent. of types with a wider distribution the following have not been found later than the Ruin Island period:

Harpoon blade of flint,
arrow head with blade seating, no barb,
tubular ferrule,
knife handle in two halves,
drill bit of flint
atypical flint scrapers
flint flake
trapeziform (triangular) scraper handle
sewing needle of bone (?)
Dorset "spatula"
small, deep, triangular-oval lamp without ledge,
ladle of musk-ox horn,
worked mica,

in all 13, or over 5 per cent. of the total. Together with the types singled out above they represent the forms that are especially peculiar to the early Thule culture of the Thule District.

The early transitional period.

In this I have collected a number of find groups that are difficult to reconcile with the fully developed Inugsuk culture, and which also differ so much from the early Thule culture on Inglefield Land that it would be reasonable to keep them apart from both in order to enable the lines to be drawn up more clearly. The point that decides the placing of the transitional period in the chronological order is that at the localities in question there occurred Norse relics or objects showing that we are within range of Norse influence (tub staves, ornamental bodkin), even

---

[1]) Mirror, see I p. 276.

if it has not yet succeeded in asserting itself in these parts. Furthermore, the houses placed in this group have no separate kitchen, as is observable in Thule's Inugsuk period proper—a negative feature which brings them towards the early Thule culture. Cape Russell is placed by the side of Cape Kent chiefly because there is greater mutual conformity between the architecture of the houses there than between these and any of the other groups.—However, we shall now endeavour by means of statistics to obtain a hint of the special relation of the period to the other periods that have been set up, and to see whether the theory can be justified. Of special features there are:

> Flat harpoon head with open socket, two oblique line holes with a common orifice in the dorsal side, a blade and three dorsal spurs,
> (whaling-harpoon foreshaft),
> heavy socket piece with cleft butt,
> w-shaped drag-line handle,
> salmon-spear side prong with V-groove,
> fish decoy of bear tooth,
> (kayak paddle),
> harpoon rest for kayak, with tenon,
> whetstone with groove (for baleen lashing)
> bone maul,
> hand-pick of antler (crude),
> cutting board of baleen,
> thimble holder with two unilateral hooks,
> (fire drill),
> (fire-drill top piece),
> lamp of crude stone,
> lamp-stool,
> (handle for lamp trimmer)
> tub stave with groove in both ends,
> ladle of hollow stone,
> small bone hook (pot hook?)
> amber bead,
> comb with narrow handle.

In all, 18 types out of 277, or $6^1/_2$ per cent. The following are shared exclusively with the Dorset middens:

> Small socket piece with triangular butt,
> arrow head with knobs, two unilateral barbs, no blade,

that is to say not 1 per cent.

The aforesaid 9 types (p. 65) were shared exclusively with the Thule culture of Inglefield Land, in this connection over 3 per cent. Of course it is probable that some of the above special features were also known in the Thule period; but it is impossible to say which when we have to confine ourselves to the material before us.

Shared exclusively with the Ruin Island group are:

whaling harpoon,
sledge angle brace.

Of whale harpoons we found a foreshaft in Thule f and a harpoon head in the midden in front of Thule House 19. One of the sledge angle braces is from Cape Russell.

Shared exclusively with the subsequent Inugsuk are:

Harpoon arrow head with two opposite barbs,
harpoon blade of baleen,
sealing-stool leg of bone,
arrow head with scarf face,
salmon-spear side prong with two holes,
flat heart-shaped ferrule,
bone "bolt",
snow knife with bent back,
snow-shovel blade of scapula,
bow-drill mouthpiece carved of bone,
adze handle with one hole,
cutting board of wood with "head",
small hollowed-out wooden box (Pl. 34.17-18),
ulo blade of slate,
lamp with ledge, open at ends,
ladle of soapstone,
blubber stick of bone with barbs,
ajagaq of seal humerus,
(top pivot)
doll with arms,
toy lance of baleen,
- side prong for bird dart, baleen,
- sledge cross-slat, baleen,
- umiaq, wood,
- lamp with knobs,
- cooking pot, crude,

This gives 25 types or 9 per cent. If we also include the 9 features which occur in the Ruin Island group too:

Bone toggle,
quiver handle with hole from side to side,
sledge cross-slat of wood,
adze head with horizontal holes
lamp with ledge
spoon of antler
(drill bow)
(boot)
baleen snow beater, narrow handle end with hole,
peg ornament,
Norse relics

the number is increased to over 12 per cent. as an expression of the particular similarity to the time immediately following. In comparison with the 3 per cent. particular similarity with the previous period this means that this transitional period is orientated well forward. This becomes still clearer when we see how many types have their upper limit here, and how many their lower. In the former category there are 11 in all, viz. the 9 special features shared with the Thule period and the two shared with the Dorset period. But of types whose earliest occurrence lies in the transitional period there are 104, not including the 18 special features of the transitional period. This, in addition to the $6^1/_2$ per cent. special features, gives about $37^1/_2$ per cent. pointing forward, as against only 4 per cent. pointing backward. There remains 52 per cent. to connect both with the past and the future. There can be no doubt but that this is really a time when the old is disappearing and the new is coming in.

Of the new forms that now begin to appear there is reason to single out the following:

Thule-2 harpoon head with blade and lashing holes,
Thule-1 harpoon head,
Thule-3 harpoon head with the spur in continuation of the butt end.
flat harpoon heads,
short cylindrical socket piece,
lance head (or knife) with blade slit,
toggle for towing line,
small toggle with oblong hole (Pl. 16.8),
arrow head with scarf face,
salmon-spear side prong with two lashing holes,
sledge cross-slat of wood
trace buckle with holes at right-angles,
harpoon rest for kayak,
knife with end knob,
baleen shave,
cutting board with "head",
compound ulo,
two-handed scraper of bearded-seal tibia,
ornamental bodkin,
anchor-shaped thimble holder,
lamp with ledge,
lamp with vestigial ledge,
lamp trimmer with groove,
tub stave,
edge mounting,
comb with concave or double-convex sides,
ajagaq of seal radius,
drum of bone,
peg ornament

and the following objects of baleen:

trout needle,
trace buckle,
whip handle,
knife,
saw,
platform mat,
snow beaters, various forms,
top disc,
toys, various.

There is evidence that whaling is now beginning to play a predominant part, that the kayak technique is in a state of rapid development, and that impulses from the south are beginning to assert themselves in the implement culture, presumably in conjunction with renewed influence from the west through new immigration.

The Ruin Island group.

This characteristic group comprises the 7 houses on Ruin Island itself and Houses 16 and 19 at Thule. Of special features found solely on Ruin Island there are:

Barbed harpoon head with vestigial spur and more than two barbs,
drag-line handle with carved figures,
drag-line handle with carved bear's head,
sledge runner of walrus ivory,
bow drill (?) with four points,
adze blade of iron,
flint flaker with separate, curved handle,
two-handed scraper with carved head,
bird-skin coat,
ornamental disc with face,
top-disc of walrus ivory with "eyes",
amulet bundle,

12 types in all, or about 11 per cent. of the 106 found on Ruin Island. Apart perhaps from the bird-skin coat they are also types that look foreign in Greenland. A flint flaker of somewhat similar type, but with a straight handle, was found earlier at Sermermiut in Disko Bay[1]); the others have never previously been found in Greenland, while the carved two-handed scraper and the curious bow-drill are the first to be recovered anywhere. It may be said that with few exceptions these are not important things, but rather curiosities; but having regard to the relative poverty

---

[1]) Th. Thomsen in Greenland II, p. 298, fig. 8 (Mus. No. L: 5798).

of mediaeval Greenland in artistically fashioned objects, it is surprising to find so many within one small area.

To the above, however, we shall add the types which occur only in Thule Houses 16 and 19 and those that are common only to these two houses and Ruin Island (the latter are marked with an *):

*Thule-2 harpoon head with vestigial spur,
toggle harpoon head with vestigial spur,
— — — — — — and vestigial side-blade grooves,
(whaling harpoon head),
*stopper for harpoon line with spike at the middle,
small socket piece with cleft butt,
heavy socket piece with triangular butt,
sealing-stool seat of bone,
drag-line handle with curved hole,
arrow head with two bilateral, slender barbs,
heavy swivel of baleen,
pick-axe,
scraper with bow-shaped handle,
*marrow-extractor (?) of wood,
"winged" pendant,
bird figure,
doll of baleen,
toy whip handle of baleen,
- kayak of baleen,
- lamp with vestigial ledge.

Together with the first list this makes 31 types, or $16^1/_2$ per cent. of the total of 186 found within this group. This then is the highest percentage of special features we have yet encountered, for the Dorset middens had 8 per cent., Inglefield Land's Thule culture had 11 per cent. and the transitional period 6.5 per cent.

The only objects shared exclusively with the transitional period were the whaling harpoon and the sledge angle brace (about 1 per cent.), with the early Thule culture 3 types: Thule-2 harpoon head without blade, with vestigial barbs and slots, quiver handle with carved figures, and flint flaker of walrus ivory, making about $1^1/_2$ per cent., and with the Dorset middens: concave flint scraper, bear figure and oval lamp of sandstone (about $1^1/_2$ per cent.).

A number of types are shared solely with these three early culture periods, but not with the Inugsuk period:

Harpoon blade of flint,
arrow head with seating for blade, no barbs,
tubular ferrule,
knife handle in two halves,
bow-drill bit of flint,
adze blade of flint,

atypical flint scraper,
flint flake,
trapeziform scraper handle,
sewing needle of bone (oval cross-section),
Dorset "spatula",
small, deep, triangular-oval lamp without ledge,
ladle of musk-ox horn,
worked mica.

Here we have 14 types or barely 8 per cent., of which over 2 per cent. are shared with the Thule culture and the Dorset middens, and about $5^1/_2$ per cent. are shared with the Thule culture and the transitional period. Thus there is not much specific likeness to the two earliest periods and only a little more with the transitional period, which we have placed nearest. Altogether we get about 12 per cent. specific similarity to the early culture phases of the Thule District.

If we now examine the closer association with the time that followed, and consequently omit things which at the same time connect with the early period, we get the following (* indicating items shared exclusively with the Inugsuk period):

```
 Oval mending disc with groove, of wood,
  wooden shaft for cylindrical socket piece,
*wound pin of baleen,
*whip handle of bone,
*kayak deck beam of bone
*snow probe of baleen
 stone axe with baleen handle
*adze head without separate blade,
       —     without holes,
       —     with vertical holes,
*adze handle with 3—4 holes,
 ulo handle with thin blade part,
 (fire-drilling hearth)
*lamp of clayey mass,
*cooking pot with projecting inside rim,
 oval drying rack of baleen,
*foursided drying rack of wood,
 blubber fork of baleen,
 thong buckle with bust,
*comb with trapeziform handle,
*dog figure,
 toy bladder-dart head (?) of baleen with many barbs,
 toy whip handle of wood,
*hollowed-out toy kayak,
*toy lamp with ledge, open at ends,
 drum of baleen,
 drum-stick of baleen,
 four-strand plaited baleen.
```

This gives a total of 25 types or about $13^1/_2$ per cent. as an expression of the close association with Inuksuk and later culture in the Thule District, and 13 or 7 per cent. of the specific likeness to the Inugsuk time proper—a figure very close to what was found for the similarity with the transitional period. Thus we have $16^1/_2$ per cent. of special features, 12 per cent. pointing backward and $13^1/_2$ per cent. pointing forward in time; consequently it is impracticable to give the early or the late period precedence. Ruin Island is midway between with its many foreign features, which indicate that the people there must have immigrated from the outside recently; but the 58 per cent. of neutral common features are clear evidence of the mutual relationship of all the parties. Actually it would have been very difficult to establish the time at which such a foreign group came in if, as mentioned earlier, there had not been the fortunate coincidence of two circumstances, that in the Ruin Island group we found Norse objects but no demonstrable Inugsuk culture within the same period (Norse influence), and that both the Ruin Island group and the Inugsuk-period houses at Thule have well-developed kitchens, whereas no such development was found on Inglefield Land. With this the period in which the new people arrived is narrowly limited; it must have been after connection with the Norsemen had been established, but before the new house type at Thule had become common, i. e. uppermost in the transitional period.

Of the new elements added to the culture in the Thule District particularly many are connected with baleen technique; the new people are great whalers. On the other hand they must be people who quickly have their characteristics worn off—or they leave the District again, as of course the many special features disappear in the Inugsuk period. The latter's all-powerful culture, which even then had already gained a firm footing in the Thule District, seems quickly to have absorbed the more outstanding features of the strangers' culture.

The Inugsuk period.

The period so designated is limited downwards by the occurrence of houses with a kitchen in conjunction with a number of characteristic types of implements which now occur in unusual numbers or begin to appear for the first time. One might exemplify Thule-2 harpoon heads with lashing holes, toggle harpoon heads with an open socket (Thule 3), flat harpoon heads with a closed socket, knives with a side blade, tub staves, and a number of baleen objects. Upwards the limitation may seem somewhat arbitrary, it being determined solely by the occurrence of genuine Norse objects. This, however, has proved to be practical, as by this means one excludes later types like the arrow head with the screw tang and the ituartit harpoon.

Within the period thus delimited we found a total of 451 types according to the classification employed here, which means about 73 per cent. of all types within the total material. To these may safely be added eight types found immediately before and after, but not within the Inugsuk period itself, so that we have 459, or 74 per cent. If to these we add the 31 special types of the Ruin Island group the number grows to 490 and the percentage to 80. These figures are direct evidence that the Inugsuk period in the 14th—15th centuries in the Thule District represented a culture culmination.

Of special features within the Inugsuk period in the truest sense, i. e. excluding the Ruin Island period, we have the following 94 types:

Thule-2 harpoon head without blade, with vestigial barbs and lashing holes,
Thule-2 harpoon head with blade parallel to the line hole, 2 unilateral spurs, holes,
Thule-2 harpoon head with blade at right-angles to the line hole, holes,
Thule-3 harpoon head with blade at right-angles to line hole,
flat harpoon head with open socket, blade, horizontal line hole (transitional type),
flat harpoon head with two line holes, one behind the other,
harpoon blade of slate,

Swivel with open back,
mending disc of wood, no groove,
loose foreshaft with 3 holes,
small socket piece with conical butt,
cylindrical socket piece, short type,
lance head without separate blade,
reserve lance head (closed socket),
harpoon rest of baleen,
seal scratcher,
sinew-twister of wood,
quiver handle with holes at right angles,
carrying handle with longitudinal grooves,
salmon-spear barb with holes and projecting back,
leister prong of baleen,
fish hook of bone,
stone sinker,
bone sinker,
ice-scoop of baleen, cornet-shaped,
—   —   racket-shaped,
gull hook with inserted barb.

Sledge upstander of bone,
(dog harness),
umiaq rib of wood,
harpoon rest for kayak, low, of wood,

harpoon rest for kayak, low, of baleen,
— 　　　— 　　, with foot, wood,
harpoon rest for kayak rack,
bone stud for kayak thong.

Knife with end blade and ornamental nails,
knife with row of side blades and end blade,
flint flaker of walrus rib,
large boat-shaped box, of wood,
foursided, compound box,
ulo of slate,
ulo of baleen,
ulo handle of wood, passing smoothly into thick back,
(handle of bone for compound ulo),
concave side scraper of stone (not flint),
handle for flint scraper,
narrow scraper of wood,
two-handed scraper, caribou tibia,
— 　　　　, musk-ox (?) tibia,
— 　　　　, walrus rib,
— 　　　　, — penis bone,
— 　　　　, bear femur,
— 　　　　, — ulna,
— 　　　　, — radius,
cup-shaped scraper of walrus cranial bone,
lamp trimmer of stone,
— 　　of asbestos,
cooking pot with outside ornamental line,
— 　　rounded-foursided with outside ridge,
— 　　with inside ear,
foursided drying rack of wood,
(cup-side of baleen),
small ladle of wood,
small spoon of antler,
spoon of antler with slender shank,
sucking tube,
blubber stick of wood,
handle (?) of wood,
tubular bead with transversal lines,
tubular button,
brow-band of antler,
— 　- brass,
bead of soapstone,
snow beater of bone,
— 　　of baleen, concave butt end with hole,

Ivory with etched drawing.
gambling bones carved in walrus ivory,
string for string figures,
top disc of bone,
whale figure,
fox figure,

doll representing Norseman,
doll of soapstone,
toy arrow, pointed,
- sling handle of baleen,
- sledge upstander of wood,
- umiaq, baleen,
- ulo handle,
- snow knife of baleen,
- lamp with ledge at back,

drum handle of wood,
amulet stone,
split bear's jaw,
kayak-shaped amulet box,
skin cap,

dot and circle ornament,
seal-tail (?) ornament.

This gives about 21 per cent., that is to say a still higher percentage of special features than for the Ruin Island group. If to these we add the 13 features that are shared exclusively with the Ruin Island group—and which of course must be regarded as characteristic of that time—the number of special types rises to 107 and the percentage to almost 24.

Of the 100 types registered either before or after Inugsuk plus the Ruin Island group, 74 belong to the earlier and 26 to the later period. The 74 types which entirely disappear are thus in the Inugsuk period not only made up for by others, but there is an influx of 33 new types. Which types disappeared has already been shown in the foregoing when dealing with the three periods in question; the others will be accounted for in the following.

Here we need mention only those types which date back to the Thule and the Dorset period, but which have their upper limit in the Inugsuk period—the types which the latter shares exclusively with the early transitional period having already been listed on page 68, while the types which stop at the Ruin Island group are shown under that heading on page 71. Taken all together these types help to characterize the early culture in the Thule District. The types to be added are the following 59; those shown in brackets are not counted, as it is directly obvious that their limited occurrence is due to accident.

Thule-2 harpoon head without blade, with slots,
— — — — —, with holes,
Thule-3 harpoon head with holes, oblique spur and sharply-cut socket (hexagonal type),
toggle harpoon head with closed socket and lateral keel, the blade parallel with the line hole,

Thin toggle harpoon head, closed socket, no blade,
— — — —, — — , blade parallel with line hole, modern type,
flat harpoon head, closed socket, blade, curved line hole, single dorsal spur,
similar, but with two bilateral spurs (Pl. 4.25),
loose foreshaft with separate, flat butt-piece,
hollow scraper with iron blade, modern type,
toy side prong for bird dart, wood,
- sledge upstander, modern type,

In all 8 types, or over 8 per cent.

In conclusion I shall show the lower limit for some types that occur up to recent time and are not included in any of the foregoing groups.

Lower limit in early transitional period:
Thule-1 harpoon head (with holes),
Thule-3 harpoon head, concave socket, spur continuing line of butt end,
lance head (or knife), blade slit,
small toggle with oblong hole,
toggle with 2—3 holes (for towing line),
(salmon spear, middle prong),
sledge shoe of antler,
whip handle of baleen,
harpoon rest for kayak, with foot, bone,
blunt bone knife,
knife with end blade and unilateral end knob,
bow-drill shank, bone,
ulo with separate blade part,
stone scraper, dolomite,
lamp trimmer of wood, with groove,
oval cooking pot with transversal holes,
tub stave,
baleen snow beater with asymmetrically curved butt,
ajagaq, seal radius,
foursided toy cooking pot,
drum, bone.

Lower limit in Inugsuk and Ruin Island period:
Thule-3 harpoon head, undercut socket and oblique spur,
Thule-3 harpoon head, spur continuing line of butt end, widened fore end,
Thule-3 harpoon head, widened fore end and deep line grooves rearwards,
harpoon-sledge runner,
sealing-stool leg, wood, with constricted neck,
compound sledge runner, bone,
sledge shoe, walrus ivory,
snow knife, knob on back,
knife handle, bone, lateral end-blade,
knife with side blade at one side,
— — — — at both sides,
knife with row of side blades,
knife-handle butt with scarf face,

atypical stone knife with ground edge,
ulo handle, bone, broad and low,
toy lamp, no ledge.

There remain now only those types that were encountered right from the ancient Thule culture on Inglefield Land up to recent time and therefore can tell us nothing whatever as to the chronology. On the other hand they provide a rough reflection of some of the most primary and constant elements in the Eskimo culture. These are:

Thin harpoon head, closed socket, single dorsal spur,
foreshaft for icehunting harpoon,
ice pick with scarf face,
  - — — triangular butt,
side prong for bird dart, inside barbs,
baleen bow,
bow brace of antler,
arrow head with knobs,
arrow shaft,
sling handle of wood,
barb for salmon spear with scarf face,
leister prong,
gull hook with oblique groove,
sledge runner, bone,
sledge shoe, narwhal ivory,
  — — , bone,
  — — , baleen,
  — cross-slat, bone,
trace buckle, ovoid, parallel holes,
hand-drill shank, bone,
bow-drill shank, wood,
bow-drill mouthpiece, caribou astragalus,
whetstone,
hammerstone,
wedge of bone and the like,
marline spike, round, pointed,
stone scraper, blunt,
lamp trimmer, wood,
cooking pot with inside suspension holes,
  — - , foursided with rounded corners,
meat tray, wood,
baleen bowl, oval,
baleen cup,
meat stick of rib,
large hook, antler,
bone rim with row of holes (for skin vessel),
ribs for skin vessel (?) wood,
bone mountings, sundry,
thong buckle,
comb with angular handle,
gambling bones,

doll with flat face, no feet,
— — — —, with boots,
— — — —, with hood and coat,
toy sledge cross-slat, wood,
baleen line with knots,

making 46 types in all and forming the regular features of the implement culture within every period ascertained in the Thule District— though with some reservation as regards a few types of recent times and possibly of the Dorset period too.

House types of the various periods.

The excavations have been unable to throw any light upon the question of how the houses of the Dorset period looked; for the present, then, we must assume that they resembled those of the Thule culture, as indeed seems to appear from Jenness' description from Cape Dorset and Coats Island[1]).

The excavated houses in the Thule District, dated up to the close of the Inugsuk time, are all partly dug into the ground and built on slightly sloping terrain, which permits of the minimum amount of soil to dig out, the longitudinal section of the house being stepped: passage-floor-platform. This is of practical importance, as the ground is often frozen to just below the surface, a circumstance that must also be borne in mind in connection with the entrance passage, the depth of which seems to vary somewhat. As a consequence of the sloping ground the front part of the house consists of a wall of stone, or stone and turf; the latter was certainly the case in the least well-preserved houses. At the back it would seem that the masonry was often confined to a line of stones to support the turf wall, and in many instances the chances are that there was not even this line of stones, but merely a low wall of turf. This of course would suffice in a domed house.

As to the construction of the roof, nothing definite could be ascertained; but in view of the frequent occurrence of large whale ribs inside the houses there can scarcely be any doubt but that whale bones often provided the material. On the outside the houses had a thick wall of turf, and it is possible that in less solidly-built houses these walls formed a necessary part of the bearing construction.

In the majority of cases the houses were more or less rounded, though several consist of two, three or more houses with a common passage, whereby angular and more or less clover-leaf shaped houses appear. In several cases, however, there are rectangular corners, and

---

[1]) Jenness 1925 p. 430 f.

some of the houses are distinctly foursided (rectangular) in plan. Disregarding the latter for the present, the houses in the Thule District as a whole correspond to the round houses in West Greenland described by Mathiassen.

Mathiassen regards these "round houses" as the whale-bone house of the Thule culture transplanted to the soil of Greenland. No doubt can indeed be entertained of the existence of a close relationsship; nevertheless the question is: how did the change connected with it take place, and what on the whole was the course of the historical development? The houses Mathiassen excavated on the 5th Thule Expedition were in most cases in such a state of collapse or obliteration that their shape could not be ascertained in detail; but his drawings and descriptions show that most frequently the houses were circular or oval, i. e. genuine round houses. In the Greenland houses, even those of earliest days, this form is modified in so many instances that it is justifiable to ask what caused this modification—the material, foreign influence, or a more indeterminable "evolution"? And when and where did it begin?

It has never been shown beyond question that the foursided houses in Greenland were due to Norse influence—at any rate not exclusively. It is true that the rectangular houses found in the Thule District must be placed to a time when Norse influence theoretically was able to assert itself; but it is curious that these houses were found only on Inglefield Land and not down in Thule (apart from House 16). Matters appear most clearly at Cape Kent; but Inf. Houses 3 and 11, presumably closely related in time, are also rectangular, and the same applies to Inf. Houses 12, 14 and 16, which are presumed to be somewhat earlier. The houses pictured by Simmons in Ellesmere Land are also foursided[2]). The earliest Inuarfigssuaq houses are more or less rounded, but in Houses 8, 18, 20, 21 and 29 there are certain rectangular corners with distinct masonry, so that all doubt about the shape there is precluded. In the latter case there can be no question whatever of Norse influence, and as regards the other houses mentioned, it is scarcely credible that the shape of the house would be the first victim of a new influence. The stone material at Cape Kent is excellent for permanent wall building, which undoubtedly is the reason why these houses are in such a good state of preservation; but it is improbable that this alone is the reason why an absolutely rectangular house suddenly made its appearance. In conjunction with the rudiments seen in some of the early houses it is presumable that tradition or a more remote influence lies behind.

---

[1]) Mathiassen 1934 p. 170 ff.
[2]) Simmons 1905 fig. 6.

But with our present knowledge of the house forms in Canada it is impossible to follow the trail farther along that line.

Conditions are somewhat blurred in the Inugsuk time proper at Thule. Here we find both rounded and foursided erections, in most cases a cross between both, and in addition there is the separate kitchen; and in the subsequent period, indicated especially by Houses 4, 7 and 22, greatly rounded forms seem to get the upper hand. Between these latter houses and the group consisting of Inf. Houses 4, 5, 6 and 7, however, we find the curious similarity that the passage leads well into the house, the foremost rooms being built forward on each side of the passage. In Inf. House 5 there was even a platform above the inner part of the passage. Whether this was the case in the other houses of this type could not be determined; if anything one must say it is improbable; in House 5 the inhabitants would seem to have been pinched for room and to have utilized the space to the utmost.—However, it looks as if it is this type of spacious house that continues up through the Inugsuk period and is combined with features from the Ruin Island houses, especially their kitchen; and when kitchens again fall into disuse, the original house tradition becomes even more distinct. In between, but prior to the appearance of the kitchen, we have the foursided houses at Cape Kent and Cape Russell. Another characteristic feature of the latter is the small, rectangular offshoots at the front, often with a low stone table, where neither soot nor slag was observed in any case and which accordingly can hardly have contained a fireplace. Similar offshoots are to be seen at several of the Inuarfigssuaq houses too.

It would thus appear that a development in the direction of foursided houses culminated with the Cape Kent houses, whereafter it was interrupted by another current which leaves its mark upon the houses of the following period. However, that this does not signify the close of the saga of the foursided house is very evident from the youngest houses at Aunartoq with their thick masonry, cantilever stones and flagged roof. There, however, the rounded forms had not been entirely abandoned either, and history shows that in the end it was these that held the field in the typical "pear-shaped" Cape York house of recent time. It would thus seem that this latter type was not a direct derivation of the round house. Through the centuries in the Thule District there was apparently some wavering between the two principles, round or foursided, as between harpoon heads with an open or a closed socket.

It is deserving of notice, however, that this hesitation as to type is observable on Ruin Island itself; there in fact we find all transitional forms from oval to foursided, and it is interesting to see that the most foursided houses (Ruin Island House 6 and Thule House 16) happen to be those which we have had to interpret as qagsse's. It is quite incredible that a cult house owed its shape to the Norsemen; on the contrary, there must be an ancient tradition behind it.

In Baffin Island, and indeed among the Central Eskimos, we find round qagsse's of snow[1]). W. Thalbitzer, who has made a special study of the Eskimo cult house[2]), assumes the snowhouse qagsse ("the playing house built of snow mentioned by Poul Egede") to be a secondary development and that there was a "primary arctic type of more solid qashes for the earliest immigrants, no doubt continued side by side with the snow qashes right down to and after Egede's time"[3]).

The fact that such solid qagsse's were used in Greenland appears from Mathiassen's excavations in the Julianehaab District, where House 2 on Tugtutûp isua and House 22 on Igdlutalik can scarcely be anything else[4]). They are round, whereas those at Thule are foursided. It would thus seem that there are at least two ancient qagsse traditions represented in Greenland, the round one pointing more in the direction of the Central Eskimos, whose round snowhouse Birket-Smith considers as belonging to the earliest Eskimo form of house[5]). There may perhaps also be reason to think that the snowhouse qagsse is primary in relation to the stone house—if not in Greenland, then at any rate within Canadian Eskimo culture. This question, however, is connected with that of whether the earliest Eskimos on the whole knew of the qagsse institution, or whether it reached the Central Eskimos from the west at a relatively late point of time in conjunction with the higher development of the Thule culture—a question that is difficult to settle. In the latter case it is possible that the first round qagsse was of stone; but the very significance of the qagsse to these Central Eskimos engenders the suspicion that it is a culture element dating far back among the original inland Eskimos.

The foursided qagsse points farther to the west, towards Alaska, and this can hardly be unconnected with the fact that several other features on Ruin Island clearly point in the same direction. For the present, however, we must simply establish the fact that foursided houses are an ancient element in the Eskimo culture; and conditions in the Thule District show indeed that there is no reason for assuming otherwise than that the earliest known foursided house constructions in Greenland are also in conformity with ancient Eskimo tradition.

---

[1]) Boas 1888 p. 600.
[2]) Thalbitzer 1925.
[3]) Thalbitzer 1941 p. 669.
[4]) Mathiassen 1936 p. 21 fig. 5; p. 50 fig. 24.
[5]) Birket-Smith 1929 II p. 48.

III. THULE IN RELATION TO THE REST OF GREENLAND

Inugsuk.

After this examination of the forms of culture in the Thule District and of the chronology, which simultaneously has been a kind of cross-check on the correctness of the conclusions drawn from the first analysis, we may now begin to turn our eyes outwards for the purpose of trying to establish a correlation with the principal earlier finds. In this connection the most natural course will be—where conditions are favourable—first to endeavour to fit the other finds into the sequence which it has been possible to establish in the Thule District, and then, on the basis of similarities or divergences thereby determined, to draw what conclusions may be possible as to the mutual relations. By this means we shall also be provided with the possibility of making a further, reciprocal correction with regard to chronology, a matter of vital importance to our comprehension of the course of developments in the Eskimo culture.

We shall begin by comparing with the material from other parts of Greenland, and accordingly it will be most natural to commence with the large collective find from the old midden at Inugsuk, excavated in 1929 by Th. Mathiassen[1]. If we employ the same detailed division into types as that used for Thule in order to preserve uniformity of treatment, we find that for Inugsuk we have in all 345 types, of which 292 occur in the Thule District as well, whereas 53 were not found there. These diverging types are:

Thin toggle harpoon head, open socket, blade, dorsal and ventral spurs.
thin harpoon head, closed socket, blade at right angles to the line hole, one barb and dorsal spur.
similar, but with two barbs,
flat harpoon head, closed socket, blade parallel to line hole, 2 barbs, 2 dorsal spurs,
flat harpoon head, closed socket, blade, no barbs, obliquely cut butt, only one line hole,

---

[1] Th. Mathiassen 1930 (a).

ice-harpoon foreshaft, wood,
toggle for harpoon bladder, wood,
bladder-dart head, one barb, blade, (Thule similar, but no blade),
reserve lance head, open socket (Thule similar, but closed socket),
wound needle, wood,
toggle for towing line, baleen,
marline spike with ornamentation,
arrow head, baleen,
arrow blade, angmaq,
wolf-killer, baleen,
side prong for bird dart, with eye for lashing,
umiaq paddle handle,
harpoon rest with foot, baleen,
kayak scraper, antler,
prismatic whetstone with hole,
bow-drill bit, angmaq,
— - , antler,
graving tool,
bodkin of bones inserted into one another,
needle case of special form,
toggle-shaped thimble holder,
spoon of wood, thin handle,
spoon of mussel shell,
ladle, bone,
oval thick box lid,
baleen basket with sharp bottom,
— — — — — , miniature,
bag, sealskin,
bag, bladder skin,
baleen door,
lice catcher,
back scratcher (?) with teeth, bone,
— — — — , baleen,
ajagaq stick, baleen,
ball, skin,
propeller, wood,
bear figure, wood,
toy harpoon head, baleen (Thule 2),
- — — , — (Inugsuk type),
- — — , — , flat, no blade,
- knife, antler,
- — , wood,
- — , walrus ivory,
- ulo, baleen,
- meat tray, wood,
- baleen platform mat,
game piece, wood,
— — , baleen,

Apart from the harpoon heads these are chiefly variations of types that have also been found in the Thule District, and in several cases it must be accidental that they were not found there; what is more, 9 of the types are only toys.

The 292 types which Inugsuk has in common with the Thule District have the following distribution there:

```
 1 only in the early Thule culture (Th.),
 4  —  -  the early transitional period (etr.),
 2  —  -  the Ruin Island group (Ru.),
25  —  -  the Inugsuk period (In.),
 4  —  -  late transitional period (ltr.)

 2 Thule and early transitional,
11 etr., Ru and In.,
 3 Ru. and In.,
19 common features with upper limit in Inugsuk,
36 etr, Ru., In. and ltr.
14 Ru., In. and ltr.

171 general distribution.
```

Thus we have in all 121 types capable of being considered in a chronological comparison. If these figures are set up with reference to the periods to which they apply we get the following table:

	ltr.		In.		Ru.		etr.		Th.
	4		25		2		4		1
				3		11		2	
		14		36			19		
Total...	18		66				34		3

It will be seen that the preponderance lies within the Inugsuk period, but that it inclines strongly down towards the early transitional period. In other words, according to this argument the Inugsuk midden corresponds most nearly to a fairly early section of what I have called Thule's Inugsuk period. Naturally, we cannot venture to assume that all the types have the same validity as evidence, and I do not regard this table as conclusive; but the figures are an indication.

In order to get somewhat nearer to the facts we may first examine the "harpoon spectrum"[1] of the various regions, a method that has proved useful in so many cases previously. For the Inugsuk midden I have made use of the figures given by Mathiassen[2]. In the following table everything is calculated in percentages (approximately) of the total number of harpoon heads for each locality.

---

[1] Mathiassen 1931, p. 73.
[2] Mathiassen 1930 (a) p. 180.

	ltr.	ltr-In.	In.	In-Ru-etr.	Ru-etr.	etr.	Inugsuk
thin, open sock., barbed ..	2	11	15	20	35	23	14½
- - - , toggle ...	57	45	40	35	17	18	12
thin, closed - , - ...	32½	36½	38	37	33	35	55
flat, open - , - ...	6½	3	2	4	12	18	3½
- , closed - , - ...	2	4½	5	4	3	6	14½
total closed	35	41	43	41	36	41	70
total flat	8½	7½	7	8	15	24	18

It will be observed at once that there is no unequivocal conformity between the Inugsuk midden and any of the groups in the Thule District. But on examining the mutual proportions of the thin harpoon heads we find that Inugsuk comes nearest to the early transitional period, though the Inugsuk harpoon head has a disproportionate preponderance at Inugsuk; and the same applies when we consider the proportions between thin and flat harpoon heads: Inugsuk is nearest the early transitional period. On the other hand the proportion between open and closed-socketed, flat harpoon heads nowhere agrees with Thule, but comes nearest in Thule's "high Inugsuk period". At no time do the thin harpoon heads with a closed socket (Inugsuk harpoon heads) attain to a corresponding preponderance in Thule, but the similarity here too is greatest in the Inugsuk period itself. In addition, besides the said harpoon heads at Inugsuk there were two with a closed socket and barbs[1]), forms that are quite foreign to Thule.

With this as a background we must conclude that developments in Thule and in the Upernavik District did not keep pace with each other through what somewhat boldly we call the Inugsuk period. The threads seem to converge most in the early transitional period, i. e. at a fairly early juncture, after intercourse with the Norsemen had been established; or rather, until then we may presume that there was a common development which, however, then divides; and even if contact is not entirely broken it is not close enough to keep the two regions on the same track.

It is evident that with regard to harpoon heads Thule is the more conservative. Throughout the whole Inugsuk period the percentage of closed-socketed harpoon heads is almost constant. In the early transitional period the number of flat harpoon heads is markedly high, but it soon falls. Apparently a development of flat harpoon heads was accelerated at an early time, but in Thule it stopped for some reason— possibly owing to influence from the Ruin Island people, who seem not to have used flat harpoon heads. On the other hand Thule again turned to the open-socketed thin harpoon heads, whereas to the south

---

[1]) Mathiassen 1930 (a) p. 183.

they retained the flat ones and evolved them in the direction of closed-socketed forms, later with barbs. It is true that towards the late transitional period, i. e. the close of the Inugsuk period, the number of flat heads grows a little in Thule, but these are open-socketed forms and they increase at the expense of the closed types.

As developments to some extent have thus gone separate ways and we know nothing of the rate of these developments at the two places, we are similarly unable to determine what in one midden is contemporary with what in the other, nor do we know how long was the time that elapsed between the separation of the two groups of people and the beginning of the two middens; the rather far-advanced differentiation of the harpoon heads suggests that the period was a fairly long one. If with Mathiassen we estimate that the Inugsuk midden dates from the 13th—14th century, the assumption must be that the early transitional period, in which the Norse relics begin to appear in the Thule District, falls in the 12th—13th century; and accordingly within this period (more likely in the 12th century) came the emigration from Thule which lies behind the formation of the midden at Inugsuk.

Matters can be further elucidated, however, by the aid of other implement types, though all the time they point in the direction indicated above. As regards the knives, the position is quite curious. For the entire stretch early transitional period—Inugsuk—late transitional period, Thule produced 97 knives with the blade at the end and 98 with side blades, and of these only one comes from the early transitional period. The Inugsuk midden had 72 end-bladed knives and only 7 side-bladed, which suggests an early, common starting point. It might also mean (as is assumed in the foregoing) that Thule's fully developed Inugsuk culture is later than the Inugsuk midden, viz. mainly in the 15th century. The Inugsuk midden presumably is more or less contemporary with the lowest part of Comer's Midden.

Thirty ice-picks from Inugsuk have a scarf face and only one (L 4: 3461 from B. 17.9) has a triangular butt. In Thule in the early transitional period the numbers are 13 — 5 (Co. A IV, 2 — 0) and in the Inugsuk period 15 — 13. The supposition I have voiced (I p. 203) that ice-picks with a triangular butt were associated particularly with walrus hunting on the ice (though the introduction of this special type must be purely historical) is supported by the circumstance that they fall into disuse in the south, where presumably there was not so much of this kind of hunting. The specimen from Inugsuk is the only one I have been able to find in the collections of the National Museum from the whole of West Greenland. It is also in line with the foregoing that the characteristic maul head of bone from Inugsuk (Mathiassen pl. 11.7) has its only parallel at Cape Kent, and two-handed scrapers of caribou metacarpus, which are common in the Inugsuk midden, were found solely on Inglefield Land and thus in the Thule District belong mainly to the early Thule culture. Furthermore, tub staves with grooves at both ends, of which Inugsuk produced three, were found only in Co. A IV at Thule, and top-discs of soapstone only in the early Thule culture.

However, opposite these things stand the great number that bear resemblance to Thule's Inugsuk period. It must be taken for granted that, in spite of the distance, there was some interchange between the two regions via Melville Bay, by which means Norse objects and types such as ornamental bodkins and spoons of antler with a slender, carved handle came to Thule. But with regard to the many new forms, especially of baleen objects, it is hard to decide how much is the result of interchange and how much mutual inheritance. It would seem that the development of baleen technique was making great strides at an early time, certainly before the appearance of the Ruin Island people; and as in this respect Thule and Inugsuk often supplement each other, there may be reason for supposing that it was due mainly to their common origin.

The Inugsuk contains no perceptible evidence of direct influence from the Ruin Islanders. The one specifically common feature is the toy kayak of baleen, and this may be due to accident; on the other hand it is possible that the curious needle-case (Mathiassen pl. 14.1) may have some connection with them; in any case it has a distinctly westerly stamp about it. It looks as if the Ruin Island people had already lost their own characteristics in Thule—if we except the house with the kitchen. Unfortunately we do not know much about the form of the houses that belonged to the Inugsuk midden.

If we disregard the Ruin Island group with its 31 special features, Thule's Inugsuk and early transitional period still has about 150 features not found in the Inugsuk midden. We know of course that the latter was only a remnant, the rest having been washed away, so there is a possibility that it contained many other types than those that were found; but if at the same time it is remembered that on essential points it displays closest association with what in Thule must be regarded as the earliest period of the Inugsuk time, it seems justifiable to inquire whether the Thule District (and Ellesmere Island?) should not rather be considered as the home of the development which Mathiassen has called the Inugsuk culture—at any rate a very large part of it. What is due to Norse influence comprises only very few forms, and at any rate there is nothing to show that the strong development of the kayak technique may not very well have begun in Thule or more to the west. The Thule District is the great stage where a numerous population, growing constantly by means of new influxes from the west and living high on productive whaling, had possibilities of raising their culture up to a considerable height according to Eskimo standards. It is a development on the Eskimo culture's own foundation that was fundamental in the Inugsuk culture and gave it its great power of expansion, even if some of its characteristic types bear the impress of influence from the Norsemen; and if particular importance has been attached to the latter, it is chiefly on account of their great value as a time-determining factor.

House Forms in West and South Greenland.

From more southerly parts of Greenland we have a quantity of systematically excavated midden material from Therkel Mathiassen's expeditions, especially to Disko Bay and the Kangâmiut region. In volume it cannot compare with the Inugsuk midden, but it put Mathiassen in a position to build up a detailed chronology for West Greenland and the coast round to Angmagssalik. In addition, we know quite a lot about the house forms, and in this connection it will be practical first to examine these and see how they compare with what we now know from the Thule District.

On several occasions Mathiassen has described the types of houses in Greenland: for Upernavik District[1]), the Kangâmiut region[2]), Disko Bay[3]) and a broader survey in "Skrælingerne i Grønland"[4]). In brief outlines the position is this: The *small round houses* (including double and triple houses) on the whole held their ground on the west coast until the middle of the 17th century, i. e. up to the time of the European whalers. In Disko Bay, however, there was a partial change to *small, foursided houses* with no kitchen already in the 16th century. At Kangâmiut and in the Julianehaab District these foursided houses apparently made their real apearance only in the middle of the 17th century, soon to be replaced by the *long communal houses* which remained in use throughout West Greenland till well into the 19th century, when *small foursided houses with no sunken passage* came into use. In the Julianehaab District, however, we find a gradual change-over to foursided houses as early as in the earliest period, from about 1350 to 1650[5]). Of these house types only the first two have been found in the Thule District—though the last one too gained some popularity in most recent years, a fact that may be disregarded in the present connection.

Of the four types of houses referred to above, only the last two seem to be quite stable in West Greenland. The early small foursided

---

[1]) Mathiassen 1930 (c) p. 11.
[2]) Mathiassen 1931 p. 55 ff.
[3]) Mathiassen 1934 p. 170 ff.
[4]) Mathiassen 1935 p. 120 ff.
[5]) Mathiassen 1936 p. 84.

house with its sunken passage seems stable too, but the transition to this form is so graduated that one should rather call it a final result which is quickly abandoned for the long communal house. Now it would seem that the small foursided house is the fundamental element in the communal house, by virtue both of its shape and the time of its appearance; but the idea itself, of uniting a row of small houses into one large one, appears to date farther back.

In 1909 Steensby had some plans drawn for him of Polar-Eskimo houses[2]), of which a double house of a kind similar to Aunartoq House 11 induced him to set up the hypothesis that this was the prototype of the West Greenland communal house. I am inclined to believe that Steensby was right in that theory—not that the Polar-Eskimo pear-shaped house was the prototype of the one in West Greenland, because for chronological reasons that would seem impossible, as the type is evidently of relatively late date in the Thule District; but in Mathiassen's material, both the published and the unpublished measurements of houses in Disko Bay and the Julianehaab District, which he has kindly placed at my disposal, there are many houses of just that type, from which both the double houses in the Thule District (cantilever construction) and the West Greenland communal houses may have been evolved.

Steensby considered that the foursided Greenland house and the pear-shaped Cape York house were both descendants of the Point Barrow house, the material in each case having determined the form[2]); but the position obviously is not so simple as all that. Nor will the available material permit us to say with certainty whether the particular form of double house, "parallel houses", originated south or north of Melville Bay.

With regard to the "small round houses", Mathiassen himself points out that this term comprises a wealth of variations, some with a kitchen, others without, "some are very small, round houses, others are large complexes with two, or more rarely three, rooms built together and with a common passage. The shape of these rooms also varies a good deal, some of them being round, others oval or irregularly angular, but never a regular rectangle"[3]). Thus through West Greenland's Inugsuk period we see the same wavering as to house form as that observed in Thule, where we might also add the whole of the earliest period, the time of the Thule culture. In actual fact only a minority of the houses are round or oval in plan, even if most may be said to be more or less rounded.

Whether or not a house of this kind in principle is round is a

---

[1]) Steensby 1910 p. 322, fig. 15.
[2]) Steensby 1916 p. 196.
[3]) Mathiassen 1934 p. 171 ff.

question which technically can best be decided by the aid of the roof construction. Thule-culture houses with a roof constructed mainly of whale ribs may be assumed to be round in principle, and if the builders erected a dome-shaped roof of ribs placed radially, one need scarcely doubt that there was a "round" tradition behind it. In houses of recent times in the Thule District the principle seems to be a similar one, as all the big tikutit stones (cantilevers) on top of the wall point in towards the middle of the house. One of these houses with an entire ring of tikutit is to be seen in the National Museum in Copenhagen, and I have a sketch of a similar one from Kangerdlugssuaq (Inglefield Gulf). Naturally the weight of these stones requires a very solid base, which is undoubtedly the reason why the masonry in the more recent Aunartoq houses is so enormous compared with their size.

It is hard to say, however, whether in the last instance there is a direct connection with the tradition of the whale-bone house, as the Aunartoq houses in the first place are rather foursided, and secondly, in principle they seem to have had only two tikutit, one on each side. So on this basis we cannot decide whether this construction originally was associated with a round house or a foursided one. However, Knud Rasmussen found similar tikutit constructions at Malerualik, and these houses seem to have been round or oval[1]), though he says that they were in a bad state of collapse and difficult to measure. This suggests that the knowledge of this ingenious roof design dates rather far back and really is related to the radial whale-bone roof; and also that the ancient tradition in the Thule District entered into a sort of compromise with the foursided house form, whereby it became possible to reduce the number of tikutit to two. Later, when no doubt people became more expert at employing this form of architecture, they went back to the use of an entire ring of cantilevers, by which means it was possible to make the house more spacious in conjunction with the rounded form that is characteristic of the "pear-shaped" house. Where and when this construction originated it is impossible to decide; but the evidence indicates that it was not forgotten—even after periods such as the Inugsuk time, when presumably there was ample whale-bone material to be had—if the method is at all so old. For it must be admitted that we are ignorant of the entire course of the development of roof forms, and there is something in the argument that the use of stone cantilevers is connected with the decline of whaling, first of course in localities unfavourable to that form of hunting, and conditioned by the fact that driftwood was hard to procure.

It is of interest that in one of the aforesaid houses at Malerualik (House 4) there were fireplaces "a little above the height of the platform

---

[1]) Mathiassen 1927 I p. 308.

inside the house, built upon a large flat stone; similar fireplaces have been found in other houses here". This makes one think of the Cape Kent houses, where there were niches with stone tables, though no fireplaces, and of the later houses in Thule with fireplaces at the front wall. There seems to be an historical connection between these phenomena even if it cannot be traced satisfactorily at the moment.

Access to driftwood provides the possibility of a roof with a thick longitudinal (or transversal) beam. In conjunction with whale ribs the result would be a kind of barrel vault, and for a long foursided house like Cape Kent House 1 this would seem to be a natural explanation. In the rounded houses it is more probable that the roof was an intermediate type, there being a principal beam (or more than one in double or triple houses), from which smaller timbers, or perhaps whale bones, were placed fanwise out to the walls, the same principle as that employed in the Eskimo screen-shaped tent. Presumably something of the same kind was to be found in the houses with two cantilevers. Naturally, this method is also applicable to constructions of whale bone alone, and a long whale bone with a very thick baleen lashing at one end, found in Ruin Island House 2, might suggest that it actually was in use. In House VIII at Qilalukan Mathiassen also found several whale bones with baleen lashings. In the whale-bone houses of the Thule culture it is probable that the Eskimos often had to adopt the expedient of lashing the beams together out of two or more ribs. On the whole, in its construction this type of house seems to be a modified form of an earlier, "purer" type which via another route found complete expression in the spiral-built snow house.

However, we know nothing of how much the material, especially access to driftwood, may have influenced the roof construction, and through this the form of the houses in the Thule District. As far as Alaska is concerned Collins demonstrated that the material was of subordinate importance[1]. It was also mentioned above that the occurrence in Greenland of houses which must be regarded as qagsses, suggests a *tradition* of both rounded and foursided houses, so much the more as the round form has been found in the south where there are ample supplies of driftwood, whereas the foursided one is from the Thule District. Tradition and material must presumably have worked hand in hand. At any rate in the Thule District there is nothing to show that the material alone determined the one or the other form of house, such as seems to have been Steensby's main idea[2]. Meantime the result in Thule was a rounded house and in West Greenland a foursided one;

---

[1] Collins 1937 p. 284.
[2] Steensby 1916 p. 196.

the fact that the latter gained so firm a footing may then have some connection with a knowledge of the houses of the Norsemen.

Accordingly it has not been possible to establish any particular form of house as being typical of the houses of the Inugsuk period in Greenland (up to about 1650). It is another matter when we consider a not inessential feature of the house, viz. its kitchen or fireplace. In itself of course it is something of a revolution suddenly to install an open fireplace inside the house; that in Greenland it must have been introduced rather suddenly appears with great clarity from conditions in the Thule District, where the properly built-out kitchens—and fireplaces on the whole in the houses—make their appearance only well into the Inugsuk period. It may be that here they were chiefly associated with the very element of the population that introduced them.

A glance at the house plans now available, in conjunction with Mathiassen's descriptions, makes it evident that houses with a kitchen or a fireplace were common in the West Greenland of Inugsuk time, if not the commonest; and houses in which no fireplace has been observed are often among the poorest preserved, as well as circular or oval in shape; in other words, they are among the earliest of the houses. This applies for instance to Igdlorssuit in Disko Bay Houses VI and XVII (13th—14th century); in the Kangâmiut area Utorqait Houses 14 and 21, Igdlutalik House 1 and perhaps House 5, and at Ingik possibly some of Houses 6, 7 and 9—13, in the Julianehaab District Tugtutûp isua Houses 1, 2, 3, 5 (?), 21 (?) and 24, Narssarssuaq House 5 (?), Igdlutalik House 22, and possibly Ûnartoq Houses 1 and 2. Except for the last two these are single houses, and their condition indicates that they may be numbered among the very earliest at their particular localities.

Of the houses which Mathiassen himself regards as among the earliest are some with no kitchen, but with an undeniably foursided form, e. g. Igdlutalik in Disko Bay House VIII (11th—12th century) and House IV (presumably 13th—14th century). In the Julianehaab District there are several: Tugtutûp isua Houses 4 and 10, Narssarssuaq House 1, and Igdlutalik Houses 7, 9, 10, 13 and 20. It is thus impracticable to differentiate chronologically between round and foursided; the two principles run side by side from the earliest time and often overlap, so that intermediate forms arise, until the purely foursided form predominates in the 17th century.

This of course agrees very well with conditions in the Thule District; but then the question is: how old are the *houses with kitchens in West Greenland*? As already stated, I take it for granted that in the Thule District they came with the immigration of the Ruin Island people, and from Thule the kitchen made its way southwards. On the whole, then, the Inugsuk period houses with a kitchen in West Greenland must be later than those on Ruin Island—unless one prefers to assume that they originated independently at each place, which would be a rather improbable explanation having regard to the migration southwards which took place just in this period. I have previously pointed out that Ruin Island of course does not necessarily represent the very first of these newcomers, and we know nothing definite of how long the immigration time lasted. Prior to that immigration there must have been a more peaceable time, when coopering technique etc. succeeded in transplanting itself to the Thule District, and at some time in this period the Ruin Island people or their predecessors began to appear. It even looks as if now it was these strangers who formed the connecting link between Thule and more southerly parts. To the south we find evidence of them in the houses with a kitchen; on the other hand this seems to be the only evidence.

However, we hear nothing of the Norsemen's acquaintance with the Scraelings in Greenland until towards the close of the 12th century[1], and from other records it appears that in this first period intercourse was not particularly intimate. We are told that in 1266 a journey was made farther north than usual, but no Scraeling were seen elsewhere than in Krogsfjordshede (possibly Disko Bay?); and on a subsequent journey still farther north—possibly to Melville Bay—traces of Scraelings were observed at two places[2]. Finally, the rune-stone at Kingigtorssuaq is presumed to date from 1333. Although this does not say much about the Eskimo settlement in North Greenland, and nothing at all about trade between the Eskimos themselves, the inference is that Norse objects cannot have reached the Thule District until some time in the 13th century, and consequently the Ruin Island people must have come about the year 1300 at the earliest. On the other hand, it is just in this period that the pressure southwards is intensified and, about the middle of the 14th century, leads to the destruction of the West Settlement. It is natural to combine these events, and the result is that houses with a kitchen in West Greenland at the earliest can date from the beginning of the 14th century.

In so far there is nothing improbable in this; but the consequence is that at any rate some of the old houses on Igdlutalik in Disko Bay, which Mathiassen considers as representing the time previous to the Inugsuk culture (presumably 10th—12th century)[3], cannot well be earlier than about 1300, for they are furnished with a kitchen placed

---

[1] Historia Norvegia; Mathiassen 1941 p. 45.
[2] Nørlund 1934 p. 124.
[3] Mathiassen 1934 p. 85.

almost like those on Ruin Island. They might be a little earlier if we assume that the Norse objects in the Thule District came in along a direct route—by the medium of the Norsemen themselves on an expedition right up to these regions. This is a thought which cannot lightly be dismissed, but the bases of such a hypothesis are so frail that it will scarcely be profitable to pursue it; and at any rate there is hardly any prospect of getting beyond the 13th century.

On the other hand, Mathiassen places most of the earliest houses at Igdlorssuit, also in Disko Bay, to the 13th—14th century, that is to say contemporary with the Inugsuk midden, though he voices the possibility of some being earlier[1]). Farther south the chronological indications are affected less by the above arguments. In the Kangâmiut area the use of rounded houses coincides with the two earliest periods, estimated by Mathiassen to lie between 1350 and 1650[2]), and something of the same applies to the Julianehaab District[3]).

The already observed wavering between round and foursided houses continues in the houses with a kitchen. These are so irregular in shape that in most instances it is impossible to decide whether to place them in the one or in the other category. Those that are more rounded are Igdlutalik in Disko Bay Houses VII and IX, Igdlorssuit (Disko Bay) Houses VIII, X and presumably XII and XVIII, and in the Julianehaab District Tugtutûp isua House 20 and presumably Ûnartoq Houses 3 and 11. The foursided ones are, in Disko Bay, Igdlutalik House X and Igdlorssuit House VII, in the Julianehaab District Tugtutûp isua Houses 6 and 9, Igdlutalik Houses 11, 12 and 21, and Ûnartoq House 12. Of the others some are more nearly five or six-sided like Narssarssuaq House 2, Igdlutalik House 6, and Ûnartoq House 10, all in the Julianehaab District.

The character and position of the kitchen also vary, some of the houses having a painstakingly built-out kitchen with access from the house like Igdlutalik Disko Bay Houses VI, VII, IX and X, and in the Julianehaab District Tugtutûp isua Houses 6, 8, 9 and 20, Igdlutalik Houses 8, 19 and 24, and Ûnartoq Houses 3, 7, 10 and 12. In a few the entrance to the kitchen is from the passage, as in Igdlorssuit in Disko Bay Houses VII, XII and XVIII, and in Igdlutalik (Julianehaab District) Houses 6 and 11. Both the latter, and Igdlorssuit House VII, also have fireplaces inside the house. In some cases the kitchen seems to be arranged more perfunctorily in a small recess or outward turn of the wall, as in Igdlorssuit (Disko Bay) Houses VIII, X and XIV,

---
[1]) Mathiassen 1934 p. 157.
[2]) Mathiassen 1931 p. 125 f.
[3]) Mathiassen 1936 p. 84.

and in the Julianehaab District in Tugtutûp isua Houses 7 and 16, Narssarssuaq House 6, Igdlutalik House 12 and Ũnartoq Houses 9 and 11. Thus we see that here again conditions in West and South Greenland are exactly the same as those we found in Thule.

It is more remarkable, however, to find fireplaces right back in the house, where normally the platform is situated. This is the case at some places in the Julianehaab District, viz. in Tugtutûp isua Houses 12 and 15 and Igdlutalik Houses 6 and 21. The first two houses were almost obliterated, and perhaps the possibility cannot be rejected that the fireplaces are later; but in the other two they seem to have been used at any rate in conjunction with the houses. These four houses also lie within the period 1350—1650, Igdlutalik House 6 towards the end, as it contained a blue glass bead[1]).

In the Thule District there was no definite find of a fireplace in the back of a house. In Inuarfigssuaq House 6 it is true were the remains of a fireplace in the north side; here, however, conditions were very chaotic and it really seemed as if the fireplace belonged to an earlier habitation. However, Greely drew a house at Lake Hazen on Ellesmere Island which is not without interest in this connection—provided the drawing is trustworthy[2]). It is an oblong house with its greatest dimension at right angles to the passage and with a side room at one side of the passage. Both at one end wall of the house and at the back wall, vis-à-vis the entrance, Greely shows small recesses in which he found fireplaces. This involved a peculiar arrangement of the platforms, for one fireplace of course lies where the platform should be, and one side room has been given two side platforms instead of one main platform. Apparently the house has some resemblance to the Ruin Island houses, and, as regards the platform arrangement, one can discern a slight similarity to Ruin Island House 3A. The latter also contained the remains of a fireplace, but apparently in the turf wall itself, and at the front there was a carefully built kitchen. The greater part of the house was obliterated and difficult to define with any accuracy. Consequently it is not impossible that earlier there was another house here with a fireplace inside, and we must take into consideration the possibility that once it was a more general practice to have such fireplaces inside the houses. In this connection I would also recall houses in Northeast Greenland with fireplaces (at the front wall)[3]), and similar ones at Malerualik[4]). And is it possible that there may also be a connection between Greely's

[1]) Mathiassen 1936 p. 45.
[2]) Greely 1886 Vol. I p. 382.
[3]) H. Larsen 1934 p. 58.
[4]) Mathiassen 1927 I p. 308.

fireplaces and the small lamp-recesses at the rear ends of the platforms as illustrated by Wissler?[1]).

This review has given no complete clarification of the question of the forms of houses; but we have ascertained that the vagueness in West and South Greenland is common to the Thule District and consequently *must be rooted farther back in time*.

However, one thing has been touched upon only lightly as yet. Among the early houses in the Thule District the compound houses are all angular, the platforms of the two or three rooms in most cases forming a right angle to each other. In West Greenland, however, we see time after time that in the double house the platforms are parallel, or rather in a line but separated by a partition; this brings us back to Steensby's theory.

In Disko Bay there are such parallel houses in Igdlutalik Houses VI, VII and VIII and Igdlorssuit House VII, in Julianehaab District Tugtutûp isua House 4, Ũnartoq House 7 and presumably Houses 2 and 3. In the latter was a lamp with knobs, which indicates that this form of house goes rather far back in time; on the other hand, however, there seems here to be a question of a special West Greenland development— at any rate judging from the material so far available. In the Thule District this form of house occurs in more recent time, as already stated, and as long as excavations in the south part of the district have produced no other evidence, we must take it that in Thule it is the result of influence from the south. Wissler indeed illustrates some houses of this type excavated by Captain Comer[2]), but there is nothing definite to show how old they are. Judging from the detailed drawings of the platform arrangements we must assume that they are not very old.

The transition from these parallel houses to the oblong communal house seems natural once they have assumed the foursided form, as of course only the partition needs removing; and the possibility of constructing the roof in one lies in the easier access to driftwood. Thus both the shape and the principle of the oblong, foursided communal house was already latent in the earliest houses of the Inugsuk period. The advantages of it are obvious, from a technical point of view, as it means a great saving in both material and labour to be content with a house of simple form instead of quite a row of small houses. Besides this, however, social considerations may have played some rôle.

The long communal house did not reach Thule; at any rate we know of no trace of it. In advance we knew that intercourse with West

---

[1]) Wissler 1918 p. 159.
[2]) Wissler 1918 p. 159.

Greenland must have been broken off before the colonization started; but the appearance of the communal house now pushes the time down to about the beginning of the 17th century; and the absence of glass beads in the excavated houses points in the same direction. Nevertheless, the small blue bead found on the beach at Thule signifies that intercourse did not ebb out until after the appearance of the whalers—unless the whalers themselves took it up there. Still, there can scarcely have been any close cultural connection in the 17th century.

We are still without any adequate explanation of the foursided houses at Cape Kent. Apparently they bore the stamp of early Thule culture, but closer examination revealed that they must lie near the Inugsuk period; on the other hand the absence of fireplaces indicated that they were of a date prior to the year 1300. However, it must first be pointed out that not all the Cape Kent houses are foursided, and next, that they are not contemporary either, even if no culture difference was demonstrable. What is more, those in the poorest state of preservation, Houses 3, 6 and 8, are almost regularly oval in shape, so that in actual fact we have here reflected in one single settlement what was established above in regard to all West Greenland: a development from round towards foursided houses.

The characteristic feature of the small, foursided offshoots in the front wall or one of the front corners reappears in a number of houses farther south—though these have a fireplace. This is most clearly seen in Disko Bay, Igdlutalik House X, and at Igdlorssuit in the original House VIII and Houses X and XV, in the Julianehaab District at Igdlutalik House 24 and somewhat less prominently in House 8, as well as Tugtutûp isua Houses 9 and 10. As for Disko Bay, these are houses which Mathiassen estimates as dating at the latest from the 13th—14th century, which of course agrees very well with the assumption that the Cape Kent houses are 13th century. It also suggests that even in the 13th century developments were moving fast towards foursided houses in Greenland; but the immigration of the new people with the kitchen houses about the year 1300 put an end to this quiet evolution for a long time—just as seems to have been the case with the flat harpoon heads in the Thule District.

In connection with the above it is also interesting to observe that the peculiar double house at Cape Russell, with the two rooms forming an acute angle which is halved by the axis of the passage, recurs in Igdlorssuit House IX, which is 13th—14th century too, while Narssarssuaq (Julianehaab District) House 1 bears a marked resemblance to Inuarfigssuaq House 30 with its small wall projection dividing the two rooms, whose platforms, however, lie at right angles to each other. The remarkable break in the line of the front wall of Ruin Island House 5 is repeated in Ûnartoq House 12, and there is a similar one, but in the back wall, in Ûnartoq House 10 and Igdlutalik (Julianehaab District) House 6. Features such as these suggest a very close connection between the houses in these widely separated regions, and consequently also that there must have been a fairly rapid migration southwards. Furthermore, in Ûnartoq House 12 there was a pit in the floor near the front wall. Similar pits were found in Thule House 10 and Inuarfigssuaq House 7.

East Greenland.

The excavations of Th. Mathiassen in the Angmagssalik District and on the southern east coast in 1931—32[1]) have proved that the first demonstrable settlement of Southeast Greenland came by way of an immigration from the south, characterized by Inugsuk culture, probably in the latter part of the 14th century[2]). The houses are of the same form as those in West and South Greenland, i. e. in the early period alternating from round to foursided. It would seem, however, as if the foursided type had already asserted itself at an early date and possibly predominated in the 16th and 17th centuries[3]). In the 18th century we find it together with the large communal houses, which are assumed to have come to East Greenland only with a later immigration in the early part of the 18th century[4]). Thus the evolution of the house types in Southeast Greenland appears to be closely associated with the same movement in West and South Greenland, with the sole difference that the small foursided house dominated for a longer period.

In addition, the kitchen apparently was not so common. In the Angmagssalik District itself Mathiassen mentions only cooking-niches, i. e. small offshoots containing ashes or slag, at Sŭkersit (Houses 1, 5, 7 and 8), but on Frederik den VI's coast at Auarqat Sydfjord (House 6), Igdlorssuartalik, Itsarnisarmiut (Houses 3, 5, 6 and 7) and Skjoldungen (House 4). On the other hand, the only locality with well-built kitchens seems to be at Itsarnisarmiut[5]). It would thus seem that the use of a kitchen fell off quickly on the east coast, and conditions there indeed argue that the houses in East Greenland are more directly connected with the foursided houses in the Thule District than it has been possible to demonstrate anywhere in West Greenland. In the relatively isolated

---

[1]) Mathiassen 1933 and 1936 (b).
[2]) Mathiassen 1933 p. 61.
[3]) Mathiassen 1933 p. 65.
[4]) Mathiassen 1933 p. 107.
[5]) Mathiassen 1936 (b) p. 31, fig. 16.

localities the early traditions were more viable, and the newer forms of houses with a kitchen apparently had not yet taken root at the time when the first immigration to the east coast took place.

Northeast Greenland.

The types of houses in Northeast Greenland have been discussed in detail by Helge Larsen[1]). Some few houses on Clavering Island, including double houses, are classified as "rounded houses" and are thought to have come from the south. According to Glob these "oval" houses were not found in Kempe and Kong Oscar Fjord more to the south[2]); nor have they been observed more to the north, in the area covered by the Danmark Expedition[3]).

Helge Larsen's Group 2 consists of houses of "varying forms" from rounded, with the greatest width in front of the platform, to four-sided, with rounded corners, often with the greatest dimension at right angles to the direction of the passage—forms similar to those which characterize the more northerly region. And most of Glob's earliest houses in Kempe and Kong Oscar Fjord are grouped among these. A prominent feature in these houses is the blubber pits in one or both of the front corners, often in a bulge of the wall or a recess, where in several cases there were partly charred bones and seal flippers. Helge Larsen says; "the significance of these pits is not quite certain. The layer of grease, which recalls what is found on lamps and cooking pots, would indicate a cooking place"[4]).

The third group consists of rectangular or trapeziform houses with their greatest dimension in the direction of the passage. They are not sunk so deep into the ground and on the whole are in a better condition than the foregoing, though in most respects they resemble them closely, except that they are smaller and always have sharp corners at the back[5]). In the Danmarkshavn area the houses which Thostrup considers to be the latest most closely resemble Larsen's Group 3. Groups 2 and 3 together correspond to Thomsen's Northeast Greenland type[6]).

On the latest houses in Kempe and Kong Oscar Fjord Glob writes that they are very different from the latest houses in Dødemandsbugt on Clavering Island; some are large houses with widened corners at the front, and others are quite small houses, which Glob considers were

---

[1]) H. Larsen 1934 p. 52 ff.
[2]) Glob 1935, p. 79.
[3]) Thostrup 1911 Pl. II.
[4]) H. Larsen 1934 p. 56.
[5]) H. Larsen 1934 p. 60.
[6]) Th. Thomsen 1928 p. 288.

evolved by means of a reduction of the former type. However, the houses on Konglomeratnæs, which culturally are placed together with Helge Larsen's Group 2, are rectangular and in shape correspond to Group 3. Glob thinks this may be due to the use of tree trunks in the walls, or possibly that the foursided house type came from the south and only later reached Clavering Island[1]). The latter sounds very probable.

In the foregoing we saw that rounded, more or less foursided houses occur as it seems promiscuously in all other parts of Greenland up to the 17th century—in Thule in fact much later; therefore it is not surprising to find the same thing in Northeast Greenland, so that on this basis alone it is impossible to say whether house forms were influenced from the south or the north. The same may be said of the dimensions. Helge Larsen's Type 2 is usually longest at right angles to the passage, in contrast to Type 3; but as this is no constant phenomenon, and as otherwise it does not affect the arrangement of the house, it may perhaps be justifiable to regard it as individual, depending on the size of the family or a supply of sufficiently long driftwood. Something of the same kind was observable in the houses—including those of the early period— in the Julianehaab District, and in the Thule District we encounter the same, as Cape Kent House 1 differs from the others there in being longer than it is deep.

It seems to be a more characteristic trait that the Northeast Greenland houses as a whole are widest at the front, whereby they acquire a certain resemblance to the "pear-shaped" Cape York house, to which reference is often made and which it is generally assumed influenced the form of house in Northeast Greenland[2]). Next come the blubber pits, which Helge Larsen after all considers are kitchens which have replaced the side platform of the Cape York house, where otherwise the lamp had its place[3]).

With regard to the resemblance to the Cape York house it is acknowledged by Helge Larsen that the characteristic constriction at the platform has not been observed in Northeast Greenland; this, however, may be because it is unnecessary, there being driftwood supplies and consequently the cantilever construction is not needed[4]). With this, however, the argument loses much of its weight, for the only real special element left in common with the Cape York house is an almost symmetrical form. Among the earliest houses in Greenland, both in the Thule District and to the south, there are several with the greatest width at the front, just on account of the larger or smaller bulge in one or both

---

[1]) Glob 1935 p. 79 f.
[2]) H. Larsen 1934 p. 62.
[3]) H. Larsen 1934 p. 58.
[4]) H. Larsen 1934 p. 57.

front corners—whatever may have been their use, blubber store or fireplace; in most cases these bulges have given the house a somewhat unsymmetrical shape. What is more, blubber pits, often separated by stones from the house floor, are fairly common in the Thule District and cannot be dated to any definite period. On Ruin Island too there are separated blubber pits *together with* a separate kitchen, for instance in House 2.

Unfortunately we know nothing certain of when the Cape York house acquired its symmetrical pear-shape; but the available material suggests that it was rather late. The cantilever construction and the marked constriction occur in the houses at Aunartoq (Houses 9, 10 and 11), which seemed to be rather recent—presumably 19th or 18th century. These houses, however, with their disproportionately thick and angular masonry give the impression of belonging to a **relatively** early phase, from which the well known, more elegant, rounded pear shape was evolved. Accordingly there is not much probability that it was this particular type of Cape York house that formed the prototype of the Northeast Greenland house. It is true that these Northeast Greenland houses are supposed to belong to the very period which, as far as Thule is concerned, has been least well elucidated, i. e. the 17th—18th century; but if the house form of that period had been able to assert itself in Northeast Greenland, one would also expect to find other distinct evidence of the connection. But there is none. And why do we not find the characteristic blubber pit in the later Polar Eskimo houses? Nowadays meat and blubber are kept in the same place, in a corner nearest the passage, but they are laid on a stone or, in most cases, are hung up. The blubber pit in the floor is more likely a reminiscence of the days when there was plenty of whale blubber, which was burned in suitably arranged open fireplaces. I can hardly think that the blubber pit itself was used as a fireplace; Helge Larsen found partly burned bones and seal flippers in the pits; but is it not likely that they were fuel remains—perhaps from fires outside the house— put away to prevent the dogs from eating them; I imagine there was every reason for economizing with the fuel.

However, it is no longer strictly necessary to resort to the traditional Cape York house to find parallels, as the houses at Cape **Kent** and Cape Russell closely resemble the Northeast Greenland houses in many respects. Some of them are foursided, mostly with the longest dimension in prolongation of the passage, and above all the small offshoots at the front wall are one of their characteristic features. What is more, they are so regularly built that the sense of symmetry is conspicuous; Cape Kent House 1 is the most outstanding in this respect. Otherwise, none of the Northeast Greenland houses illustrated are strictly symmetrical, neither in Larsen nor in Glob, so for that matter they might just as well be related to others among the early houses on Inglefield Land with widened front corners or a small offshoot. On the other hand, Thostrup's plans are so regular that one cannot get rid of the thought that they are at any rate somewhat schematical.

But having gone so far, we must also acknowledge that the probabilities of an influence on the form of the house from the north or the south are about equal, so much the more as it looks as if settlement in Northeast Greenland on the whole is not so very old[1]). The earliest fundamental culture observed is the Inugsuk culture, and, as we have seen, this involves the possibility of practically every imaginable combination of round and foursided house types. And if the Inugsuk culture came to Northeast Greenland from the south—and there is every reason to believe it did after Mathiassen's investigations in the Angmagssalik District—there is no urgent reason for assuming that the house forms did not come along the same route too. Nevertheless I am inclined to believe in a more direct connection with the Cape Kent houses north about Greenland, mainly because of the presence in Northeast Greenland of certain other culture elements which in all probality must have travelled that way—a matter to which we shall presently revert.

Implement Culture.

Hitherto we have been looking mainly from Thule southwards. We shall now see if there are possibilities of cultural influences from the other side, from the south northwards to Thule. A few things have been touched upon, such as Norse objects, tub staves, ornamental bodkins and the parallel house, and the conclusion was arrived at that connections southwards must have ebbed out in the 17th century; but there is still lacking an account of other implement types capable of throwing light on the question of connections between Thule and West Greenland in the preceding time. The comparison with the Inugsuk midden revealed that on the whole there was great agreement between the two regions, but in certain respects it was not so great as might have been expected. We shall therefore proceed farther south and see what the relation is with the culture in Disko Bay and the Kangâmiut area.

Igdlutalik (Disko Bay) Houses VI—X[2]). Of 75 implement types from these houses, which Mathiassen considers to be the earliest at Igdlutalik, only 5 were not found in the Thule District:

    thin harpoon head, closed socket, two barbs, separate blade,
    harpoon socket-piece of wood,

---

[1]) H. Larsen 1934 p. 55.
[2]) Mathiassen 1934 p. 71 f.

bladder dart head with three holes,
gouge of stone,
blubber pounder of wood.

The harpoon head is of a type similar to one of those already mentioned from Inugsuk[1]) and shows that the combination of barbs and closed socket began already at an early Inugsuk stage. Whether or not the bladder dart head with three holes was known in Thule is not known, as we found nothing but broken fore ends; but it is possible that a specimen described as a foreshaft with three holes was once a bladder dart head (I p. 199). The gouge-shaped scraper seems to be a special West Greenland type[2]), whereas blubber pounders of wood have also been found in Northeast Greenland[3]). The remaining types are of such a character that they do not furnish many criteria for a close comparison. It may merely be pointed out that the harpoon rest Mathiassen pl. 1.10 is exactly the same as the one from Cape Kent (pl. 18.22); and on the whole the finds seem to correspond to an early stage of the Inugsuk period in Thule, presumably the 13th—14th century, as was also pointed out on the basis of the house types (p. 101).

Igdlutalik (Disko Bay) Field A, lower layer[4]).

This midden contained somewhat more material for comparison. Of the 119 types from there 16 were not definitely found in the Thule District; of these, however, five are playthings. Furthermore the harpoon blade of stone with a lashing notch, recorded from Field A, is a type which I have identified as a knife blade; but I admit the possibility that some of the specimens from the Thule District may have been used as harpoon blades. On the other hand, harpoon heads with a lashing groove corresponding to a stone blade of this kind are extremely rare in Greenland. From Southampton Island there are harpoon heads with a lashed-on stone blade of this kind[5]), and Boas figures a similar one, possibly from Baffin Island[6]); here the blade is lashed on to one side of the head, and its butt end is more like a tang than on the knife blades from Thule. Lamps with a partition at the middle (towards the back), which also occur in Field A, recur in Thule in the form of toys (Pl. 43.12). Thus there remain 9 types, or barely 8 per cent., as an expression of the difference from the Thule District. On making a similar reduction of the 53 foreign types in the Inugsuk midden we get 40 out of 345, or

---

[1]) Mathiassen 1930 (a) p. 183.
[2]) Mathiassen 1930 (a) p. 76; Solberg 1907 figs. 4—8.
[3]) Thalbitzer 1909 fig. 44; H. Larsen 1934 p. 124.
[4]) Mathiassen 1934 p. 85 ff.
[5]) Mathiassen 1927 I pl. 74.1.
[6]) Boas 1888 fig. 423; 1901 fig. 87.

about 11$^1/_2$ per cent. Thus the earliest part of Field A at Igdlutalik seems to come a little nearer to Thule than the Inugsuk midden did.— The deviating types from Field A are:

flat harpoon head, closed socket, no blade or barb,
flat harpoon head, closed socket, barbed,
sealing net, baleen,
lanceolate arrow head of stone,
angakoq stone,
propeller of wood,
game piece, of wood or bone
mica ball,
implement of wood (Mathiassen pl. 7.20).

Of these in fact only the first four may be said to be of much importance, and indeed it is not impossible that the sealing net was known in the Thule District, having regard to all the thin baleen cords with knots. Those of the remaining types that are directly comparable with corresponding types from the Thule District are distributed as follows:

```
 1 only the Thule period
 6  —   Inugsuk
 1  —   the late transitional period

 1  —   etr — Thule
 2  —   In — etr — Thule
15  —   ltr — In — etr — Thule
 7  —   In — etr
23  —   ltr — In — etr
 3  —   recent time — ltr — In — etr
 5  —   ltr — In
 1  —   recent time — In

33 general distribution.
```

If the figures are set up according to the period to which they apply we get the following

rt	ltr	In	etr	Th
	1	6		1
		15	2	1
	3	23 7		
	1	5		
In all	10	51	3	1

This shows that there is relatively most resemblance to Thule's Inugsuk period, especially its earlier part, and therefore it will not be far wrong to say that the lower part of Midden A at Igdlutalik mainly corresponds to the same culture phase as the early Inugsuk period in the Thule District. This becomes still clearer when we compare some of the most outstanding types. It is evident that coopering technique became a good deal more common in Disko Bay than it was in the Inugsuk midden, where tub staves represented only about 1.3 per cent. of the total finds compared with over 3 per cent. in Disko Bay. For Co. A IV the percentage is about 1.8 and for Thule House 21, midden, 2 per cent., whereas for Co. A III it is only 0.33 per cent. This means that notwithstanding Thule's more remote situation tub staves in this period are relatively more common in this period than in the Inugsuk midden, which on other points too had an earlier stamp about it; however, Thule does not reach such high figures as Disko Bay, where presumably coopering culminated.

If we take the knives, the lower part of Field A contains three with an end blade against 16 with a side blade, i. e. about 16 : 84 per cent. In the Inugsuk midden the figures are 91 : 9 per cent., and in Thule in the late transitional period plus the Inugsuk period about 50 : 50 per cent., wheras for House 21, midden alone they are about 37 : 63 per cent. The latter thus comes nearest to Field A. It is also noteworthy that the flat stone scrapers with a slightly ground edge, which are common in Field A, now begin to appear in the Thule District[1]).

These things indicate rather strong culture influences on Thule from the Disko Bay region at a certain juncture, and all the evidence argues that this juncture was fairly early in Thule's Inugsuk period, i. e. in the 14th and the beginning of the 15th century. Next, these influences were associated especially with the houses with a kitchen, particularly the complex 21. E—W, which again suggests that it is connected especially with the doings of the Ruin Island people. Evidently these people represented both a more mobile and a less conservative element of the population than the permanent Polar Eskimos.

In this connection I would also mention the harpoon heads of Thule type that were found in the bottom of Houses II and IV at Igdlutalik. Mathiassen's Pl. 8.2 has 2 × 2 barbs, a form not previously found in Greenland[2]). Now, however, we have a fragment from Ruin Island (pl. 3.5); and even if the specimen from Igdlutalik had acquired a blade, a rounded socket and lashing holes, all features that evidence a more advanced time or acclimatization, it is reasonable to assume that the type was introduced by the Ruin Island people—which may possibly be an example of the influence of these people on the implement forms of West Greenland. Mathiassen's pl. 8.1 is another very unusual form of thin barbed harpoon head, for it has two unilateral spurs; the fore

---

[1]) A similar one was also found at Qilalukan House VIII; Mathiassen 1927 I p. 143.

[2]) Mathiassen 1934 p. 125.

end is defective, and it has an extra, no doubt secondary line hole right forward between the barbs. From Thule we have two harpoon heads of similar type, both with the blade parallel to the line hole, one from House 21. E (pl. 3.19), the other from Co. A III; on the latter the spurs are bifurcated, a feature which otherwise is common only to the flat harpoon heads from Thule.

Mathiassen places the lower part of Field A to the 15th century[1]), which of course will agree very well with the first appearance of the Ruin Island people about the year 1300; they then move down the west coast in the course of the 14th century, and during this time new impulses flow northwards to Thule, where they become most perceptible in the houses with a kitchen dating from the latter part of the 14th and the beginning of the 15th centuries.

But as now conditions suggest that Co. A IV is somewhat earlier than the characteristic kitchen houses, and Co. A III on the other hand must be later, we encounter a chronological difficulty which, however, may be only apparent. If what has been said in the foregoing is right, the early transitional period, which has no kitchen, and at any rate the lower part of Co. A IV, must for the most part be placed in the 13th century and perhaps a little way into the 14th; in that case the transition to Co. A III must be "stretched" in order to make room for the kitchen period which, having regard to the large midden in front of House 21 in Thule, cannot have been so very short in duration. But if we look back at the table for Comer's Midden on page 22, we shall find that this stretching must if anything refer to layers 11 and 10, where the disproportionately high percentage of wood was attributed to the new culture movement, and where on the whole there were irregularities. Nor can it be without importance to our understanding of these things that there was a change of residence in the kitchen-house period. This alone argues that in this period Comer's Midden was less frequently inhabited—perhaps by some few families of the old population, whereas the newcomers preferred to build their large kitchen houses on the plain a little way from it. It is only when the great majority of the new arrivals have been absorbed by more southerly regions and things have quietened down again, that Comer's Midden once again begins to grow, and this time much more quickly.

Igdlutalik (Disko Bay) Houses I and partly II, House V, and the upper part of Field A[2]). Of the 119 types occurring in the lower part of Field A, 22 have now disappeared here; six of them are only toys, however, and as regards some of the other 16 it is evidently accidental

---

[1]) Mathiassen 1934 p. 119.
[2]) Mathiassen 1934 p. 85 ff.

that they were not found; this applies for instance to the harpoon wing, seat for a single-legged sealing stool, seal net, umiaq fragment, adze head, side of baleen bowl, ladle, and ajagaq of seal radius. The position is different with regard to the open-socketed flat harpoon head, bola ball, flint-flaker of rib, baleen shave of stone (:scraper with convex side edge), baleen basket and sling handle; by this time these elements may have been on the retrograde. On the other hand, there is an addition of 57 types, though at least 25 of them are not new. It will be profitable to examine the remaining 32 with regard to their occurrence in the Thule District.

Eleven of them were not found in the Thule District, viz:

Harpoon blade of stone, no notch or hole,
bladder dart head with belt of barbs,
bird-dart head with screw,
kayak scraper,
shark-tooth knife,
thong smoother,
boot-creaser of stone,
scraping bench,
bone bead,
ajagaq of seal tibia,
toy knife with side blade,

The others are:

Ituartit harpoon,
wound plug of wood,
neck-piece for towing line,
arrow head with screw,
ferrule for bird dart,
toggle-shaped gull hook (gorge),
fish hook,
racket-shaped baleen scoop,
ferrule for kayak paddle, segment-shaped,
bone stud for kayak thong,
one-edged knife blade of stone,
boot-creaser of bone,
lamp without ledge,
lamp trimmer of asbestos,
foursided drying rack,
pot-hook of antler,
blubber-stick of antler,
blubber pounder of antler.
baleen wool
ajagaq of seal penis bone,
drum frame of bone.

Of these, the wound plug of wood, ferrule for bird dart, one-edged knife blade, boot creaser, hook of antler, and baleen wool date back to the Thule period, and the neck-piece for towing line, blubber stick of antler with barbs and the drum frame of bone to the early transitional period—first and last at any rate to Co. A IV. The blubber pounder is more uncertain, as it is recorded only as having been found at various places around Etah, but not in Comer's Midden[1]). The toggle-shaped gull hook, fish hook of bone, baleen scoop, ferrule for kayak paddle, bone stud for kayak thong, lamp trimmer of asbestos, and foursided drying rack were found in the Inugsuk period, mainly in houses with a kitchen. Co. A III produced only the scoop of baleen. Thus it would seem that here these types go back at any rate towards the year 1400.

Matters are otherwise with the ituartit harpoon, arrow head with screw, and lamp without ledge; they have not been found prior to the late transitional period, the first two only in Co. A II, and they are only very weakly represented, as the first two are unique fragments and the last a toy. It would thus seem that here we have the limit of the cultural influence from the south. It is true that the ledgeless lamp afterwards became the prevailing form in Thule, but it assumed a shape different to that in West Greenland—or rather, it retained the ancient segment form, while the ituartit harpoon and the screw have quite disappeared. The bladder-dart head with the belt of barbs does not seem to have reached Thule at all. Thus there can only have been a peripheral contact at a time that corresponded to Co. A II. But when was this?

Mathiassen judges these particular finds at Igdlutalik to date mainly from the 16th century, comparing them with the 2nd culture phase in the Kangâmiut area. Thus there is reason for assuming that Co. A II dates from about the year 1600, and with this the connection southwards is closing down—the same result as that to which our consideration of the oblong communal house led us.

If we maintain it as being most probable that Co. A IV has its upper limits within the 14th century and thus, taking it all round, is contemporary with the Inugsuk midden, Thule's real Inugsuk period will in the main fall within the 15th and 16th centuries. In that case the period for the kitchen houses will have been in the first part of it, as indeed we concluded before, and Co. A III and the large houses with fireplaces at the front wall rather in the latter part. The latter have been placed in the late transitional period, as no true Norse objects were found; but of course there is no sharp delimitation from the Inugsuk period. Both periods, divided here merely for practical reasons, must together occupy the period from about 1400 to 1600.

The old houses at *Igdlorssuit* in Disko Bay bear a remarkable likeness to the Inugsuk-period houses in Thule, as both the well-built kitchens and the more casually arranged fireplaces at the front wall are represented. They have been estimated as dating from the 13th—

---

[1]) Wissler 1918 p. 142.

14th century[1]), but I scarcely imagine that the 13th century can come into consideration except for the small house VI with its many whale bones, which undoubtedly date far back in time. According to what I have said in the foregoing the others are more likely 14th—15th century, the parallel house, House VII, which presumably is relatively late, also pointing in the same direction.

The finds from the *Kângamiut area*, which were of fundamental importance to Mathiassen's chronology for Disko Bay, are only of indirect significance to conditions in the Thule District. The more characteristic types are closely associated with the special West Greenland development, and those of them that were capable of contributing to the establishment of the chronology of the Thule District have already been referred to above. Nor do we get much assistance in this connection from the more sparse finds in the *Julianehaab District*.

Northeast Greenland. The investigation into the house types in this region with regard to the question of cultural communications from north or south gave no definitive result. In addition to the Cape York house, however, Helge Larsen enumerates ten culture elements which, owing to their absence from West and South Greenland, must be supposed to have immigrated to Northeast Greenland from the north[2]):

Thule-2 harpoon head,
heavy socket piece (with scarf face),
side prong for bird dart with int. and ext. barbs,
toggle for towing line,
snow knife with two shoulders,
double drill bit,
snow-beater of wood,
baleen handle,
swimming bird,
pyrites.

To these we may add with as much probability the two-handed scraper of bear femur, assumed to be a local form[3]) but now found in Thule, toggle of walrus molar with carved bear head[4]), reserve lance head of slender type[5]), and possibly the cup-shaped scraper as well[6]), which, however, occurs in the Inugsuk midden, and finally the mica mirror (see I p. 276).

From Helge Larsen's list I consider it right to omit the snow beater

---

[1]) Mathiassen 1934 p. 157.
[2]) H. Larsen 1934 p. 103.
[3]) H. Larsen 1934 p. 85.
[4]) H. Larsen 1934 p. 132.
[5]) Glob 1935 p. 48.
[6]) Glob 1935 Pl. 6.56.

of wood. It has not definitely been found in the Thule District, but there is a specimen from the southeast coast with an edge mounting and ferrule of bone[1]). The toggle for towing line seems rather doubtful, too (where does H. Larsen describe it?). The baleen handle has not been described definitely from West Greenland, but among the many baleen objects from Inugsuk midden there are several narrow strips whipped with baleen[2]), and from Thule we have several indubitable baleen handles. However, this mainly northern occurrence may perhaps mean that Helge Larsen is right.

Of the other elements the double drill bit has been found only at Qilalukan[3]) apart from Northeast Greenland, whereas the remainder occur in the Thule District. They are mostly old types, but they are not rare in Thule's Inugsuk period and therefore do not tell us so much as to in what limited period an immigration to the northeast coast can have taken place. The snow knife with two shoulders, of the characteristic Northeast Greenland type, was not found in Thule, however—a type that bears much greater resemblance to forms of the Canadian Thule culture[4]); nevertheless we recognize it in a toy snow knife of baleen from Inugsuk[5]). However, there are other things which may perhaps provide us with a hint. For example, no bow-drill mouthpiece of caribou astragalus was found in Thule's early Inugsuk and early transitional period, but three made of bone. But before and after that period we do find the caribou astragalus. In Northeast Greenland a form made of walrus skull bone was found; Helge Larsen reckons it to be a local type[6]), but together with the Polar Eskimos' less characteristic form it stands as a contrast to the early form of astragalus, so that there is also some probability that the Northeast Greenland form dates from early Inugsuk time. Its appearance in this time also indicates that it is due to an impulse from the west; thus the mouthpieces from Thule are very reminiscent of one from Naujan[7]).

One more parallel is to be seen in the salmon-spear barb with a neck, one of which was found by the Danmark Expedition on Maroussia[8]); this Canadian type too appears in the Thule District in the Inugsuk period (pl. 13.14). Finally, attention may be drawn to the fact that apart from two pieces of drilled bone of the earliest time, this technique does not seem to have gained a footing in the Thule District until some time

---

[1]) National Museum No. L 16: 7104.
[2]) Mathiassen 1930 (a) p. 264.
[3]) Mathiassen 1927 II p. 79; I pl. 63.13.
[4]) Mathiassen 1927 II p. 65.
[5]) Mathiassen 1930 (a) pl. 21.26
[6]) H. Larsen 1934 p. 163.
[7]) Mathiassen 1927 I pl. 22.14.
[8]) Th. Thomsen 1917 fig. 17.

in the Inugsuk period; there are only two specimens from Co. A IV but 17 from the kitchen houses and 16 from Co. A III. On the other hand, drilling was never so common in Thule as in Northeast Greenland, no doubt a result of the easier access to iron at Thule which made it possible to make good knives.

The objects named might well suggest that at any rate a culture influence reached Northeast Greenland—very likely round about the 14th century. If this is correct, however, the probability also increases that there was a connection between the Cape Kent houses and those in Northeast Greenland—a question which without doubt would be much better illuminated by means of excavations on Ellesmere Island, where Simmons illustrates a similar foursided house[1]). In that case however, there is also a possibility that a number of types which are placed to the Inugsuk culture passed along the same route and *need* not have gone via Cape Farvel. This holds good of the knife with a side blade, the edge mounting and the ornamental bodkin, which in fact are the only ones of the 15 types from III House I on Clavering Island from which it is possible to conclude that the culture here is Inugsuk[2]). But as already stated, we have besides the two-handed scraper of bear femur and presumably the two-handed scraper of bear radius, which in Northeast Greenland was found not far from Danmarks Havn[3]).

Nor must the fact be overlooked that it is just at this time that the flat harpoon heads begin to appear in the Thule District, where they quickly culminate. There is no form corresponding exactly to those in Northeast Greenland, but in principle it is the same type, flat with a closed socket, two dorsal spurs, with or without a separate blade. The type with a blade was not found by Helge Larsen in the early houses (house type 2), but Glob has it from the early period in Kempe and Kong Oscar Fjord[4]). Arrow heads with a scarf face also occur in the Thule District in the early part of Inugsuk and the early transitional period, and it may be that there is a connection between these and the Northeast Greenland type with a wedge-shaped butt. Wedge and scarf at any rate are more closely related than wedge and knobbed tang. However, the arrow head with a wedge-shaped butt is not entirely unknown in South Greenland. A specimen from Igdlutalik in the Julianehaab District (L 15: 857) with opposite barbs is only 5.7 cm. long and had almost the appearance of a toy; another from Ûnartoq (L 15: 1655) is round and 8.25 cm. long. Nevertheless it is doubtful if either of these had any close connection with Northeast Greenland.

---

[1]) Simmons, Ymer 1905 fig. 6, p. 191.
[2]) H. Larsen 1934 p. 84 f.
[3]) Th. Thomsen 1917 pl. XXVI.5 and p. 445.
[4]) Glob 1935 p. 81.

Neither flat harpoon heads nor salmon-spear barbs with a projecting neck seem to have any close association with the Ruin Island complex, and the arrow head with a scarf face is chiefly confined to the early transitional period. Thus new impulses came to Greenland not only with the Ruin Island people, but also with people with a somewhat different culture—and possibly both before and after the Ruin Island people. The latter had leanings particularly towards the south, West Greenland; and conditions indicate that more to the north, on Inglefield Land, Ellesmere Island and in Northeast Greenland there was a region where the culture evolution to some extent followed its own paths, conditioned first and foremost by the direct line from the ancient Thule culture, but with supplements from the west of forms which doubtless reached more southerly parts of the Thule District, but which were unable to establish a footing in West Greenland. In this way do we arrive at the most feasible explanation of how the foursided houses and the foresaid implement types reached Northeast Greenland so to say round behind the Ruin Islanders and less affected by the stronger— or at any rate the different development which took place at the same time more to the south in the Thule District. In so far Helge Larsen seems to be justified in saying that the cultural influence which came north about to Northeast Greenland can at most have merely touched the Thule District[1]. On the other hand it would be nothing remarkable if some few of the characteristic forms of the Inugsuk period travelled by the same route, even if the culture of Northeast Greenland for the most part was the result of immigration from the south.

The discussion of these matters has not resulted in the complete clearing up of the Northeast Greenland problem. Indeed it has rather become more intricate, because it has transpired that the Inugsuk culture pressed close up on either side of the region in question. However, if as Helge Larsen thinks[2] the earliest immigration to Northeast Greenland (Dødemandsbugten) came via Angmagssalik, it must be dated rather late (15th—16th century). But if it came north about Greenland it was more likely in the 14th century; and as both the foursided houses and various implement forms suggest this latter time in the Thule District, there may perhaps be reason for assuming that *the first immigration* did in fact pass round the north of Greenland, carrying the Thule culture with it. And now that we know that the small round houses were also characteristic of the early Thule culture on Inglefield Land, there is no difficulty in explaining the almost obliterated sites which Helge Larsen found on Clavering Island, and there is no reason what-

---

[1] H. Larsen 1934 p. 164.
[2] H. Larsen 1934 p. 86.

ever for calling them a "transitional type"[1]); rather do they suggest that there were people in Northeast Greenland even before the 14th century.

Our investigation of culture developments in the Thule District and the comparison with the rest of Greenland have now thrown some light upon the population movements that took place in Greenland, though we cannot say that all the questions arising have been answered. One thing appears from it all, however: the movements in Greenland are closely connected with similar movements more to the west; it was on American soil that the great Eskimo migrations took place, presumably along several different routes and at different times—a theory which Mathiassen advanced earlier[2]). Some of these waves reached Greenland direct, of others perhaps only the after-swell, and Mathiassen undoubtedly is right too when he says that "the West Greenland culture seems to be a rather involved edifice"[3]).

---

[1]) H. Larsen 1934 p. 53.
[2]) Mathiassen 1927 II p. 195.
[3]) Mathiassen 1927 II p. 169.

IV. RELATIONS WITH THE DORSET AND THULE CULTURES IN CANADA

Having now consolidated the chronological structure for the Thule District as far as is practicable, we shall see whether it is possible by its aid to advance a step farther in the chronology for Canada than has hitherto been feasible. The fundamentals were achieved by Th. Mathiassen and Birket-Smith, whose publications and theoretical treatment of the material collected by the Fifth Thule Expedition signified a turning point in Eskimo research as a whole, and the following investigations are based preponderantly on these works, there being no other publications of other systematically excavated material from these parts. First and foremost I refer to Mathiassen's "Archaeology of the Central Eskimos" I—II. In that work Mathiassen was able to establish a relative chronology for the various finds belonging to the Thule culture; but owing to the lack of connecting links with the Greenland chronology the two could not be coupled together with certainty. Excavations in the Thule District have now remedied some of these defects, and it is fortunate that there we have finds that extend through several centuries. Our task must therefore be to correlate them with the Canadian finds in order to join the two together into one great whole.

The Dorset Culture.

Unfortunately it is impossible to bring the Greenland Dorset phase into direct connection with the finds in Arctic Canada, the latter not having been datable in relation to known phases of the Thule culture with even approximate certainty. It is regrettable that Mathiassen had not more time for systematic investigations at Button Point, as excavations there would undoubtedly have brought matters on to a more certain track. All the same, there is agreement on the whole that the Dorset culture belongs to an old stratum in relation to the Thule culture.

On the Fifth Thule Expedition it was impossible completely to segregate the Dorset culture from the Thule culture, and therefore

Mathiassen was most inclined to regard it as a peculiar, local phase of the Thule culture[1]). Subsequent investigations in eastern Canada have shown that it is justifiable to speak of a relatively independent Dorset culture[2]); but its relation to the Thule culture has been nothing like cleared up. On the origin of the Dorset culture Jenness set up the following hypothesis:

> "The unbroken sequence of Eskimo remains around Bering Sea shows that there have been no movements between Asia and America, except of Eskimo, for 2000 years. Probably the latest movement was that of the Athapascan peoples, who introduced the snowshoe complex into America about the 1st millenium B. C. The Eskimo may have entered earlier and some remained near Bering Sea while others penetrated into Central Canada and intermarried extensively with Algonkian Indians. These eastern Eskimo split into two; one group became Caribou Eskimo, the other evolved the extinct Dorset culture which left its traces even in Greenland. Dog-traction and whaling originated, perhaps, in northeast Siberia, spread to north Alaska in the 1st millenium A. D., and were carried over the whole American Arctic by the Thule Eskimo. The old Bering Sea Eskimo acquired their peculiar art, perhaps also pottery, from the southwest, ultimately from China. For the proto-Eskimo home, where they adopted a coastal life and the hunting of sea mammals, we should seach the Arctic shores of Siberia. Proto-Eskimo remains ought to reveal a clear relationship with epipalaeolithic cultures of Europe ..."[3]).

I quote this at such length because later there may be occasion for reverting to some of the opinions expressed in it. I shall not question the possibility that the Dorset people were distantly related to the Caribou Eskimos. But according to Jenness this means that the Dorset culture was evolved out of an inland culture; whereas even if the slender harpoon heads suggest life on lakes and rivers, the fact remains that so far we know the Dorset culture only as a coastal culture. Some of the implements are of antler, may be, but a very large number are of walrus ivory. Finally, the whole question is bound up in the problem of how high an age we must attribute to the Dorset culture.

How old the Dorset culture is in Greenland it is beyond our power to say exactly, but here we have somewhat firmer ground under our feet. A few Dorset types were found in the Inugsuk period, viz. the harpoon head with a closed socket, cleft butt, two line holes and a blade (pl. 1.5-6) and the heavy type (pl. 1.7), as well as the knife with a side blade. These were known at any rate in the 14th century and perhaps in the beginning of the 15th. On Ruin Island we found a "spatula", oval sandstone lamp and ornamental plate with a face, though the latter perhaps is rather problema-

---

[1]) Mathiassen 1927 II p. 165.
[2]) Jenness 1925 and Nat. Mus. Can. Bull. 56 (1929) p. 38.
[3]) Jenness 1939 p. 296.

tical as a Dorset element. Presumably these two date from the 14th or the latter part of the 13th century.

The relation of the Dorset culture to the Thule culture on Inglefield Land is not quite clear, as the Dorset types found there may have come from the early settlement. But if we put the date of the Thule culture there at the 11th—12th century, the Dorset phase dates from a time before or about the year 1000. If really there is anything in the account in Are Frode's *islændingebog*, that when the Norsemen came they found traces of Scraelings, there is at any rate a probability that these were Dorset people. This however has not been demonstrated archaeologically. But if they were Thule people, the Dorset period must have been still earlier. Collins cautiously asks "might it not be possible that some of the non-Thule types of the "Stone-age" as described by Solberg would represent a mixture of Dorset types—or special Greenland variants of these—and of later Thule types"[1]. This I think can now be confirmed without hesitation, though there need scarcely be any question of a mixing with later Thule types, just in view of the fact that in the Thule District flint technique so very distinctly is confined to the Dorset period. In the earliest small houses excavated by Mathiassen in West Greenland the finds are also extremely sparse, so that they do not contradict it, at any rate. One of the foremost tasks for West Greenland archaeology must be to see whether—for instance at Sermermiut south of Jakobshavn—it is possible to find remains of Dorset settlement lowest of all.

At *Button Point* on Bylot Island[2] we encounter some types of harpoon heads (Mathiassen pl. 61.17-21) and a few other implements such as facetted scrapers of flint (Mathiassen pl. 61.13), slate blade (pl. 61.15), needle case (pl. 62.19), thick bone needle (pl. 62.2) and a quantity of ornamented objects which were not found on Inglefield Land; on the other hand a number of other types were found at the latter place. From Button Point, however, there are also artefacts of a more pronouncedly Thule stamp: bone maul head, snow shovel, soapstone bowl, bone hook and disc (top-disc?) of soapstone. In Greenland all these have been found within the Thule period and early transitional period i. e. about 1000—1300, so that with some degree of probability the Button Point find would seem datable to within that period.

As regards the finds at *Kuk* on Southampton Island[3], there is very little to go upon. Nevertheless, a harpoon head was found in House

---

[1] Collins 1937 p. 336.
[2] Mathiassen 1927 I pl. 61—62.
[3] Mathiassen 1927 I pl. 73.1-7.

XVII, which chronologically occupies a midway position, i. e. it is somewhat later than Naujan[1]).

At *Naujan* itself only one object, which looks like a foreshaft[2]), was found of distinctly Dorset type, and at *Malerualik* a harpoon head which had had a lashed-on blade, apparently of slate or the like[3]). Here we seem to be at the western limit of the Dorset culture's association with the Thule culture; but it is impossible to decide whether this faint Dorset sprinkling is based upon the influence of time or of geography. Nevertheless it may be that we have a slender guide after all, as the harpoon heads from Malerualik of types Thule 2 and 3 (Mathiassen pl. 82.1-2) have lashing holes, a feature which in the Thule District does not appear until towards the close of the Thule culture period, i. e. presumably about the year 1200. It does not tell us much, however, as long as we do not know more of the history of the Dorset culture or whether there may be earlier houses with Dorset artefacts at Malerualik.

More or less the same argument applies to the finds from *Cape Dorset*, which Jenness described[4]), though there the find-combinations are more uncertain. Jenness's fig. 5d and e are apparently two harpoon heads of Thule type 2 with lashing holes and the bottom of the socket rounded, that is to say relatively late Thule forms. All the same they are undoubtedly the oldest of the non-Dorset types illustrated; but whether they are contemporary with, earlier or later than the particular Dorset types is not known, unfortunately.

There is a striking difference between the finds from Inglefield Land on the one hand and Button Point and Cape Dorset respectively on the other, as open-socketed harpoon heads at the latter places are relatively common as compared with Inglefield Land, where we found only one. This in itself says nothing about the time difference between these finds; in any case open-socketed Dorset harpoon heads need not be earlier than the others, as the open socket may well be a feature that was borrowed from the Thule culture. The open socket is in marked contrast to the whole character of the Dorset harpoon head, as the point of it of course lies just in the fact that a closed socket is easy to cut out in the two spurs themselves (I p. 194). Therefore if the open socket is not so common in the Thule District, the explanation may be that the Thule culture there did not influence the Dorset forms so much and that the particular group of people belonged to an earlier phase of the Dorset culture; this of course would agree very well with what was said above as regards Malerualik and Cape Dorset. The fact that

---

[1]) Mathiassen 1927 I p. 260.
[2]) Mathiassen 1927 I pl. 5.8.
[3]) Mathiassen 1927 I pl. 82.3.
[4]) Jenness 1925 figs. 5—7.

it reached so much farther north also points in the same direction. At any rate I am inclined to think that on Inglefield Land we have a find of Dorset culture earlier than those referred to from Canada.

Mitimatalik.

The ruin excavated there yielded a total of 54 types[1]), and only three of them were not found in the Thule District, viz. the heavy form of fixed lance head (like Naujan pl. 6.6), adze blade of slate, and cylindrical bead of narwhal ivory. The ulo handle with a concave underside has not the characteristic form of that at Mitimatalik, but three specimens (L 3: 3282, 6976 and 7223), all of the Inugsuk period, bear a slight resemblance to it. If we include the latter we get 51 common features divided as follows:

```
 2 only in Thule culture
 4  —  In

 1  —  etr — Thule
 8  —  In — etr — Thule
10  —  ltr — In — etr — Thule
 4  —  In — etr
 1  —  ltr — In — etr
 3  —  ltr — In
 1  —  recent time — ltr — In

17 general distribution.
```

If we arrange the figures again (leaving out the 17 from which we can learn nothing) according to their chronological weight, we get the following row:

ltr		In		etr		Th
1	3	5	14	8	1	2

It will be seen that the preponderance lies between the early transitional period (etr) and the Inugsuk period (In), that is to say, nearest the 14th century. This of course is not saying that the Mitimatalik find is necessarily datable to that time, but it would be most reasonable to seek its date round about there. Apart from the fact that all the types are not of equal weight, the distance between the two localities must also be taken into consideration; and in this respect one would be inclined to assume that, everything else being equal, Mitimatalik lies a little farther back in time than Thule. This need not be so, however, as it is also within the bounds of possibility that the strong development

---

[1]) Mathiassen 1927 I p. 135.

taking place at this time in the Thule District was capable of spreading back on to Canadian soil, and of course the distance is no greater than between Thule and West Greenland. However, none of the artefacts from Mitimatalik suggest any close connection between the two places, as the types that are common only to Inugsuk and the late transitional period are the whaling harpoon head, harpoon blade of slate, knife with side blade, harpoon blade of bone, snow knife with one shoulder and straight back, loosely knotted baleen net presumably from a drying rack, and ulo with concave underside. None of these lend themselves to the assumption that they are of Greenland origin; rather did they come to Thule from the west. Furthermore, the heavy lance head displays a clear association with Naujan.

A few individual features may serve to define the position of the Mitimatalik find in relation to the Thule District a little more clearly. In the Thule District the long cylindrical socket piece for the harpoon is known only from the early Thule culture, whereafter it is evidently replaced by the characteristic short type (pl. 6.9—upside down) which was also found at Qilalukan (Mathiassen pl. 41.5). Furthermore, one of the Thule 2 harpoon heads from Mitimatalik has a triangular line hole, a feature which in the Thule District was found only in the early Thule culture and on Ruin Island. All in all this suggests a culture phase prior to the Inugsuk period in the Thule District, so that with great probability its upper limit may be put at about the year 1400.

Qilalukan.

Direct comparisons can be made with the finds from House I, III, XXIV and VIII and the middens A and C[1]), Parson's collection from House VIII not being included, as Mathiassen does not consider them likely to provide a quite reliable chronological picture. The find spots are shown in the chronological order set up by Mathiassen; but as they evidently lie fairly close together in time—House III for instance corresponds fairly well to the lower part of Field A[2])—there is no reason for treating them separately here.

Of a total of 167 elements 38, or about 23 per cent., do not occur in the present material from the Thule District (though the blubber pounder of antler and the swimming bird of walrus ivory are known from previous finds), and 31 are types of general distribution. The remaining 98 are distributed as follows:

---

[1]) Mathiassen 1927 I p. 140 ff.
[2]) Mathiassen 1927 I p. 160.

3 only in Thule culture
2 — - etr
13 — - Inugsuk
1 — - ltr

1 — - etr — Thule
16 — - In — etr — Thule
27 — - ltr — In — etr — Thule
6 — - In — etr
10 — - ltr — In — etr
9 — - ltr — In
4 — - recent time — etr
5 — - recent time — ltr — In
1 — - recent time

This gives the following row:

rec	ltr	In	etr	Th			
1	6	13	23	33	18	1	3

As at Mitimatalik, most weight falls between Inugsuk and the early transitional period, but there is a characteristic difference in the distribution of the figures. If we calculate the values as percentages for the sake of comparison and gather them in groups on both sides of the principal value, we get:

	%	%	%
Mitimatalik	17	26	21
Qilalukan	26$^1/_2$	20	13$^1/_2$

This shows a perceptible displacement upwards in time for Qilalukan, and the same is indicated by the relatively large number of types that are shared only with the Inugsuk period in Thule. These are:

Thule 2 harpoon head with more than 2 barbs (Ruin Isl.),
Thule-2 harpoon head with blade at r. angles to line hole,
thin-flat harpoon head with closed socket,
harpoon blade of slate,
harpoon rest of baleen,
seal scratcher of wood,
low harpoon rest for kayak, wood,
knife blade of copper,
ulo of slate with baleen whipping,
adze handle with three holes,
trapeziform comb,
top-disc of bone,
fire-drilling hearth.

That the latter was found only within this period must be accidental. The other types, however, are of such a character that we must suppose there really was a close connection between the culture phases in Thule and Qilalukan. What is more, a comb from Qilalukan is ornamented with incised designs of kayak and umiaq. In Thule such designs are found only in the Inugsuk and late transitional periods.

The two types that are shared only with the early transitional period are the W-shaped drag line handle and the fire-drilling stick, the latter of which can scarcely be credited with much importance. Objects shared exclusively with the Thule culture on Inglefield Land are: long cylindrical socket piece, thimble-holder of skin, and mattock handle. Of these the last two must have had a wider distribution.

The six types shared with Inugsuk and early transitional period are:

adze head with horizontal holes and curved groove,
ulo blade of slate,
salmon-spear side prong with lashing holes,
quiver handle with horizontal holes,
spoon of antler,
metal of European origin.

These elements too indicate a more intimate cultural connection between Qilalukan and Thule. Whereas the elements in themselves and conditions in general argue that the movement was towards Thule, the curious metal object from Qilalukan (Mathiassen fig. 60) makes it possible that there was an opposite movement too. With the knowledge we now have of Norse relics in the Thule District it is highly probable that this metal is of Norse origin. On the other hand it is imaginable that the Norsemen themselves had been in the neighbourhood of Pond Inlet. The relatively great special likeness between Qilalukan and the Thule District's Inugsuk and early transitional periods means that the Qilalukan finds may be placed to about the 14th or, perhaps, beginning of the 15th century; this however would preclude the possibility of access to European metal along other routes.

Theoretically of course there is no reason why Qilalukan should not be of later date and have retained its early character; for we have no definite knowledge of when the new impulses from the south, from the Iglulik Eskimos, began to be felt. Consequently we must also look at the elements that are shared with the later time in Thule. From the late transitional period and Inugsuk we have:

Arrow head with knobs and one barb,
knife with bilateral rows of side blades,
lance blade of slate,
gorge (of bird bone),
adze head without holes,
ulo handle with thick back and thinner blade part,
scraper of diabase with worked edge,
stone axe with baleen handle,
fixed lance head with blade slit.

None of these types make it necessary, however, to assume that Qilalukan is later than Thule's Inugsuk period. Only the stone axe with its baleen handle and the gorge of bird bone were missing at Naujan, a find which Mathiassen supposes is earlier than Qilalukan. The corresponding knives from Naujan have only a unilateral row of side blades, but that does not necessarily mean that the one from Qilalukan was the result of an impulse from Greenland.

The only elements that are shared solely with recent time—ltr—Inugsuk are:

Knife with unilateral row of side blades,
knife with single side blade,
knife with side blade at the end,
ulo handle, low and broad, of bone,
sledge shoe of walrus ivory.

Of these only the third was not found at Naujan; this form of knife ("crooked knife"), however, is known from Punuk time in Alaska[1]). Finally, there is from Qilalukan a small flat toy harpoon head with a closed socket and dorsal spur, which seems to have a blade slit[2]). In Thule the corresponding full-sized type was found only in the upper part of Comer's Midden; but as similar types, except that they have two spurs, date back to the early transitional time, there is hardly any reason for attaching much importance to this simple miniature.

Thus there is nothing to show that Qilalukan is necessarily later than was first assumed; indeed, most of the elements point farther back in time. It is therefore reasonable to assume that the Qilalukan finds are about 14th century.

This signifies that Qilalukan is later than the period when the Ruin Island people were in the vicinity; and as a matter of fact there is no clear sign of them in the finds. The one object that might suggest a connection with them is the Thule 2 harpoon head with more than two barbs; but the curious features about these harpoon heads: vestigial spurs or barbs, do not occur at Qilalukan, nor do we observe the special "style" that marks the finds from Ruin Island. The numerous outstanding features combined with the close resemblance to Naujan also indicate that the Qilalukan finds came from a permanent population which was based on the Central Thule culture and in addition developed a certain local character. We see from Mathiassen's description of House VIII[3]) that indoor fireplaces were used; but for the present we know very little about the history of these fireplaces.

---

[1]) Collins 1937 p. 231.
[2]) Mathiassen 1927 I p. 149.
[3]) Mathiassen 1927 I p. 142.

Through the medium of the considerable specific similarity displayed by Qilalukan to the time round about Thule's Inugsuk period it is now possible to pick out at least some of the new cultural elements that came to Thule up towards the Inugsuk period and possibly prior to the advent of the Ruin Island people. These must include at least some of those enumerated above, for instance flat harpoon heads, harpoon rest of baleen, seal scratcher, stone axe with baleen handle, slate technique (cp. Northeast Greenland), scraper of diabase with ground edge, incised design on walrus ivory, and presumably platform mat of baleen and several other things which begin to appear in the early transitional period. It may also be mentioned that the ornamentation on a comb from a grave find at Qilalukan (Mathiassen pl. 63.4) recurs in a somewhat more simple form on a scraper handle from Inuarfigssuaq House 4 (pl. 23.12), which is one of the later houses with early Thule culture.

Arrow heads with a scarfed butt do not occur in this material selected from Qilalukan, but they do occur in Parson's collection from Houses VIII and XXIV, and Mathiassen remarks that they may be due to later intermixtures[1]. However, arrow heads of this kind do actually occur—if sparsely— in the early transitional period, that is to say at the same time as the other elements that point to a close cultural connection with Qilalukan. If these arrow heads are the result of influence from the south, the necessary conclusion to be drawn is that this influence must already have begun as early as in the 13th century—the very time when the development of the flat harpoon heads is accelerated. This agrees very well with Jenness's assumption that the expansion of the inland tribes began about the year 1200 A. D.[2].

Naujan.

It being particularly Mathiassen's finds at Naujan that form the basis of the definition of the Thule culture, it will be particularly interesting to see how those finds compare with the culture in the Thule District. A calculation of the elements found, based upon Mathiassen's publication[3], and made according to the same principles as those employed in the foregoing, gives a total of 235—which is very nearly the same as that for Inglefield Land's Thule Culture (243), somewhat less than for the early transitional period (277) and much less than for the Inugsuk period including the Ruin Island period (504). From this it may perhaps be concluded that the Naujan find belongs to a "quiet" time with no violent impulses from the outside—or at any rate a time

---
[1] Mathiassen 1927 I p. 154 f.
[2] Jenness 1937 p. 34.
[3] Mathiassen 1927 I pp. 23—82.

when developments had settled down to a calm course. The relatively small number of types of harpoon heads from Naujan in itself suggests the same.

Of the 235 elements—whose taxonomic value of course varies greatly—58 or almost 25 per cent. were not found in the Thule District. This apparently is evidence of a fairly wide gap, which one might explain for instance by the purely geographical remoteness; but on going through these elements their importance becomes considerably reduced. Three are harpoon heads of transitional type between thin and flat and with closed socket. One is an unusual form with the blade at right angles to the line hole; the other two occur in the Thule District but have an open socket, and similar forms were found at Inugsuk[1]). These three types of harpoon heads came from the latest houses at Naujan.

The bladder-dart head with two opposite barbs was found in Thule in the form of a toy (pl. 48.18). As regards the mouthpiece plug of walrus ivory Mathiassen admits that his identification is not quite certain[2]). Harpoon, ulo and adze blades of copper and harpoon blades of jade are partly conditioned geographically and at any rate are not common; nevertheless the harpoon blade of copper has also been found in Greenland[3]). Weapon shafts of bone presumably are the result of wood scarcity, and the same may hold good of the bow made of bone. It is possible, however, that some of the unidentified bone objects from Thule may have been weapon shafts (e. g. L 3: 11743 from Co. B). The holed wound needle occurs in Northeast Greenland, where it is true the hole is drilled through the head of the needle[4]), but the object was presumably the same, viz. to enable the wound needle to be carried on a string together with other implements for ice-hunting. Sinew-twisters of bone are common in Greenland, but in Thule the only specimen is of wood. As regards arrow blades of flint, it is possible that some of the small triangular flint blades pl. 2.1-4 were used in arrows, and arrow blades of slate with a tang have been found in Northeast Greenland[5]) and West Greenland[6]).

The wolf killer of baleen was found at Inugsuk[7]). The salmon-spear side prong with a hole for the barb is known from Angmagssalik[8]), and possibly pl. 5.26 from Co. A 15 layer 9 is a barb for one of these spears.

---

[1]) Mathiassen 1930 (a) p. 184.
[2]) Mathiassen 1927 I p. 30.
[3]) Knuth 1940 p. 120.
[4]) Mathiassen 1933 pl. 5.30; H. Larsen 1934 p. 144.
[5]) H. Larsen 1934 pl. 3.11.
[6]) Mathiassen 1934 pl. 3.17.
[7]) Mathiassen 1930 (a) p. 198.
[8]) Mathiassen 1933 p. 82; pl. 5.44.

The simple salmon-harpoon head is rather common in Greenland, as is the compound fish hook. The toggle for the sledge draught line, of antler, has been found in Northeast Greenland[1]), and the method of lashing a snow knife together out of two pieces, apparently common at Naujan, occurs at any rate in Thule (L 3: 2776, from Thule House 1). The snow knife of baleen may be problematic[2]). The whetting tooth of musk-ox molar has not definitely been found in Greenland, but it is possible that such teeth found in houses in Inglefield Land may have been used in the same manner. The adze head all of stone is common in Northeast Greenland, and the chopping block of whale vertebra is known from Inugsuk[3]). Drill bits of slate are common in Greenland outside the Thule District. The scraper of antler with the handle at an angle occurs at Thule, but not with a separate blade; the latter has been found at Chesterfield Inlet, however[4]). The bone marrow-extractor was found at Inugsuk[5]), the blubber pounder of antler in the Thule District on earlier occasions, and cylindrical bone beads in Northeast Greenland[6]). "Swimming birds" have previously been found in the Thule District[7]), the nuglutang in Northeast Greenland and Angmagssalik[8]), and "game men" of bone and baleen, as well as the peg with a groove for the bird dart, at Inugsuk[9]). Toy sledge runners of baleen were presumably known in Thule, as there we have sledge cross-slats of baleen (pl. 49.28). I consider that the remarkable baleen "bird" from Naujan[10]) is a scraper, as the broad edge is distinctly rounded by wear; it has not been met with outside of Naujan, however.

As all the above elements (with the exception of the last) may be assumed to have passed through the Thule District, so that it may simply be accidental that they were not found there, we have left 21 characteristic elements, or 9 per cent., which distinguish Naujan from the Thule District with Greenland on the whole as a background. In comparison it may be said that the Thule culture in Inglefield Land had about 11 per cent. of types that were not common to the Thule District as well. Of the 21 it is presumable that some are more or less local forms, whereas others undoubtedly signify a real difference in culture phases. These special elements are:

---

[1]) H. Larsen 1934 pl. 5.13-14.
[2]) Mathiassen 1927 I p. 47.
[3]) Mathiassen 1930 (a) p. 217.
[4]) Mathiassen 1927 I p. 113.
[5]) Mathiassen 1930 (a) p. 240.
[6]) Th. Thomsen 1917 pl. XI, 10.
[7]) Mathiassen 1927 II fig. 10.7.
[8]) H. Larsen 1934 p. 153; Mathiassen 1933 pl. 9.20.
[9]) Mathiassen 1930 (a) pp. 315, 262; pl. 8.15, p. 200.
[10]) Mathiassen 1927 I fig. 14.

Harpoon foreshaft, conical butt, lateral hole (pl. 3.2-4)[1]),
tension piece, symmetrical (pl. 5.6-7),
reserve lance head, open socket (pl. 6.8-9),
arrow head with cleft fore end (pl. 8.7),
bird harpoon head (pl. 10.8-11)[2]),
arrow blade of bone,
arrow of baleen (pl. 35.3),
salmon-spear side prong of wood (pl. 12.1),
back-piece for salmon spear (pl. 12.15),
toboggan of baleen,
edge mounting for snow shovel (pl. 16.6),
adze head with blade in both ends (pl. 22.5),
hand-drill shank of bone for bits at both ends,
spoon of musk-ox horn with slender shank (pl. 28.9),
meat fork of walrus ivory (pl. 33.10),
club of walrus penis bone,
buttons or buckles with carved figures (pl. 29.6-8),
bear tooth with carving (page 71),
drop-pendant, unusually long (pl. 30.16-17),
drop-pendant with human figure (pl. 30.21),
ajagaq of walrus ivory (pl. 33.9).

The other implement types shared with the Thule District have the following chronological distribution:

```
 7 only in Thule period
 4  —   - early transitional period
24  —   - Inugsuk period
 2  —   - late transitional period

 3  —   - etr — Thule
25  —   - In — etr — Thule
34  —   - ltr — In — etr — Thule
12  —   - In — etr
14  —   - ltr — In — etr
 9  —   - ltr — In
 5  —   - recent time — ltr — In — etr
 4  —   - recent time — ltr — In

34  —   - general distribution.
```

Omitting the latter we get the row:

	ltr		In		etr		Th
6	14	38	46	29	3	7

This again means that the preponderance lies somewhere between the early transitional period and Inugsuk, but nearer the latter; and

---

[1]) The plate numbers refer to Mathiassen 1927 I.

[2]) It may be that two small harpoon heads from Thule Houses 10 and 19 should be regarded as bird-harpoon heads (I p. 189).

the 24 elements that are shared solely with Thule's Inugsuk period point very distinctly towards this time. It will also be seen that no fewer than 74 elements, or about 31 per cent., have their lower limit in the early transitional period or later. Thus in all essentials Naujan must be said to correspond to a culture phase which in the Thule District is to be found in the 14th century, and accordingly Naujan would be almost contemporaneous with Qilalukan.

A comparison of the groups calculated in percentages gives:

	rec.	ltr		In		etr		Th	gen. dist.	special elements
Naujan		$2^1/_2$	6	16	$19^1/_2$	12	$1^1/_2$	3	$14^1/_2$	25 (9)
Qilalukan	$1/_2$	4	8	14		20		11	$1/_2$	2	17	23
Mitimatalik		2	6	$7^1/_2$		26		15	2	4	$31^1/_2$	7

The resemblance between Naujan and Qilalukan is obvious; but, if we can venture to read so much from the figures, Qilalukan displays a slight displacement upwards in time at the expense of the lower end—corresponding to the fact that Mathiassen considers Qilalukan to be a trifle later than Naujan[1]). The figures included for Mitimatalik suggest that the finds from there are somewhat earlier than both Qilalukan and Naujan; here, however, more regard must be paid to the smaller compass of the material, which makes the conclusions less certain.

The distance between Naujan and the Thule District of course means that one cannot say off hand that corresponding culture phases are of the same date; and indeed the number of special elements in these two places shows that there were local developments. But in addition there are so many points of mutual resemblance that it must be justifiable to assume a cultural relationship so near that the results shown above will presumably hold good within fair limits.

By putting such a late date to the Thule culture as we have hitherto known it, it is now easier to understand why the knife with a side blade, which has played a certain rôle in the relative chronological determinations, makes its first real appearance in the Thule District in the Inugsuk period—a phenomenon which otherwise has been difficult to explain in a reasonable manner.

The finds from *Malerualik* in King William's Land[2]) are so very like those from Naujan that there can scarcely be any great time difference between them; at any rate we cannot expect to make any finer differentiation with the aid of the chronology of the Thule District.

---

[1]) Mathiassen 1927 I p. 197.
[2]) Mathiassen 1927 I p. 306 ff.

Kuk, Southampton Island [1]).

The finds from here are not numerous, and on the whole come so near to Naujan that we cannot really distinguish between them by means of a numerical comparison. For Houses VI, IX, XVI and XX, which according to Mathiassen are the earliest[2]), there are out of 26 elements:

3 special elements

1 only in Inugsuk

5 — - In — etr — Thule
6 — - ltr — In — etr — Thule
2 — - ltr — In — etr
1 — - recent time — ltr — In — etr
1 — - ltr — In
1 — - recent time — ltr — In

6 general distribution.

This gives the row

	ltr		ln		etr	gen.	spec.
	1	2	3	6	5	6	3
in percentage....... ca.	4	8	$11^{1}/_{2}$	23	20	23	$11^{1}/_{2}$

As one would expect, a comparison with the figures for Naujan and Qilalukan shows that on the whole the cultural picture is the same. Six types here have their upper limit in the Inugsuk period, i. e. snow-shovel blade of walrus scapula, salmon-spear side prong with lashing groove, scraper of caribou scapula, Thule 2 harpoon head, triangular harpoon blade of flint, and mattock blade with a shaft hole—whereas only 2 have their lower limit here: adze head with vertical holes, and knife with unilateral side blade. This indicates that these finds more nearly are contemporaneous with early Inugsuk or early transitional period—13th-14th century. The special elements do not tell us much: salmon-spear side prong, barb with elongated, cut holes, and ornamented button of walrus ivory.

The next group, consisting of Houses VII, XVII and XVIII, gives 91 types, distributed as follows:

23 special elements

1 only in early transitional period
7 — - Inugsuk,

---

[1]) Mathiassen 1927 I p. 224 ff.
[2]) Mathiassen 1927 I p. 253 ff.

```
13 only in In — etr — Th,
15  —   - ltr — In — etr — Th,
 5  —   - In — etr,
 4  —   - ltr — In — etr
 2  —   - recent time — ltr — In — etr,
 3  —   - ltr — In
 4  —   - recent time — ltr — In
```

14 general distribution.

From this we get the row:

	ltr		In		etr	gen.	spec.
	4	5	11	20	14	14	23
in percentage...... ca.	4	$5^1/_2$	12	22	15	15	25

In comparison with the foregoing this shows that the cultural picture becomes a little more concentrated about the Inugsuk period, and at the same time the local character becomes more marked. Here too are 7 types which are specifically shared with Thule's Inugsuk period, viz. harpoon head like the Inugsuk head, but with the blade at at right angles to the line hole, heavy socket piece with triangular butt (but differing a little from the ordinary type), harpoon blade of slate, salmon-spear barb with holes and projecting neck, snow-shovel of scapula, flint-flaker of walrus rib, and two-handed scraper of bear ulna—the only two-handed scraper found during the excavations of the Fifth Thule Expedition[1]). For the most part these are types on which one may safely base a dating. Furthermore there are 25 types, or about $27^1/_2$ per cent., with their upper limit in Inugsuk period, and 7, or about $7^1/_2$ per cent., with their lower limit in the same period, besides the 7 elements that occur only in the Inugsuk period. The elements with lower limit in that period are: fixed lance head, adze head without holes, snow-goggles, Thule 3 harpoon head with holes and oblique spur, knife with row of side blades (converted into a salmon-spear side prong—Mathiassen pl. 71.2), knife with unilateral side blade, and low, broad ulo handle. On the whole these too are elements which, as conditions in Thule show, are good dating factors. Thus with fairly complete certainty we have narrowed this house group down to the Inugsuk period, i. e. 14th—15th century; and if we take the local special types into consideration, it is most reasonable to assume that these finds date more nearly to the latter part of the period, i. e. the 15th century. This means that this period saw the advent of the more highly developed flint technique and the use of limestone flags for lamps and cooking pots[2]).

---

[1]) Mathiassen 1930 (a) p. 223.
[2]) Mathiassen 1927 I p. 255.

Of the types which in the comparison with the Thule District I have singled out as special elements there are several that Kuk has in common with Naujan; but on the subject of the mutual relationship between these finds—and the Fifth Thule Expedition's finds on the whole I must refer to Mathiassen's publication.

House III, which Mathiassen regards as the latest[1]), partly on account of its general appearance, yielded only 23 elements, which have the following distribution:

8 special elements,

1 only in Thule culture,
2 —   - Inugsuk,
2 —   - In — etr — Thule,
4 —   - ltr — In — etr — Thule,
1 —   - In — etr,
1 —   - ltr — In — etr,

4 general distribution.

This gives:

	In		etr	Th	gen.	spec.
	3	5	2	1	4	8
in percentage ca.	13	22	9	4	17	35

Compared with the foregoing the material here reveals an increased specificity, whilst the cultural picture on the whole assumes an earlier character—a circumstance which, in the additional light of historical conditions, may be interpreted as meaning that an initial development of some of the implement types fell into stagnation when Southampton Island became isolated. The new types, which were common to the surrounding localities, failed to gain a firm foothold and were abandoned in favour of a more local development, based chiefly on the old stock of types. Something of the same kind took place, as we have seen, in the Thule District after the Ruin Island phase; and here, as in that case, we find once again that one can build upon statistical methods only with the exercise of all due criticism and constant reference to the concrete types and the actual conditions.

As long ago as in 1918 Wissler drew the conclusion—but from a much more slender basis—that the lower layers of Comer's Midden are contemporary with the earliest settlements on Southampton Island[2]). It is interesting to observe, however, that among the finds in Thule he mentions "a large stone slab with ridges of cement around the edges,

---

[1]) Mathiassen 1927 I p. 256.
[2]) Wissler 1918 p. 150 f.

suggesting a lamp of the Southampton Island type. The shape of this piece also suggests the Southampton Island lamps. We may therefore feel reasonably certain that this same type of built-up lamp was known to the inhabitants of Comer's Midden".

However, I am disinclined to believe that the people of the Thule District were very familiar with these lamps. The find would seem to indicate that a group of people with Southampton Island culture reached Thule at some time within the Inugsuk period, and there they had no need to make lamps in this fashion any longer. Other signs may be read as meaning the same thing, for instance the flint flaker of walrus rib, which in Thule occurs only in what is assumed to be late Inugsuk period (Houses 8 and 10). In House 8 there were also two roof supports of stone as in Houses III and XXII on Southampton Island, and a store room at the front side of the house, as in XXII, seems to be common in the houses in Thule which correspond to House 10. Furthermore, the two-handed scraper of bear ulna in Thule is confined to the Inugsuk period (Co. B). It is also possible that there is some connection between the spatula-shaped boot-creaser (?) (Mathiassen pl. 69.8) and the similar implement from Thule House 20 (pl. 1.15), which merely has a longer handle. Again, the small piece of walrus ivory with an incised design (Mathiassen pl. 72.5) is very similar to the one from the midden in front of Thule House 21(pl. 36.33). It is more doubtful if there is any connection between the lamps of Southampton Island and the one found by Mathiassen at Angmagssalik, "formed of a slab of gneiss, and along the back there has been an edging of clay"[1]), and estimated as being 18th century.

---

[1]) Mathiassen 1933 p. 92.

V. RELATION BETWEEN THE THULE CULTURES OF INGLEFIELD LAND AND CANADA

The result arrived at from the foregoing investigation is that the classical Thule culture of Arctic Canada, such as it is described by Mathiassen, prevailed mainly in the 14th century, and presumably in part of the 13th, contemporaneously with what has been called the early transitional period and the Inugsuk period in the Thule District. We have also seen that the large collective find from Naujan contains a much smaller wealth of elements than that from Thule's Inugsuk period, so that there can hardly be any doubt but that the strong development which characterizes the Inugsuk period only reached its culmination in Greenland. It should be added, however, that the adjacent regions on the west are almost unknown archaeologically, and the finds at Qilalukan prove that the aforesaid development had already begun to gather speed on American soil.

The consequence of this must be, however, that the Thule culture of Inglefield Land, with its upper limit round about the year 1200, represents an earlier phase of the Thule culture than that known to us from Naujan. It will therefore be of interest to consider the cultural picture in Inglefield Land on the background of the Canadian Thule culture; in other words, we must see what elements occur in Inglefield Land but not in the Canadian Thule culture. In this connection the Dorset elements will also be taken into consideration.

The elements that are characteristic of Inglefield Land are:

Dorset elements:
Harpoon head, open socket, no blade, one line hole,
— — , closed socket, blade, one line hole, square-cut butt (D),
— — , heavy type,
sling handle (D),
knife handle, wood, side-groove at end (D),
knife with side blade,
adze head (D),
hatchet head of walrus ivory (D),
spatula-shaped implement,
wood stick with ornament (D),

((D): occurs only in Dorset middens).

Thule elements:
Thule-2 harpoon head, slots, vestigial barb, no blade,
* — — —, —, blade parallel to line hole,
toggle harpoon head, thin, closed socket, oblique spur, blade parallel to line hole,
keeled harpoon head, blade parallel to line hole,
barrel-shaped swivel,
stopper for harpoon line with end-spike, no holes,
flat, oval bladder mouthpiece,
fastening peg for bladder, wood,
— - - —, baleen,
small mending disc with groove, walrus ivory,
loose foreshaft with two holes,
stiletto handle of wood,
wound plug of wood,
*seat of antler for one-legged sealing stool,
sealing stool leg of bone,
bow brace of wood,
— — - antler,
quiver handle with groove at ends,
— — — carved figures, horizontal holes,
sling handle of baleen,
two-pronged leister,
ferrule, long conical or cylindrical,
*ferrule with end-concavity (for bird dart etc.),
— tubular (open ends),
bone peg with head,
sledge runner of wood,
sledge shoe of narwhal ivory,
*sledge upstander of antler,
trapeziform trace buckle,
trace buckle with hole obliquely from the side,
(kayak stem, gunwale and rib),
*snow knife with hole-handle,
knife handle of wood with slit for end blade,
* — — - — with seating for side blade at end (Dorset type?),
knife with side blade (ulo?), broad blade part, thin handle,
whetstone of asbestos,
hand pick, rib,
— —, antler, with teeth,
* — —, antler with transverse handle,
moss spade,
flint flaker, walrus penis bone,
— —, antler,
— —, walrus ivory,
marline spike, flat, slender constricted fore-end,
cutting board, bone,
arrow straightener,
ulo handle, bone, even transition to broad back,
— — with end projections on blade side,
*convex-edged scraper blade of stone (not flint),
— side scraper of flint,

concave side scraper of flint.
broad scraper, bone or antler,
— antler with projecting handle (no blade),
trapeziform scraper handle,
*side scraper, antler, open at ends,
two-handed scraper, caribou metacarpus,
*thimble holder, hook shaped,
boot creaser,
*pyrites with handle,
lamp, small, oval, sandstone (Dorset type?),
lamp, small, deep, triangular-oval, no ledge,
*coiled basket of osier,
ladle, musk-ox horn,
*spoon (?), walrus ivory,
bone strip with row of holes (for skin vessel?),
thin wood stick with flat point (rib for skin vessel?),
gut-skin coat (or pane),
baleen wool,
mitten,
thong buckle with hole and groove,
tubular buckle, "winged",
bead of fish vertebrae,
comb with hexagonal handle,
*mica mirror in skin frame,
gambling bones,
*top-disc, soapstone,
doll, wood, with toupé,
—, —, with boots,
*human figure of walrus ivory, naturalistically carved,
toy arrow with widened fore end,
- sling handle, wood,
- sledge cross-slat, bone,
- — — , wood,
- kayak paddle, narrow type,
- lamp with ledge,
miniature baleen knife (amulet?).

This makes a total of 95 elements, or no less than about 37 per cent. of the 258 found in the Thule culture of Inglefield Land plus the Dorset period. Not one of them was found in the Canadian Thule culture, and even if this in several cases may have been purely accidental, there can be no question but that this is really another culture phase. Of the 95 elements 16 (marked *) are types which in the Thule District have been found only within the Thule culture of Inglefield Land. Ten are Dorset forms, and of these six (marked D) were found only in the Dorset middens; it is possible that the others also originate from the Dorset settlement, but not quite certain, and in any case we must assume that they are forms that were also used in the Thule period.

With regard to the 85 Thule types, some are variants of well known elements; but quite a number are more or less independent culture elements, for example: the barrel-shaped swivel, peg for holding a bladder, mending plug with groove, stiletto with wood handle, wound plug of wood, two-pronged leister, sledge upstander, hand pick, arrow straightener, hook-shaped thimble holder, basket of osier, ladle of musk-ox horn, bone strip with row of holes, gut-skin coat, baleen wool, thong buckle with hole and groove, tubular "winged" buckle, gamling bones of seal metatarsus, kayak paddle with narrow blade, and the small baleen knives— 20 elements in all. This number is so high that it would be remarkable if at any rate some of them had not appeared in the Central finds, if they really had been in use there.

Naturally it must be taken into account that some of the elements are locally developed types; to enable us to form an idea on this point it is necessary first to see what elements occur outside of the Canadian Thule culture—among the Western Eskimos, the present Central Eskimos, or perhaps among Indian tribes south of the Eskimo territory. (In this connection we may disregard the other parts of Greenland, as occurrence there must be secondary in relation to Inglefield Land). However, for the region with which we are mainly concerned the only systematic, archaeological investigations published are in Alaska, where conditions on St. Lawrence Island especially have been revealed through the excavations made in 1930—31 by Collins, Ford and Chambers and published by Collins[1]). In that work Collins demonstrates characteristics of the Old Bering Sea and the Punuk cultures and makes a detailed account of their relation to the later Eskimo culture in Alaska. However, valuable help is also to be found in Birket-Smith's comprehensive work "The Caribou Eskimos", to the second part of which reference will often be made in the following.

In the Old Bering Sea and Punuk cultures we recognize:

Wound plug of wood (no screw),
two-handed scraper,
knife handle, wood, with slit for end blade,
side scraper, antler, with open ends,
hand pick,
concave scraper of flint,
convex-edged scraper of slate or the like.

The wooden wound plug occurs in the Old Bering Sea, Punuk and modern Western Eskimo cultures[2]) and on Baffin Island[3]), and the similar form but with screw threads is widespread among the Central Eskimos. In Old Bering Sea the two-handed scraper is usually of dog femur, but one was found of caribou metatarsus[4]). It is also recorded

---

[1]) Collins 1937.
[2]) Collins 1937 p. 357; pl. 35.11-14, 75.11.
[3]) Boas 1901 fig. 18.
[4]) Collins 1937 pp. 166, 356; pl. 30.12-14.

from Pt. Barrow[1]) and from the Aivilik Eskimos[2]). Knud Rasmussen mentions a two-handed scraper, "sharp on one edge" from the Copper Eskimos[3]), and Birket-Smith states that among the Caribou Eskimos it is said to be of musk-ox, or bear bone or of walrus penis bone[4]). The latter forms must undoubtedly have been borrowed from the coastal tribes, originally no doubt of caribou or musk-ox. Two-handed scrapers of tubular bones are also recorded from a number of Indian tribes just south of the Eskimo region, from the Tahltan in the west to the Naskapi and Beothuk in the east, as well as other tribes as far south as the old Pueblo regions[5]). Altogether this shows that the wooden wound plug and the two-handed scraper of tubular bone must be ancient elements common to Eskimo culture.

The knife handle of wood with a slit for a blade at the end was found in the Old Bering Sea and Punuk cultures[6]). The knife handle with a side blade towards one end also occurs in Old Bering Sea, but there the blade was also fitted into a slit and not on to a seating as in the case of those from Inglefield Land. The concave scraper from Old Bering Sea is figured by Collins pl. 41, where fig. 22 is the most typical. These scrapers seem to disappear in the Punuk time, when polished slate objects gain predominance[7]). The convex scraper with an edge at the end, of other stones than flint and the like, also occurs in Old Bering Sea, and some of the side scrapers illustrated by Collins have more or less convex scraping edges. The side scraper of antler (pl. 27.15), which must be regarded as a variant of the cup-shaped scraper (fat scraper) has been found only in the Punuk culture[8]), but it must be related to similar scrapers of walrus ivory in Old Bearing Sea[9]).

Finally, there is the simple hand-pick of rib, which seems to be quite the same as Collins' "bone rubbing tool"[10]), but which I, on account of the wear marks, presume must have been used as a moss-pick or the like, in the same manner as the corresponding forms of antler with teeth, transversal handle, or the broader moss spades. I have seen Polar Eskimos hacking turf off with a knife wielded in the same manner as the above tools must have been. The hand-pick of rib occurs in both Old Bering Sea and Punuk, and Mathiassen illustrates an implement of whale bone of similar character, but more carefully made, from

---

[1]) Murdoch 1892 p. 299 fig. 299.
[2]) Boas 1901 fig. 132.
[3]) Knud Rasmussen 1932 p. 103.
[4]) Birket-Smith 1929 I p. 244.
[5]) Birket-Smith 1929 II p. 357 f.
[6]) Collins 1937 pp. 144, 232.
[7]) Collins 1937 p. 232.
[8]) Collins 1937 p. 351; pl. 78.14.
[9]) Collins 1937 pl. 51.8-9.
[10]) Collins 1937. p. 163, pl. 48.10-13.

Pt. Hope; it is said to have been used for splitting the fat from the skin when making harpoon bladders[1]). Mathiassen calls the implement an "ivsvugat", no doubt corresponding to a form given by Jenness from Barrow, which presumably can be spelt "ivzRutaq" (-zR- representing Jenness's velar, voiced spirant) and meaning "mattock for turf"[2]) (cf. Greenlandic "ivssoq": turf). I have been unable to find this simple implement described from the Central Eskimos, but it is evidently related to the moss spade reported as being used by the Caribou Eskimos[3]), Copper Eskimos[4]) and Aivilingmiut[5]); it must be assumed to be an ancient element common to all Eskimos.

The *mica mirror* has not been observed among Eskimos, but de Laguna mentions that it was used by Salish tribes in the interior[6]).

Of culture elements with a wide distribution in the modern Eskimo culture we have:

Barrel-shaped swivel (Alaska-Baffin Island)[7])
sledge runner of wood,
arrow straightener (Alaska-Baffin Isl.)[8])
gut-skin coat,
mitten,
boot creaser (Alaska-Labrador)[9])
gambling bones (Pt. Barrow, Netsilik, Caribou, Polar Eskimos)[10])
coiled basket.

These too must be assumed to be very ancient elements, even if direct archaeological evidence is lacking.

As regards the swivel, the earliest forms are quite barrel-shaped with a hole in the side, through which they were hollowed out, whereas the forms commonly known have a large opening at the back and make their first appearance in the Inugsuk period. Coiled basketry is known from Pt. Barrow[11]), Netsilik Eskimos[12]) and Labrador. Hawkes draws attention to the close resemblance between coiled basketry from Alaska

---

[1]) Mathiassen 1930 (b) fig. 20, p. 65.
[2]) Jenness 1928 (a) p. 46.
[3]) Birket-Smith 1929 I fig. 19.
[4]) Knud Rasmussen 1932 p. 100, "talugLitit".
[5]) Boas 1901 p. 102.
[6]) de Laguna 1934 p. 186.
[7]) Birket-Smith 1929 II p. 259.
[8]) Birket-Smith 1929 II p. 284.
[9]) Nelson 1899 pl. XLIV, 41—51; Knud Rasmussen 1932 p. 104; Hawkes 1916 pp. 43, 46.—Furthermore Dr. Birket Smith informs me verbally that the boot creaser is also in use among the Netsilik Eskimos, two specimens (15709 from King William Island and 15743 from Ukjulingmiut) belonging to the Gjöa collections in Oslo.
[10]) Birket-Smith 1929 II p. 291.
[11]) Murdoch 1892 p. 326 f.
[12]) Birket-Smith 1937 p. 223, 1927 p. 201, illustration.

and from Labrador, compared with Indian work, the nearest parallels being from California[1]). The ladle of musk-ox horn is known from all Central Eskimos[2]).

Elements found only among the Western Eskimos are:

Small mending disc with groove,
quiver handle with carved figures,
hatchet head of walrus ivory,
hook-shaped thimble holder.

The small mending discs of walrus ivory from Inglefield Land correspond to Nelson's pl. LVI a.5, where we also recognize the conical shape at one end similar to that on the specimens from Inuarfigssuaq House 20 (pl. 5.21). Quiver handles exactly like those from Inglefield Land are not illustrated by Nelson, but the motif of an animal head at each end is seen employed in pl. XLIII.5,15,21. The hatchet head which was found in the Dorset midden, agrees in form with the "root picks" of the Western Eskimos[3]). The hook-shaped thimble holder has been found only at Pt. Barrow and Bering Strait[4]).

Elements known exclusively from Baffin Island are:

Mouthpieces for bladder, of flat, oval form[5]),
loose foreshaft with two holes (for bladder dart)[6]).

It is presumable that the Thule culture included the bladder dart with a loose harpoon head similar to those from Baffin Island, and no doubt the long mouthpieces with a flat underside (pl. 5.14) were used with them. The small, deep, triangular-oval lamp with no wick ledge also seems to have persisted on Baffin Island[7]), and possibly there is a relationship between thong buckles with a hole and groove (pl. 38.6-8) and those which Boas describes as having been used for the sledge draught line[8]).

Trace buckles with a hole running obliquely from the side to the end were found on Southampton Island[9]), and finally the sledge upstander of antler is used by the Baffinlanders[10]) and Iglulik Eskimos[11]).

---

[1]) Hawkes 1916 pl. XXX p. 103 f.
[2]) Birket-Smith 1929 II p. 241.
[3]) Nelson 1899 pl. XXXIII b. 3.
[4]) Birket-Smith 1929 II p. 282; Murdoch 1892 fig. 328; Nelson 1899 pl. XLIV
[5]) Boas 1888 p. 493; 1901 fig. 21.
[6]) Boas 1888 p. 494, fig. 429 c.
[7]) Boas 1901 fig. 56 a.
[8]) Boas 1901 fig. 48.
[9]) Boas 1901 fig. 96 a.
[10]) Boas 1888 fig. 482, p. 529.
[11]) Mathiassen 1928 (b) fig. 42.

The sledges of the Old Bering Sea and Punuk cultures are very small and low, and we have no evidence at all that dogs were used for drawing sledges in these periods[1]). Accordingly there is reason for believing that the sledge with upstanders is peculiar to the Thule culture and that upstanders were not used by the inland Eskimos, their occurrence today among the Iglulingmiut and Baffinlanders being explained most readily as a relic from the Thule culture.

As regards the four elements that are shared solely with the modern Western Eskimos, they are of such a special character that one must necessarily assume an intimate association; but these isolated elements tell us nothing certain about the nature of this connection or by what route it travelled. The artistic fashioning of implements nowadays is particularly characteristic of Alaska; all the same, we must not overlook the East Greenlanders, and strictly speaking it would be unjustifiable simply to conclude that the motive necessarily originated a thousand years ago, or even more, in Alaska and was transplanted to the east, even if circumstances as a whole no doubt may suggest something of the kind. In this case too the reverse must at any rate be taken into consideration — so much the more as Collins has advanced weighty reasons in support of the theory that the Thule culture, in the form known to us from the Canadian finds, came to Alaska from the east at a relatively late period[2]). If this is so, one would naturally connect this movement with the pressure from the Central Eskimos which drove the people of the Thule culture northwards. On the other hand we can say very little about what happened during the early phase of the Thule culture.

There is no doubt that the Dorset phase in Inglefield Land is connected most closely with Baffin Island and Labrador, and the elements named above might also be taken as evidence of a special easterly orientation; on the other hand there were features that indicated that the early Thule culture signified a new immigration into Greenland. In as far as the Dorset forms found in that culture really formed a part of it, they may, however, have been acquired in the region round about Pond Inlet, whereas the people themselves with their special form of Thule culture may well have come from the regions north or west of Hudson Bay. Further excavations alone can clear up this point. Nevertheless, on the basis of the elements that have proved to be shared with the late Central Eskimo culture, but not with the Canadian Thule culture, the fact can be established that the early phase of the Thule culture found in Inglefield Land in some respects is somewhat nearer to the Inland Eskimos than is the later Thule culture.

It is possible to mention other circumstances that support this

---

[1]) Collins 1937 p. 338 f.
[2]) Collins 1937 p. 364.

argument—for instance the occurrence in Inglefield Land of toy kayak paddles with a markedly narrow blade, whereas the broad-bladed type does not appear until the following period. A paddle with a similarly narrow blade was figured by Nelson from King Island[1]), and Boas illustrates two more, described as Aivilik sea-paddle and Kinipetu paddle respectively[2]). There is thus a possibility that the Greenland type of narrow-bladed paddle now in use dates far back in time, but for a while was superseded by the more broad-bladed type of the Thule culture and the Inugsuk period. Here we must also recall the toy kayak with the long beak, from Inf. House 3 (pl. 42.15), apparently intended to represent a form of kayak resembling most of all that of the Caribou or Netsilik Eskimos.

Finally, there is the remarkable absence of graves in Inglefield Land. At Inuarfigssuaq we found only one, arranged inside a passage, and this may well be of later date. The fact that not a single grave except this was found in the vicinity of a settlement of this size must mean that the people did not use the substantial graves that are common in the Canadian Thule culture and throughout the rest of Greenland. Knud Rasmussen records a Polar Eskimo legend explaining the origin of the name Inuarfigssuaq, "the fjord of the great massacre" (literally: the place of the great human slaughter). The legend has it: "and all the dead lay black against the white ice, just like seals basking on a spring day. How long they killed no one knows..."[3]). Is it not likely that a legend of this kind would arise out of the later Eskimo's own astonishment at not finding any graves? Or perhaps they saw skeletal remains lying on the ground, unburied. Apparently the earliest inhabitants followed the simple custom of exposing the corpse, one that is common among the Central Eskimos and in Labrador and also known among the West Eskimos, Chukchi and Koryak[4]). It must be an ancient Eskimo form of burial[5]) and it forms a particular connection between the people of the early Thule culture and the tradition of the inland tribes.

The massive graves of the later Thule people are evidence that new spiritual movements have also begun to assert themselves—perhaps in conjunction with the advance from the west of the developed form of shamanism, revealed by Thalbitzer's thorough-going investigations[6]). In this connection it is strange that we found no definite remains of drums datable to earlier than the lowest layer of Comer's Midden, i. e.

---

[1]) Nelson 1899 p. 225, fig. 71b.
[2]) Boas 1901 fig. 107, b and c.
[3]) Knud Rasmussen: Grønland langs Polhavet p. 186.
[4]) Birket-Smith 1929 II p. 293 f., 379 f.
[5]) Birket-Smith 1929 II p. 122 f.
[6]) Thalbitzer 1926 p. 74; 1928 p. 426 ff.

from about the time of the Inugsuk culture. I would not venture to say that drums were not known earlier; but they would scarcely be so common, and it is justifiable to assume that *qilaneq* (head-lifting conjuring) played a greater rôle in the cult than it did later on—just as indeed the drum is called *qilaut* (*qila*-implement). We still find something of the same thing among the Caribou Eskimos, where outwardly the shamanistic technique is not nearly so highly developed as among the coastal peoples[1]. It may also have something to do with this fact that the people of Southampton Island are alleged to be in ignorance of the drum[2]. If it was never of much importance, its disappearance would be so much the easier.

In the foregoing we have succeeded in tracing at least 29 of the elements enumerated; none of them can be purely local to Inglefield Land. As regards the remainder, matters are less clear; but the majority are forms of implements of such a character that it is difficult to believe that they were confined to Inglefield Land, so much the more as the people there immigrated from the west; it would therefore be justifiable to expect that similar forms will be found if new excavations are made in Arctic Canada.

However, the approach to the inland culture raises another question, viz. what position this early phase of the Thule culture occupies in the development of the Eskimo culture as a whole. The answer to this question must be deferred a little while yet, however.

---

[1] Knud Rasmussen 1930 p. 54.
[2] Birket-Smith 1929 II p. 117.

VI. POSITION OF THE RUIN ISLAND PEOPLE IN THE ESKIMO CULTURE

It still remains to examine the background of the people of Ruin Island, who seem to have played such an important part in the mediaeval history of the Greenland Eskimos. Of the 30 special elements enumerated on pp. 70—71 we know only of the following in the Canadian Thule culture, and from Naujan alone:

Heavy socket-piece with triangular butt (Mathiassen pl. 3.10),
"winged" pendant (Mathiassen pl. 30.20),
doll of baleen (Mathiassen pl. 32.10).

Naujan also produced a socket-piece with a cleft butt, but of heavy type[1]), whereas a corresponding specimen from Ruin Island is small, apparently for a fish harpoon or a small bladder dart (pl. 6.7) Mathiassen also makes mention of an implement of walrus rib "resembling in shape the flint flakers used in Alaska; this classification is, however, uncertain"[2]). The characteristic curved handle that is supposed to belong to it and was found on Ruin Island was not found at Naujan.

Accordingly, there is not much to show for a close connection with the Canadian Thule culture, which, by the way, as we have seen proved to be somewhat later. The Ruin Island culture compared with it seems just as "foreign" as with the culture in the Thule District. From what we know of it so far it does not seem capable of representing a culture that has slowly spread forwards, but rather a tribal group that moved rapidly, apparently along a route which at the most merely touched the regions hitherto investigated. Here, however, we must remember that in the northern marginal regions there have been no systematic excavations whatever that can at all come into consideration, so there is a possibility that one day we shall have the opportunity of seeing a more widespread culture of similar character.

---

[1]) Mathiassen 1927 I pl. 3.11.
[2]) Mathiassen 1927 I p. 79, pl. 34.9.

One element that is especially peculiar to the Ruin Island group is the harpoon head with a vestigial spur (pl. 3.5,6,13,14), for as such the small knob at the base of the spur must undoubtedly be regarded. No such form has been found in the Central and eastern regions before; on the other hand, harpoon heads with a curious divided spur is typical of Old Bering Sea, Birnirk and Punuk cultures; and if we compare with Collins' table of forms of harpoon heads[1]), it is clear that the connection is to be found especially in Punuk and early Punuk. It is true that Collins' survey does not include exactly the same forms of harpoon heads; but the vestigial spur is observable only in Early Punuk (type III (a) y) and right down in the Old Bering Sea culture (III y). Under Punuk Collins shows a harpoon head with 2 × 2 barbs, apparently like the one (defective) from Ruin Island (pl. 3.5), except that the latter also has a vestigial spur. The characteristic Punuk ornamentation is not to be found on any of the Ruin Island specimens, but nor is it on all the Punuk harpoon heads from St. Lawrence Island. On the other hand there is close similarity in the entire exterior form, for example between the toggle harpoon head pl. 3.14 and several on Collins' pl. 70. The same applies to the harpoon heads of Thule 2 type, these lacking the marked shoulders level with or a little anterior to the line hole which are characteristic of most specimens in the Thule culture. The shape of the barbs on pl. 3.5 also agrees with Collins' pl. 70.6. Similar slender barbs are also to be seen on the arrow head from Thule House 16 (pl. 11.29) which, instead of knobs, also has a ring-shaped thickness on the tang, a common feature on Western Eskimo arrow heads (for example Collins pl. 74.6,8,14 Punuk and Modern; Mathiassen 1930 pl. 9.1-3). However, slender barbs are also to be seen in the Canadian Thule culture on harpoon heads, and precisely on types with several barbs (Mathiassen 1927 I pl. 9.9 and 72.4). Here too this feature is presumably the outcome of influence from the west—and perhaps originally just in connection with the Ruin Island people. Finally, all open-socketed harpoon heads from the Ruin Island group have slots for the lashing, as is also the case in the ancient Alaskan cultures.

Of the other harpoon heads from the Ruin Island group that with the keel and with the blade at right angles to the line hole (pl. 4.9) is the most common. This, however, provides us with no special information, the type being widespread from Bering Strait to Greenland[2]); the same applies to the whale harpoon. Nevertheless there can be no doubt that it is a western type, and moreover there is the special agreement between the keeled harpoon heads from the Thule District and from St. Lawrence Island that several have the characteristic lateral roll between the fore

---

[1]) Collins 1937 fig. 24.
[2]) Mathiassen 1927 II p. 21.

end and the line hole which Collins mentions as a feature that differentiates them from the ordinary Thule type[1]).

Besides the above the only harpoon heads found in the Ruin Island group are the thin toggle type with a closed socket, the blade parallel with the line hole and an oblique spur, and the flat toggle harpoon head with an open socket and a blade (the latter not from Ruin Island proper); both occur in the early transitional period, and the former is fairly common in early Thule time.

To judge from the harpoon heads we may thus say that the Ruin Island group is fairly closely related to the Punuk culture—at any rate more closely than any hitherto known phase of the Thule culture. It is therefore a question of whether the Ruin Island culture is to be regarded as a transitional phase of a continuous development from Punuk to Thule culture, or as an originally Thule culture which made contact with Punuk. The former presupposes only one movement in one direction, from west to east, the latter a meeting between two independently developed cultures, of which the Thule culture must then be presumed to have come from the east. Thereafter there must have been a movement in the contrary direction, as of course the result of this meeting has been ascertained only in the Thule District. In the latter case, however, it would certainly be incorrect to regard the small knobs as vestigial; they would rather be a somewhat awkward attempt to imitate the more complicated forms of spurs. This is improbable, partly for general psychological reasons, but especially because we have seen a distinct developmental series through Old Bering Sea and Punuk towards forms with spurs that become more and more simple, and it is just one of the later, but not the latest, stages that are met with in the Thule District. Consequently it seems most reasonable to assume a third possibility: that it was people from the west with Punuk culture who wandered eastwards and on their way encountered the already developed Thule culture. They did not allow themselves to be quite overwhelmed by it, however, as witness the fact that the unmistakable Punuk stamp of the harpoon heads persisted all the way to the Thule District. In actual fact we have evidence from Alaska that the Punuk culture extended northwards from Bering Strait[2]); but where it encountered the Thule culture—already in North Alaska or farther east—cannot be decided at the moment. When to this we add the fact that the qagsse of the Ruin Island people is foursided and consequently must rest on a distinctly western tradition, the immediate impression is strengthened that these people originally were a group with Punuk culture who made their way eastwards, probably up towards the 13th century,

---

[1]) Collins 1937 p. 313.
[2]) Collins 1933 p. 48.

and that by means of future excavations it should be possible to trace its route.

This is supported by a consideration of other elements of the Ruin Island group which also point direct towards the ancient cultures in Alaska. This applies to the top-disc of walrus ivory with a flat and a convex side (pl. 42.9). One of these, from Old Bering Sea, is illustrated by Collins[1]), but without the ornamental "eyes" on the one from Ruin Island. From the Punuk culture, however, there is a richly ornamented top-disc of similar form[2]), and Geist & Rainey illustrate another, from Kukulik[3]). The "eyes", which are characteristic of the specimen from Ruin Island, consist of inserted wooden pegs, in the centre of which again is a hammered-in peg of bone—a technique which dates back to Punuk[4]) and which one imagines is a special development of the "dot and circle" motif. Holes filled with baleen pegs date right back to Old Bering Sea. Mention is made in I p. 224 of a curious little sledge runner of walrus ivory, corresponding to Collins' pl. 77.8 from Punuk time—a type similar to that used to this day on St. Lawrence Island for the transportation of meat and blubber[5]). The remarkable adze or hatchet head of walrus ivory without a separate blade (pl. 28.3) also seems to point in the same direction.

Of specifically Western types used in modern times there are the flint-flaker with a separate curved handle[6]) and the pick-axe of whale bone[7]). In Alaska the blade of the latter is of walrus ivory and the implement is called an "ice pick" by Nelson. From Pt. Barrow, however, Murdoch figures three "pick-axes", two of which are of bone and supposed to be old, as nowadays they are never seen to be made of anything but walrus ivory[8]). The drag-line handle with the two walruses back to back (pl. 9.1) seems to be a Western motif too, corresponding to Nelson pl. XLIII.20, except that the animals are bears.

I have been unable to find a direct parallel to the scraper of walrus ivory with the handle carved into a human head (fig. 92); but in form and workmanship the face bears an astonishing likeness to a bust carved in walrus ivory figured by de Laguna and found at Kachemak Bay. The Indians said it was a "shaman's puppet, ja'nju (Athapascan), a representation of his guardian spirit"[9]). A broken-off head of similar

---

[1]) Collins 1937 pl. 46.10, p. 176.
[2]) Collins 1937 pl. 67.2.
[3]) Geist & Rainey 1936 pl. 72.5.
[4]) Collins 1937 p. 240.
[5]) Nelson 1899 p. 208 pl. LXXVI.1.
[6]) Nelson 1899 fig. 26; Murdoch 1892 figs. 279—281.
[7]) Nelson 1899 pl. XXXV.1.
[8]) Murdoch 1892 p. 303, fig. 304.
[9]) de Laguna 1934 pl. 52.7, p. 114.

character is from Yukon Island[1]). The similarity of these heads—in an artistic sense too—is so striking that there must be some connection between them.

The remarkable bow-drill shank with four points (fig. 106.11) is another element of which I have failed to find a parallel; the ornamentation, however, consisting of simple spur lines, has a certain Punuk stamp about it, though in itself the motif is widespread. Nor is the bird figure with the sharp, protruding breast bone (pl. 38.31) known elsewhere, to my knowledge, and the same may be said of the stopper for the harpoon line with the spike at the middle (pl. 5.12). This element is not even mentioned from Alaska and may safely be said to belong to ice-hunting technique. On the other hand the small buckle carved into a bear's head (pl. 38.5) is reported from both Alaska[2]) and the Central Eskimos[3]).

Of the Ruin Island group's special features there remain the adze blade of iron, bird-skin coat, ornamental plate with a face (pl. 1.26), bundle of amulets, sealing-stool seat of bone, handle for towing line with a curved hole (Western?), heavy swivel of baleen, scraper with a bow-shaped handle, marrow extractor (?) of wood, toy whip handle of baleen, toy kayak of baleen, and toy lamp with vestigial ledge—all things which by virtue of their character have their natural place in the Thule culture. On the other hand, as we have already seen the great majority of the elements that seem foreign in the Thule culture point directly to the west.

Finally there is the foursided house and the carefully built kitchen-offshoot. Here it must be remembered, however, that the houses of the Ruin Island group are not particularly foursided, whereas their qagsse's are. This seems to suggest that these people had learnt a new building custom, i. e. the round or rounded houses of the Thule culture. All the same, foursided houses seem to occur in the Thule District prior to the time of the Ruin Islanders, so we must suppose that the knowledge of them together with other elements had already spread eastwards from Alaska at an earlier juncture. They have not been found in the Central region, it is true, but continued excavations will presumably reveal them, perhaps especially in the northern marginal region and westwards, where so far no foursided house has been found east of the Mackenzie basin.

But what about the kitchen? Fireplaces occur sporadically in the houses of the Thule Culture, but nothing comparable to the kitchens

---

[1]) de Laguna 1934 pl. 52.1.
[2]) Nelson 1899 p. 172 fig. 46; Murdoch 1892 fig. 257c.
[3]) Mathiassen 1928 (b) fig. 8a.

of the Ruin Islanders. Are these a western element too, brought along by the Islanders, or did they develop in this almost unexplored northern marginal region?

Collins' excavations, to which in particular we owe our knowledge of the prehistoric forms of houses among the Western Eskimos, did not reveal any house directly similar to that of the Ruin Islanders, but they present features which may very well be connected with the more specific architecture of the kitchen in association with the house such as we know it in the Thule District.

It is characteristic of the Alaska houses that they are foursided—apart from the modern house on St. Lawrence Island, which is eightsided and was introduced from Siberia, presumably in the 18th century[1]). The Old Bering Sea and Punuk houses have a sunken passage and in their outline are strongly reminiscent of Greenland houses of simple form. In Alaska, however, the material is boards placed horizontally, and the extension of the floor stones right out to the walls indicates that platforms of wood were used (or sleeping places directly on the floor?). Later in the Punuk period we find houses with the passage level with the house floor and built of stone, skulls and whale bones instead of wood, and with the passage widened at one part. In some cases there is also an annex to the passage (Collins fig. 22, p. 190), which brings us very close to a form of house that often occurs in Greenland. Both in Greenland and in Alaska the annex at the passage was most often employed as a store-room or the like; in the Alaska house at any rate not a trace of a fireplace has been found, but there are separate kitchens in annexes to the passage of houses at Metlavik, north of Bering Strait (22 miles north of C. Prince of Wales)[2]); and at Pt. Barrow "opening from the passage on both sides were several small chambers or recesses used for cooking and storage"[3]). Unfortunately, nothing is known of how far these houses date back in time. There is no mention anywhere of houses with a kitchen having an entrance from the house itself. Both forms are, however, represented in the Ruin Island period, and there can scarcely be any doubt that there is a certain connection between the houses of this period, the Metlavik house and some of the Punuk houses.

No fireplaces having been observed in the offshoots of the Punuk houses, it would seem as if these annexes alone migrated eastwards—perhaps at a relatively late time, as there is no definite discovery of them in Greenland prior to the coming of the people of Ruin Island; and it was only while on the way that they developed into kitchens and in

---

[1]) Collins 1937 p. 261.
[2]) Collins 1937 p. 261 ff., fig. 26.
[3]) Collins 1937 p. 264.

some cases were connected with the house itself. Unfortunately, we know so little about the prehistoric houses in North Alaska, that we cannot say whether this change took place there or only later on, more to the east. If these particular forms of houses at Pt. Barrow and Metlavik were used only in later centuries, their kitchen like so many other features might well be placed in connection with Collins' supposed "back-wash" of Thule culture. This too is a point that will be cleared up only by means of more excavations. On the other hand we know of no such house forms in regions nearer Hudson Bay, at any rate not stone houses, and they seem to have been associated especially with the culture phase dealt with in the foregoing, one which supposedly arose out of contact between the Punuk and the Thule cultures.

However, from the Thule culture in both Canada and Greenland we know of the more casually arranged fireplaces, mostly against the front wall of the house, and the obvious course would be to regard these more primitive fireplaces as an early stage of a development which proceeded only within a narrow, as yet undefined region. Within this region the habit was formed of moving the fireplace into the passage annex which had come from the west, or into a separate room with direct access from the house itself. Conditions on Ruin Island also suggest that this was connected with a more intensive whale fishery, and with some probability at any rate we may conclude that this particular development must have taken place within the region between North Alaska and Coronation Gulf, or perhaps the parts just to the east.

Another question is: what caused the Eskimos to build fireplaces inside their houses? In Southwest Alaska it is a regular feature of the festival houses; but—"the ceremonial house was probably not an original feature of Eskimo culture" says Collins, who demonstrates a number of features with regard to both arrangement and function that connect the Eskimo *kashims* of the Bristol Bay—Yukon region with the *kivas* of the Pueblo Indians[1]). Birket-Smith considers it possible that "the dance house is an old cultural feature which survived in the marginal regions (i. e. California and the northwest coast—Bering Sea region), whereas it has all but disappeared in the centre. For special reasons again it has lost much of its importance among the Eskimo outside Alaska"[1]). In the ordinary dwelling houses of Southwest Alaska, however, there are fireplaces too, but situated towards the rear of the house just in front of the platform; we know nothing of how far this feature goes back in time, so that it is impossible to say whether it has a remote connection with the fireplaces of the Thule culture.

Ordinary reasoning would say that if the people of the Thule culture

---

[1]) Collins 1937 p. 257 f.
[1]) Birket-Smith 1938 p. 374.

at some early stage were more closely associated with the interior, it would be natural for them to cook by means of firewood, perhaps inside the house too, in which case the fireplace would be an ancient Eskimo element which had merely lost in importance in the coastal regions with their plentiful supplies of blubber. But if the spread of the Eskimo culture was essentially conditioned by the blubber lamp, it is less certain if the fixed fireplace can date so far back. However, it is interesting to find that the Caribou Eskimos build separate kitchens to their snow houses, often with an entrance from the living room[1])—in other words, in the same manner as the Ruin Islanders arranged theirs in their stone houses. This seems to indicate a mutual tradition having its root in the interior and associated especially with the regions west of Hudson Bay; at any rate, nothing similar is known in eastern Canada. Furthermore, the fact that the kitchen has not been observed in the prehistoric houses of Alaska indicates that fireplaces in this form were connected particularly with the round type of house, which is predominant outside of Alaska. That cooking over a fire, in contradistinction to cooking over the blubber lamp, is the earliest form of cooking among Eskimos has already been established by Birket-Smith on the grounds that cooking over a fire is the only generally widespread form[2]). Evidently this is an ancient Eskimo feature which developed in a special direction in the coastal regions west of Hudson Bay, and from there travelled with the Ruin Island people to Greenland without penetrating into the Hudson Bay region.

The building of a separate kitchen cannot, however, be so particularly old in relation to the Thule culture, which in advance was able to spread to Inglefield Land. This means, if the foregoing assumptions are correct, that even after the first formation of the Thule culture there must have been contacts between the inland and the coastal Eskimos in the aforesaid region, at any rate up to about the 13th century.

---

[1]) Birket-Smith 1929 I p. 83.
[2]) Birket-Smith 1929 II p. 99.

VII. CLOTHING

The theory that there was cultural contact between inland and coastal tribes at a certain time, presumably in the regions around Coronation Gulf, is supported by a consideration of the forms of clothing, made possible by the archaeological material now available. From the Thule District we have quite a collection of dolls, though most of them are of the stereotype form, unclothed and with a flat face, of more or less indeterminable sex, some with a natit. A few, however, show the clothing.

Pl. 40.18 is a person in a half-long coat, apparently fairly wide, only slightly longer front and back (these lengths being equal) than at the sides; the trousers are wide and reach to about the knees, where they have an abrupt edge below. It was found in Co. A 20 layer 1 and apparently represents a man of the Baffinlanders who immigrated in the 19th century.

Pl. 40.19 is a man in a similar half-long coat, but slightly longer at the back than at the front. It comes from Inuarfigssuaq House 12 and thus dates back to Thule times. On another doll, from Thule House 21 midden (L 3: 6448), i. e. the Inugsuk period, the coat is the same length all round. The last two provide an idea of the male dress in the time of the Thule culture and immediately after. It would seem that the coat had not the long flaps front and back described from West Greenland by earlier writers[1]), which indicates that a new fashion for men arrived in the course of the Inugsuk period. The former of the two dolls is wearing thick boots, and there seems to be no doubt that the coat is an outer one. Tied under the arms of the same doll is a sinew thread, the significance of which is not very clear (shaman belt?). The legs of the other are cut off a little way below the edge of the coat. Hans Egede writes: "Some have a flap front and back"[2]), which evidently means that not all the men wore coats with flaps. One imagines that a new form of coat with flaps was introduced by the immigrants, presumably

---

[1]) Birket-Smith 1924 p. 167 f.
[2]) H. Egede: Perlustration ed. Bobe p. 369.

the Ruin Island people, and that for a long time the various elements of the population adhered to their own forms of dress. That something of the kind really did happen is evidenced by Mathiassen's find of a doll at Qilalukan, apparently representing a man; he is wearing a coat with a short flap in front and a very long one at the back, lower than to the heels[1]). This is of particular interest, as Qilalukan, as we have seen, on many points displays unusual resemblance to the Inugsuk period in Thule. Apparently the flaps then shrank a good deal in the course of the subsequent centuries.

Four dolls with a high, fairly pointed hood are undoubtedly female, though three of them are of crude workmanship and give little information as to the shape of the coat. One of these is from the lower part of the midden in front of Inf. House 4, so that it dates from the early Thule culture or Dorset time; two are of Inugsuk time (Thule House 21 midden). The fourth, from Cape Kent, that is the early transitional period, is well made (pl. 40.27) and displays a coat with a very long flap behind; in front it is somewhat shorter and almost rectangular, in its most characteristic form nowadays worn in Labrador[2]) and Baffin Island[3]). That women affected the toupé is to be seen both from the high hoods and a number of dolls with a hair knot like that of the present-day Polar Eskimos, but placed higher up.

It would thus seem that the Thule culture dress as used in Greenland in earliest times was more or less the same as that now worn in Labrador and Baffin Land, where by the way several of the Thule culture elements have held out most faithfully[4]). In the Middle Ages, however, there was the change that some of the men also began to have flaps on their coats, a feature that nowadays is most pronounced among the western Central Eskimos: the Netsilingmiut and the Copper Eskimos—among the Caribou Eskimos only the Qaernermiut[5]). It would accordingly seem that in olden times there was a certain conformity of dress between the inland Eskimos and the more westerly coastal Eskimos, from whom the long flaps on the man's coat are supposed to have come to Greenland.

In Greenland short flaps are still to be seen on men's coats in Thule and Angmagssalik, but not in West Greenland, whereas they are still a feature of women's coats, which nowadays are also much shorter than in early times[6]). Bearskin trousers are worn only in Thule and

---

[1]) Mathiassen 1927 I pl. 57.16, p. 187.
[2]) Hawkes 1916 pl. I.
[3]) Boas 1888 fig. 528.
[4]) Mathiassen 1927 II p. 163.
[5]) Birket-Smith 1929 II p. 81.
[6]) Birket-Smith 1924 p. 169, 193 f.

Angmagssalik, but up to 1902 were worn by the Sadlermiut on Southampton Island[1]). We cannot say definitely whether bearskin trousers were worn in the time of the Thule culture or not, but it is probable. The fact that they have gone out of fashion in West Greenland must be due partly to the climate, partly to the difficulty of obtaining bear skins. The description of the long wide outer coat of the Sadlermiut also agrees closely with the dolls from Thule. Among the latter, however, we have no evidence of the long kamiks of the women; but another of Mathiassen's dolls from Qilalukan (Mathiassen pl. 57.19) seems to represent a woman wearing these long boots.

In conjunction with these Sadlermiut features mention may be made of several things that connect the people of the eastern Thule culture with the Polar Eskimos. In striking conformity with the archaeological evidence is the tale of the small lamps of the *tunit*, which they carried under their coats[2]); they were called *tumiujang*, i. e. "footprint-like". Can these be anything but the small oval lamps, some of sandstone, found in the Dorset midden at Inuarfigssuaq, on Ruin Island and in Thule House 21 midden? It will also be recalled that the identifiable lamp fragments from Inglefield Land were markedly small. It is also said that the tunit employed quartz or rock-crystal for drill bits, thus conforming with the fact that in the Thule District we found drill bits of flint only; this of course may be accidental. Whether or not the alleged tunit ignorance of the salmon spear[3]), bow and arrow and kayak-building[4]) has anything to do with these elements having fallen into disuse in Thule is perhaps problematic. But we do know that the tunit were not skilled at skin curing. This may be connected in some way with the fact that the Polar Eskimos do not employ urine tanning—a technique which perhaps was first introduced into Greenland by the Ruin Islanders together with other western features. This would at any rate explain why the Polar Eskimos, despite their living in permanent houses, soon abandoned urine tanning—or perhaps never wholly adopted it[5]), as the influence of the Ruin Islanders on the culture in the Thule District seems on the whole to have been of only limited duration.

Stories of the tunit are told as far west as among the Copper Eskimos, where, however, the "*tornrin*" tales are more legendary. We learn from them that the tornrin hunted caribou, but not seals[6]). This may perhaps

---

[1]) Mathiassen 1927 II p. 186.
[2]) Mathiassen 1927 II p. 188.
[3]) Mathiassen 1927 I p. 287.
[4]) Mathiassen 1927 II p. 189.
[5]) Birket-Smith 1929 II p. 116.
[6]) Mathiassen 1927 II p. 188.

be a reminiscence of the days when the Thule people—or part of them—
were still leading a less markedly coastal life; and indeed Mathiassen
says that the finds from Malerualik indicate a life based more on caribou
hunting than that among the more easterly Thule people; the culture
at Malerualik is poorer than at Naujan[1]).

Both the clothing and the other elements referred to here have
further strengthened the impression of interaction between eastern and
western forms of ancient Eskimo culture, which in the Thule District
became mixed or superimposed one over the other. Before we can draw
further conclusions, however, it is necessary to try to throw some light
over the relation between the Greenland chronology and developments
in Alaska.

---

[1]) Mathiassen 1927 I p. 321.

VIII. CONTRIBUTION OF THE THULE DISTRICT TOWARDS ELUCIDATING THE DEVELOPMENT OF THE ESKIMO CULTURE

Jenness holds the opinion—and I agree with him—that the Old Bering Sea culture represents the earliest form of Eskimo culture hitherto known[1]); and Collins considers that at any rate it is of a much higher age than the more widespread Thule culture[2]), which is supposed to have derived from the Birnirk:

> "We have seen that on St. Lawrence the Old Bering Sea culture gave rise to the Punuk; that on the Arctic coast it was apparently ancestral to the Birnirk, the stage from which the Thule, the dominant prehistoric culture of the central regions, was derived".[3]).

The essence of Jenness's hypothesis is that two streams of Eskimos migrated eastwards from Alaska, presumably about the year 500 A. D. One kept to the interior and got as far as the regions west of Hudson Bay, the other spread northwards in the Arctic archipelago and possibly reached Greenland, where Erik the Red found traces of them in 982 A. D. Jenness places the Naujan finds to this time. In the meantime the inland people west of Hudson Bay had also begun to send colonies out to the coasts—to Ellesmere Island, Greenland, the islands in Hudson Strait and Labrador as far as New Foundland; these are the Dorset people. What the time-relation of this latter movement is to the first flow from Alaska is not known; but it is supposed that it began several centuries before, and at places—as in Baffin Island—where the two movements converged, the Western Eskimos gained the supremacy[4]). Here, then, we have an eastern and a western culture group, but with a common origin in the west; on this latter point, however, Jenness refrains from any discussion. Regarding the Dorset culture Collins says:

[1]) Jenness 1937 p. 30.
[2]) Collins 1937 p. 382.
[3]) Collins 1937 p. 379.
[4]) Jenness 1937 p. 34.

"The Dorset and Cook Inlet cultures differ in so many respects from the Old Bering Sea that we can say little as to what relationship may have existed between them and the latter. Neither of them, however, are Eskimo cultures in the same sense as is the Old Bering Sea culture, which in spite of its specialized development in certain directions is fundamentally Eskimo, and basic, apparently, to the existing phases of northern Eskimo culture from Siberia to Greenland"[1]).

As we see, Collins does not tell us anything either about the connection between these western and eastern Eskimo cultures, and I consider he overrates the importance of the Old Bering Sea culture to some extent when, treating of Birket-Smith's hypothesis on the position of the Caribou Eskimos, he says:

"If the Caribou Eskimos do represent the ancestral type from which all others have sprung, we should expect that the farther back into Eskimo prehistory we go the more we would find the culture approaching the original Caribou pattern. We should expect that the oldest Eskimo culture that could be determined archaeologically would show strong resemblance to the supposed prototype. This, of course, is not the case. On the contrary, the oldest form of Eskimo culture that has yet appeared in the Western regions is further removed from the Caribou Eskimo culture than is that of many modern groups. It is difficult to see, therefore, how the data of archaeology can be brought to support the theory of the central origin of Eskimo culture"[2]).

On the basis of her excavations in Kachemak Bay de Laguna ventures somewhat farther back in time than Old Bering Sea, for she sets up the supposition:

"I suggest that on the Alaskan mainland, north of the Peninsula, traces of a Thule or a proto-Thule culture should be found, correlated both with the Canadian Thule culture and with the First Period of the Kachemak Bay culture. From a chronological point of view, the proto-Thule stage must have been pre-Punuk. It was, therefore, contemporaneous with the Old Bering Sea culture on St. Lawrence Island; or, if it existed on St. Lawrence Island, it was older than the Old Bering Sea culture"[3]).

As to this Collins writes:

"The Kachemak Bay culture appears to be no closer to the Thule culture than to that of the intervening sections of Alaska. I do not see, therefore, how the occurrence of these simple, common Eskimo elements at Cook Inlet can mean more than that the culture there was basically Eskimo. There is a far closer relationship between the two prehistoric culture stages on St. Lawrence Island and the Thule or for that matter between these and any other adequately known eastern form of Eskimo culture than there is between the Kachemak Bay, or the Aleutians, and any other Eskimo culture to the northward"[4]).

---

[1]) Collins 1937 p. 379.
[2]) Collins 1937 p. 380.
[3]) de Laguna 1934 p. 219 f.
[4]) Collins 1937 p. 374.

Now the Old Bering Sea culture need not have developed directly from such a Thule or proto-Thule culture, of whose physiognomy we know very little either; and, by the way, according to Collins the Old Bering Sea form is more likely associated with Siberia; accordingly, it may have been formed rather independently of contemporaneous cultures in Alaska. Indeed, with regard to the regions north of Cook Inlet Collins says: "With the latter region there has evidently been a basic early relationship, but the development of south Alaskan culture has been virtually independent of influence from the northward."

To me it seems as if Collins and de Laguna actually agree on the essentials, except that Collins perhaps pays particular attention to the late occurrence of the Thule culture in Alaska, whereas de Laguna employs the term "Thule" or "proto-Thule", evidently mindful of the fact that such an early phase of Eskimo culture must rather have been like the Thule culture. If the expression *proto-Thule* is replaced by *proto-Eskimo*, we obtain a more neutral formulation and at the same time an approximation to Birket-Smith's hypothesis, in so far as this expression signifies a primitive culture with elements of more general distribution, in association with Hatt's "coastal culture" or Birket-Smith's "ice-hunting stage". So far it will be possible on the whole to establish unanimity of views. The divergency begins when the discussion turns upon where, how and when such a culture began to assume a specially Eskimo character; but what does that mean, really?

To Birket-Smith the salient point is adaptation to the sea, as expressed in breathing-hole hunting for seals and the consequent higher development of the blubber lamp; the focus of such a development he finds west of Hudson Bay, in the coastal regions to the north of the Barren Grounds; here it was that the Palae-Eskimo culture first developed[1]), though this region must not be taken too strictly and possibly it extended a good way to the northwest[2]). When Collins says that Kachemak Bay culture rests upon a foundation that is "basically Eskimo", the meaning must consequently be—according to Birket-Smith—that it is later than the first development of the Eskimo culture in the central regions; otherwise the term "Eskimo", applied to the culture, covers two different views. In order to bring greater clarity into the discussion I therefore think it would be better to use the term "proto-Eskimo" as the common denominator of those culture phases of which we have no tangible evidence as yet;—or we should insist that the term palae-Eskimo applies only to the eastern centre of development, though this is not Birket-Smith's opinion.

However, the question is whether Birket-Smith's definition is not

---

[1]) Birket-Smith 1929 II p. 226.
[2]) Birket-Smith 1940 p. 109.

a little narrow, and whether it would not be equally justifiable to speak of other palae-Eskimo culture phases which, perhaps not to the same degree, were based upon ice-hunting on the sea. If so, the western centre in Alaska would acquire a kind of equality with the eastern centre, and an independence which perhaps it would be practical to assume until we have more concrete material. One argument in favour is the difference in the human types. The Eastern Eskimos are almost dolichocephalic, the Western brachycephalic[1]). The special anthropological peculiarities among the Eastern peoples are attributed by Jenness to intermarriage with Algonkin Indians[2]), and Birket-Smith has since accounted for the marked likeness between Eskimos and Indians around Lake Athabasca[3]). However this may be, it is obvious that it is a question of two groups which have been separated so long in time and by such distances that they have probably been able to develop their own adaptation to the coast, independently of each other. If that is so, it is actually less important which of them began first. It is a problem that will solve itself gradually as we become able to penetrate deeper into Eskimo prehistory with the certainty which archaeology alone can give for the present; in this connection we must place our hopes in the investigations made by Helge Larsen and Rainey in Alaska in recent years.

There is no doubt that the uncertainty and the different opinions on the problems connected with Eskimo culture to some extent are the result of differences in the time-perspective of the various authors, and much would be gained if it were possible to establish an acceptable correlation between Alaska and the Eastern regions. The question now is whether the last excavations in the Thule District can help to throw more light on these matters.

It was shown in the foregoing that the Ruin Island phase in the Thule District is more closely associated with the prehistoric culture of Alaska than any other Thule culture phase hitherto known, as some of the implement forms seemed almost like direct imports. The assumption must therefore be that only a limited time can have elapsed since these forms left Alaska. They may be presumed to have arrived in the Thule District up towards the year 1300 A. D., and the migration of the Ruin Islanders eastwards and northwards from Alaska must have taken place in the preceding period. How long this took cannot of course be said with any certainty, but it cannot have been many centuries. If we put it at two, I imagine we shall be fairly well on the right side. Accordingly, as some of the harpoon heads bear most resemblance to

---

[1]) Birket-Smith 1929 II p. 227.
[2]) Jenness 1937 p. 34.
[3]) Birket-Smith 1940 p. 109.

corresponding types of early Punuk, we may assume that the Punuk culture prevailed at any rate in the 11th—12th century and possibly still later, which means that Old Bering Sea would be somewhat earlier, possibly in the time up towards the year 1000.

If this is so, phases of the Old Bering Sea culture must on the whole be contemporaneous with the Dorset culture in eastern Canada and Greenland, and in any case their mutual relationship must fade out in the remote past. Jenness's eastward stream of coast dwellers should correspond to the people of the Thule culture, and according to Collins their culture was much younger than the Old Bering Sea culture. But now we have seen that the Thule culture, or an early phase of it, was dominant in Greenland, undoubtedly in the 11th—12th century, and for centuries before in eastern or central Canada, as in fact assumed by Mathiassen. Jenness in so far has estimated this too, so that the only new assumption is that the Ruin Island people draw the ancient Alaska cultures farther forward in time. The consequence of this, however, is that *it becomes more difficult to derive at any rate the early Thule culture from the old Alaska cultures. It simply cannot be done.*

As has been said several times in the foregoing, impulses from the west came to the Thule culture also in the time prior to the 13th century; the most characteristic of these impulses are the keeled harpoon head and the foursided house, and possibly the triangular butt of the ice pick. But before that there must have been a Thule culture without these elements, a culture which may briefly be characterized by Thule-2 harpoon heads, round houses and ice picks with a scarf. The round houses in particular seem to preclude the possibility that this culture is a direct derivative of the Punuk culture.

If nevertheless it was so derived, the implication is that the Punuk culture must have lasted a very long time, so long that a first wave of emigrants was first able to develop the early phase of the Thule culture, including the change from foursided houses to round; afterwards a secondary influence would be brought to bear, during which the Eskimos again began to make their houses foursided; and finally, then came the Ruin Island people with several elements from the same source. This seems to be rather an artificial hypothesis, so much the more as the round house according to Birket-Smith's exhaustive investigation must be assumed to be the earliest form of Eskimo house.

It is surely more reasonable to think that an ancient form of Thule culture—de Laguna's "proto-Thule"—prevailed in Alaska; it would then be easier to imagine that these originally round houses had been affected by foursided west-coast forms, as Birket-Smith thinks[1]), and that in time they made their way eastwards. Nothing of the sort has been de-

---

[1]) Birket-Smith 1929 II p. 47 f.

monstrated archaeologically as yet; but on theoretical grounds we must expect that such old round houses do exist, says Collins[1]).

The facts before us suggest that in several respects the early phase of the Thule culture was associated most closely with the eastern culture region, where it was dominant more or less simultaneously with the Old Bering Sea culture in the western region. As we have seen, the earliest known Thule culture in Inglefield Land in several ways indicated a connection with an inland culture, and it is presumable that this character was the more marked, the shorter was the distance to the region west of Hudson Bay, i. e. at a still earlier phase. This opens up the possibility of this culture having been derived direct from an inland culture, corresponding almost to Birket-Smith's proto-Eskimo phase; and, if we retain the term Thule Culture, that culture will thus signify one that extended right down through Birket-Smith's palae-Eskimo stratum, whereas what was originally meant by Thule culture in this connection comprises only a later phase, characterized by influence from the west. This means some blurring of the lines drawn up so sharply by Birket-Smith on theoretical grounds, but at the same time a simplification of the problems in certain respects. For we can glimpse a steady development from the proto-Eskimo phase to a coastal culture which quite secondarily is conditioned by a western centre of development on Bering Strait. This coastal culture, which would almost correspond to Birket-Smith's palae-Eskimo culture, may possibly have reached Greenland, though Birket-Smith doubts it[2]); but its characteristic implement forms no doubt bear such strong resemblance to those of Mathiassen's Thule culture that it would be almost absurd to call it anything else than Thule culture.

To begin with, this palae-Eskimo Thule culture extended—perhaps most of all—westwards to Alaska, where it established contact with the culture prevailing there, presumably at a time that corresponded to some undefined phase of the Old Bering Sea or early Punuk culture; in any case this must have happened earlier than the year 1000, as otherwise it is difficult to explain the western intrusion into Greenland in the following centuries. In this manner it is possible that the western strain was acquired before this culture reached Greenland; but this does not explain away its originally eastern character. The effect is merely that in this case we must ascribe a still higher age to the earliest Thule-impressed phases.

After this the western culture centre, signified by the Old Bering Sea culture, must be credited with an independent position, and its development must have proceeded independently of the genesis of the

---
[1]) Collins 1937 p. 284.
[2]) Birket-Smith 1929 II p. 231.

Thule culture—or, if you will, the palae-Eskimo Thule culture and its development out of an eastern, proto-Eskimo culture. Still, we can hardly doubt that at bottom there is a relationship; and if the Old Bering Sea culture in many respects bears a certain resemblance to the Thule culture, this need not be due solely to influence from Old Bering Sea to Thule; the explanation may also be that the mutual basis perhaps was not so remote from both cultures—the basis which de Laguna must mean by her proto-Thule culture. In that case, however, the structure I have outlined would seem to be in danger of collapsing. For if the proto-Eskimo culture employed as the broad initial phase was of such a character that both the palae-Eskimo Thule culture and the ancient Alaska cultures (by which we must imagine an earlier phase than the artistically highly developed Old Bering Sea) can without difficulty be made to derive from it, we must also recognize the probability that the earliest development in the direction of a Thule-impressed culture, including round houses, began already at Bering Strait, or perhaps in Siberia. At the same time, however, we must explain the position of the Caribou Eskimos; but having gone so far, we may also assume that their simple culture was the result of a specialization, perhaps in the direction of greater simplification of the proto-Eskimo common culture, as Mathiassen was most inclined to think[1]). We have a somewhat similar example, but in a coastal culture, in the culture of the Polar Eskimos, which has been very greatly simplified during the last few centuries.

As I have said, we have no definite evidence as yet as to the appearance of such a proto-Eskimo common culture, neither in the east nor in the west, and it will scarcely pay to continue very long with purely theoretical speculations, so much the more as of course there are other possibilities. By this I mean especially Jenness's idea of two emigrations from Alaska, one orientated towards the interior, the other towards the coast. This presupposes a certain differentiation—at any rate as regards disposition—already in Alaska, and it would readily harmonize with what we now know positively about the position of the early Thule culture and the supposition of its relatively close association with proto-Eskimo culture, and it also explains the necessarily high age of the eastern culture centre. But even in this case it must be maintained on the basis of the material so far available that *the Thule-characterized culture known to us suggests a more direct connection with the eastern centre with its inland stamp.*

As regards the Dorset culture, as Jenness says it must presumably have developed from the eastern centre. Whether or not it extended eastwards via Southampton Island as Jenness thinks[1]) is a matter

---
[1]) Mathiassen 1930 (d) p. 606.
[1]) Jenness 1937 fig. 1.

which future archaeological investigations must decide. Judging from what we already know of it, its centre must be in the regions around Hudson Strait, and no doubt we must also consider the possibility of a movement south about Hudson Bay, so much the more as the Dorset culture seems to have a distinctly Indian stamp about it. Presumably it reached Greenland prior to the year 1000, and therefore the first differentiation in a Dorset direction must have taken place several centuries before. But if the development of the palae-Eskimo Thule culture within the same period occupied the regions northwest of Hudson Bay, as is indicated by the conditions as we know them, there is a growing probability that the Dorset culture headed south about Hudson Bay.

The Dorset culture having proved to be the earliest traceable in Greenland, there is also the possibility, however, that it developed so early that it was able to move northwards west of Hudson Bay prior to the Thule-stamped culture; however, the extensive excavations of the Fifth Thule Expedition in just those regions seem to argue against it. On the other hand the reason may be that no Dorset ruins were found because they are totally obliterated. In that case, however, one should expect to find rather more exterior similarity between Thule and Dorset; but in those cases where Thule and Dorset types are found together, the circumstances seem to indicate mostly that this was due to a later encounter between the two separately developed branches. But matters here are nothing like clear.

The picture as it resolves itself after these speculations has the following appearance:

1) Perhaps a short time after the beginning of our present era—perhaps long before—there began an immigration of Eskimos (proto-Eskimos) via Bering Strait, Eskimos whose culture had arrived at an "ice-hunting stage" of mainly inland character, but yet to be seen under the aspect of Hatt's coast culture. The first of these immigrants adhered to their ancient customs and were perhaps particularly interested in fishing and hunting land game, which in time brought them eastwards—perhaps under the pressure of steady streams of new immigrating kinsmen. Eastwards we find at least some of them as the supposed proto-Eskimos on the Barren Grounds. They had both round, sunken houses and snow houses.

2. a) Some remained west of Hudson Bay, where they lived a purely inland existence; their descendants are Birket-Smith's Eschato-Eskimos and the Caribou Eskimos. Gradually they abandoned the earth or stone house for the snow house, which in its turn attained to a high pitch of perfection.

2. b) Others continued their migration, north or south about Hudson Bay and acquired a hunting technique—or developed the knowledge they already had—which enabled them to catch walruses and other large marine mammals, probably by ice-hunting methods. They retained the stone house, but continued to use the snow house as well. Perhaps through Indian influence their culture acquired the curious character that marks the Dorset culture, which is traceable northwards to Greenland and southwards to New Foundland.

2. c) After the separation of the Dorset people, others too became more attracted by the sea mammals and in the arctic coastal regions developed the Thule culture.

3) In the meantime, in Alaska south of Bering Strait (or in Siberia) another development had begun, trending towards the sea and governed by the particular environment and cultural impulses from the outside— according to Collins especially from the west. In time this led to the Old Bering Sea culture. In North Alaska this or a related culture made contact with the Thule culture, and a number of elements or features, especially the foursided house, passed into the latter and were transplanted eastwards, presumably in the course of the 10th—12th centuries. It may also be that the powerful development of whaling was due to this western influence (this is argued by the spread of the keeled harpoon head; but even the very first people presumably knew the umiaq or a similar vessel).

4) Old Bering Sea was displaced by the Punuk culture, which extended northwards. Under the influence of the Thule culture the Punuk people began to use whale bones in their foursided houses. A group with a culture strongly Punuk moved eastwards, where it came under the constantly growing influence of the dominant Thule culture. En route it picked up the fireplace, which was given a place in the passage annex brought from the west. This group or its direct descendants reached as far as Greenland, where they are encountered about the year 1300.

5) Almost simultaneously with the latter events the inland people on the Barren Grounds began to make their way out to the coast, where they remained. The Thule people (the tunit) were pushed north and westwards (Collins' backwash), and the Caribou Eskimos remained alone in the interior, just as some Thule people remained on Southampton Island.

6) Finally, some descendants of the last people to advance reached the Thule District in the 19th century.

The above of course is merely a very rough sketch; but in broad outlines it gives the picture of the course of events in the culture of the Eskimo as visualized on the background of the excavations in the Thule District. To a certain extent it signifies an approach to Birket-Smith's hypothesis; but as a whole that hypothesis means in effect that the Eskimo culture was derived from an inland culture, and that the Eskimos became acquainted with the coast only at a later time. I am more apt to suppose that the first Eskimo people on American soil were in some degree acquainted with coastal life. But, of course, this question is to som extent connected with that of at what stage one will separate "Eskimo" (physical type, or perhaps language) from "Eskimo culture".

In this statement the supposition which calls most for verification is that of a close connection between the earliest forms of Thule culture and the proto-Eskimo ice-hunting culture; this, however, is hindered considerably by the fact that we have no direct knowledge of a culture group known definitely to represent that ice-hunting phase as it must have appeared in the period under review. It has never been demonstrated archaeologically as a cultural whole; conclusions have merely been drawn by devious routes as to some of the elements which such a culture must have possessed[1]). As it happens, this general term of course covers many different prehistoric, mainly Eurasian culture groups, each of which may have had its own outer stamp; but the issue here is merely whether it is possible to set up a narrowly defined culture with a complex of characteristic types of implements, which may be regarded as forming a necessary but also sufficient condition for the supposition that the Thule culture in its earliest known form was derived from it direct—a complex which also in itself must have formed a sufficient basis for Eskimo life as it was lived before any real differentiation took place. This of course is not saying that such a culture must necessarily have been confined to the Eskimo group of peoples.

On looking to see what elements, or types of implements in all have been found to be common to the early Thule culture and Dorset— beyond the special Dorset harpoon heads and ornaments— we find the following (* signifying less definite Dorset finds):

Thule-2 harpoon head with slots, no blade,
*Y-ornament,
harpoon blade of flint,
*plug for bladder mouthpiece,
leister harpoon head,
foreshaft for ice-hunting harpoon (D)[2]),

---

[1]) Hatt 1916, 1933; Birket-Smith 1918 p. 215 ff., 1929 II p. 212 ff., 1930 p. 101 ff., 1938 p. 515 ff.; Collins 1937, p. 382.

[2]) (D) signifies that as regards the Dorset finds the implement is of special Dorset type.

small socket-piece with triangular butt,
*heavy socket-piece with scarf-face,
ice-pick with scarf-face,
lance head with seating for blade,
*wound plug,

*bow brace of antler,
*arrow head, small round, blunt, with knobs,
— —, — —, sharp, — —,
— —, lanceolate, no blade, with knobs,
* — —, with two unilateral barbs, knobs,
sling handle of wood (D),

sledge shoe of bone,
*trace buckle, ovoid,
bone peg,
*compound snow knife,
compound knife handle,
simple whittling knife with end blade,
knife handle of wood with seating for end blade,
— — - — — groove for end blade at side,
knife with side blade (D),
knife blade of flint,
— — - slate,
— — - iron,

hand-drill shank of bone,
drill bit of flint,
whetstone,
hammer stone,
adze,
adze blade of flint,
hatchet head of walrus ivory (D?),
mattock head with seating for handle,
*flint flaker of antler,
wedge,
*marline spike, flat with narrow fore end,
— —, round, pointed,
*pointed seal fibula,

*flat ulo handle (iron blade),
convex-edged end scraper, flint,
— side scraper, flint,
concave side scraper, flint,
atypical scraper, flint,
flint flake
blunt scraper of stone,
spatula-shaped implement (boot creaser?),

small oval sandstone lamp,
small deep, triangular-oval lamp of soapstone,
lamp trimmer of wood,
rounded cooking pot of soapstone (round or oval),

meat tray, hollowed out of wood,
*meat stick of antler,

*tubular, "winged" buckle,
*chain link,
 worked mica,
*ajagaq (stick),
 gambling bones,
 seal figure of wood,
 bear figure of walrus ivory,
 doll with kamiks,
* — — coat and hood,
*toy arrow head.

To these forms of implements, which all together provide a characteristic culture picture, we may add those from the early Thule culture, supposedly of very ancient origin by virtue of their occurrence:

wound plug of wood,
knife handle of wood with slit for end blade,
convex-edged end scraper of slate or similar,
side scraper of antler, open ends (fat scraper),
two-handed scraper of tubular bone,
hand-pick of rib.

The latter forms signify no change whatever in the picture given above.

Confining ourselves to this we certainly get a picture of a culture based upon caribou hunting and fishing and adapted to the coast by acquiring an ice-hunting technique, as is Birket-Smith's leading idea. I would not venture to assert that these earliest people knew the kayak, but it is very probable, as in the early Thule culture we have found two types of kayak (toys), one of them closely approaching the kayak of the present-day inland dwellers, whereas the other is the usual, broader type which may be assumed to be a later form, adapted more for use on the sea.

If we are content to take the absolutely certain Dorset finds (unmixed), i. e. those from Midden B. II, the list becomes somewhat shorter. However, those mainly affected will be just those items which may have been associated especially with kayak hunting, viz. plug for bladder mouthpiece and heavy socket-piece; but doubt may also be cast upon the snow knife, ulo, winged buckle, chain link and ajagaq. This, however, can only strengthen the supposition of an original ice-hunting phase for the Dorset people.

If we would go a step farther, to all the forms of the early Thule culture, the matter becomes more difficult at once, because now we cannot be quite certain that secondary western influence can be excluded.

The relationship with the Dorset culture is clear, however, but only in so far as it has to do with the ice-hunting period. One must really believe that there were two branches on the same tree, but that one grew so to say on the shady side, the other in the sun, the Thule culture having gone through a more rapid development. It is significant, however, that apparently the only harpoon head at the disposal of the Dorset people—apart from the special Dorset forms—is Thule 2; but this too appears here in a smaller and more slender form than is usual among the Thule people. Thule 2 of course is just the harpoon head that particularly characterizes the early Thule culture, and the fact that it is shared with Dorset shows that it must date back to the proto-Eskimo culture. It is still glimpsed in the ice-hunting harpoon head of the Central Eskimos, which though now with a closed socket has retained the two barbs. It is permissible in this connection to hazard the guess that it is a conservative feature or survival, in contrast to the position in Greenland, where harpoon heads of this type are used for kayak hunting, whereas ice-hunting harpoons are barbless.

The Thule 2 harpoon head does not occur in the Old Bering Sea culture, however, and this fact particularly strengthens the supposition of the independent eastern origin of the Thule culture. Several of the Old Bering Sea harpoon heads are barbed, it is true, but the barbs are quite small and close, almost vestigial; from their exterior form they seem to bear towards the Thule 3 type. It seems most likely that the Thule 2 type underlies the Old Bering Sea types, an idea that is in line with the supposition of the earliest Thule culture having descended direct from the common proto-Eskimo culture which presumably also lies behind Old Bering Sea. It is only with the Punuk culture that we encounter Thule 2 harpoon heads in Alaska[1]); but now we are so far advanced in time that it is more probable that they were the result of influence from the Thule people, that is to say from the east. It is just such forms as are met with among the Ruin Island people. With regard to the Birnirk harpoon heads, known to us especially from van Valin's collection from Point Barrow, they combine features of the Thule and the Old Bering Sea cultures. Some illustrated by A. Mason (pl. V.10-13)[2]) have at one side a powerful barb of distinctly Thule form, whereas the other side with the inserted stone blade and the divided spurs is Old Bering Sea, as both Mathiassen and Collins have shown[3]). I am inclined to believe that here again is an outcome of interaction between the two cultures, as indeed is Mathiassen's idea; and I also consider it most correct, at any rate in North Alaska, to regard the

---

[1]) Collins 1937 pl. 70.
[2]) A. Mason 1928.
[3]) Mathiassen 1929 p. 50 f.; Collins 1937 p. 366.

Thule culture as the earlier[1]). But if the Old Bering Sea harpoon heads originally are related to the Thule 2 type, no matter how distantly, the proto-Eskimo culture moves over to the Old World—if it is right as Collins says that the Old Bering Sea culture has its roots in the west; with this we are faced with still more remote phases of the circumpolar coastal culture (Hatt) or the ice-hunting stage (Birket-Smith).

Collins, however, has demonstrated resemblances between Old Bering Sea and Dorset cultures, and the only actual difficulty seems to lie in the fact that Old Bering Sea, just by virtue of its being a coastal culture, on several points seems to agree with the Thule culture. The question therefore is: can we imagine that a development out of the proto-Eskimo substratum could preserve so uniform a direction in the two separate regions, western and eastern.—But, except for those elements which probably must be attributed to an original cultural fellowship, and those which definitely signify a later cultural association, is the resemblance really so very great?—I consider the answer must be in the negative. There may be some uncertainty with regard to loose foreshafts for the kayak harpoon, as none of these have been found in the Dorset culture; but on the other hand there are many of the small leister-harpoon heads as well as a small socket piece (with a triangular butt), showing that the principle of the loose foreshaft was known. None of the other elements enumerated by Collins[2]) seem to offer any difficulty—except perhaps the umiaq and the bird dart; but these can scarcely have been vital to a culture which first and foremost had adapted itself to ice-hunting; on the other hand we must assume that the umiaq was known (the passage across the Bering Strait?); and in any case the proto-Eskimos seem to have had the kayak. The main thing is that a coastal culture with a Thule stamp had the conditions necessary for being able to develop out of an essentially inland culture, independently of the Old Bering Sea culture. To this one might add that only because as a coastal culture it met currents from the Old Bering Sea culture, was it at all capable of absorbing so easily some of its features and reforming them on the special Thule pattern.

If we go through the foregoing list of elements common to early Thule and Dorset for the purpose of picking out those which occur in the Old Bering Sea culture, and leaving out the not entirely certain Dorset features, we shall find quite considerable fundamental agreement. In Old Bering Sea there are:

(Harpoon heads)
leister-harpoon head,

---

[1]) Mathiassen 1929 p. 55.
[2]) Collins 1937 p. 362.

socket-piece with triangular butt,
ice-pick (triangular butt),
lance (loose foreshaft),
bow,
lanceolate arrow head without blade,
tang on arrow heads (but without knobs),
sledge shoe (walrus ivory),
compound knife handle,
whittling knife of bone with end blade,
knife handle of wood for end blade (blade slit),
knife handle for side blade,
knife blade of slate,
hand drill,
drill bit of flint (or the like),
whetstone,
hammer stone,
adze head,
adze blade of stone,
pick of walrus ivory,
mattock head of bone,
wedge,
pointed marline spike,
convex flint scraper,
concave flint scraper,
round lamp (clay),
round cooking pot (clay),
meat tray of wood,
bear figure of walrus ivory

to which may be added:

wound plug of wood,
side scraper with open ends,
two-handed scraper,
hand-pick.

Without doubt we may also add the flint-flaker and possibly the ulo and chain link. A similarity which may perhaps also be quoted is the frequent use of elongated, cut-out holes.

This somewhat reduced list also points in the direction of a basis in an ice-hunting culture and in itself provides quite an eloquent picture of the character of such a culture. To this it must be said that the picture is fairly neutral with regard to whether such a culture was associated with a mainly inland or coastal existence. I do not consider it strictly necessary to banish it to the interior. The very fact that it must once have passed over the Bering Strait in company with Eskimo people makes it imperative to credit its bearers with some familiarity with the sea coast; and if their migration proceeded along the tundra belt, which would doubtless seem probable, it need not definitively have turned its back on the sea in the earliest times. In this manner the further development of ice-hunting technique and sea-mammal hunting on the whole becomes easier to understand, as also the fact that almost at the same time there are two coastal cultures, quite different exteriorly, on either side of the continent, but born of the same progenitor. Among features which seem to have developed among the eastern people, the bow of antler with sinew backing and the development of the dog sledge must be considered the most important. Here perhaps contact with the "inland complex" plays a part[1]). Another peculiarity is that the tang of the arrow heads acquires knobs.

In this manner it is also possible to explain how it was that the round, sunken house persisted throughout the entire eastern region— and, at the same time, why despite its outer form and the material, the foursided Old Bering Sea house in its arrangement is so very like the eastern house forms. We must assume that the Old Bering Sea house acquired its foursided form comparatively soon after the bond connecting west and east had been severed, i. e. after the separation from the people who in the east developed the Dorset and the Thule cultures.

Nor does this view of the course of developments cause any difficulty to the comprehension of the inland culture of the Caribou Eskimos, as the original territory of the inland Eskimos is merely moved out between the timber line and the sea. This in fact agrees with their present living conditions; and just as Birket-Smith imagined that they were led out to the sea, one might just as well imagine that they were led into the interior, attracted by the caribou. *But the final proof of this is lacking too.* We need to find this proto-Eskimo culture's round stone or earth houses and powerful barbed harpoon heads in the western region, in strata which demonstrably run under the Old Bering Sea culture. If we succeed, it may be right to say that in the last instance the Thule culture, or a culture with a certain Thule stamp, came from the west; in the opposite case we must maintain that in relation to Alaska it represents an eastern culture development.

---

[1]) Collins 1937 p. 382.

SUMMARY

The archaeological investigations entrusted to me to undertake in the Thule District in the years 1935—37 have led to the following general conclusions:

The earliest demonstrable Eskimo culture in Greenland is the Dorset culture, found chiefly in three middens at Inuarfigssuaq on Marshall Bay. The largest of these middens was homogeneous in its contents; in the other two there was a possibility of admixtures of Thule culture. I was unable to find any house definitely contemporary with the Dorset middens; but under some house ruins were signs of earlier settlement which presumably was associated with the Dorset culture. This culture must be assumed to have reached Greenland prior to the year 1000 A. D.

After the Dorset culture came the Thule culture, but belonging to an earlier phase than that at Naujan. The assumption is that it arrived with an independent immigration. This early Thule culture differs from the Canadian Thule culture in that it contains a number of elements, of which some owing to their distribution are presumably very ancient, and some point towards a less pronounced coastal existence. The houses of this early Thule culture are most often round or rounded, but there are signs of a progressive tendency towards building them foursided. At Cape Kent there were rectangular houses containing Thule culture.

On Ruin Island off Marshall Bay was a habitation which on vital points differed from that on the mainland, the house being provided with separate kitchens with a fireplace. The culture was Thule in the main; but harpoon heads etc. revealed close relationship to the early Punuk culture in Alaska. Two houses in Thule (Ũmánaq) belong to the same group. In these as on Ruin Island I found Norse relics—which indeed was the case in one or two houses at Inuarfigssuaq, though it was impossible to find traces of Inugsuk culture. On the basis of this evidence it is possible to say that the early Thule culture was dominant in Inglefield Land at any rate in the 12th—13th century, and that the

Ruin Island people made their appearance towards the close of that period, presumably about the year 1300.

It is assumed that the kitchen of the Ruin Islanders originated from a combination of a western form of house and fireplaces, an element picked up more to the east in the houses of early Thule.

The Inugsuk culture, defined by the occurrence of tub-staves and other elements of Norse influence, succeeded in gaining only a slight footing in Inglefield Land, whereas it was dominant in the southern part of the Thule District in the 14th—15th—16th century. It had rounded houses and at first adopted the well-built kitchen of the Ruin Islanders; the kitchen disappeared subsequently, the Inugsuk character fading away at the same time. The conditions suggest that communication with West Greenland ebbed out about the year 1600, whereafter the culture acquired a more special, Polar-Eskimo character.

Some houses of apparently late date, presumably 18th—19th century, revealed the characteristic construction with solid wall projections and cantilever stones seen in more recent Polar Eskimo houses. These houses are both foursided and rounded in plan. As the "pear-shaped" Polar-Eskimo house is most closely related to these, it is evident that the "pear-shaped" house is a late house type, at any rate not directly derived from the round houses of the Thule culture, but closely related to them.

In West Greenland, houses with a kitchen are common in the Inugsuk period and it is probable that this is the result of influence from the Ruin Islanders who, however, left no visible trace of any other kind. This is explained by their having quickly adopted the already dominant and superior Inugsuk culture. The Ruin Island people are assumed to have been the driving force in the southward advance of the Eskimos which led to the destruction of the Norse West Settlement in the 14th century.

Relations with Northeast Greenland are not entirely clear, as the Inugsuk culture observed there may now be imagined as having come both from the south and from the north; but the resemblance of the Northeast Greenland houses to the foursided houses at Cape Kent, in conjunction with certain implement types, suggests that there was a cultural influence, or perhaps an immigration, north about Greenland, most probably in the 14th century.

The midden at Inugsuk in the Upernavik District displays no absolute agreement with any period in the Thule District, but seems to represent a local development from a basis common to Inugsuk and Thule, a basis that may be dated to about the 12th—13th century. The indubitably dominant position of the Inugsuk harpoon heads is a special West Greenland phenomenon.

The essentials of the Inugsuk culture, viz. the strong development especially of kayak hunting and its appurtenant implements, are well marked in Thule, and it seems probable that this development was accelerated already in the Thule District in the latter part of the Thule culture period, while the Ruin Islanders undoubtedly meant a great deal to the development of whaling.

The qagsse of the Ruin Islanders was foursided. As round qaggse's have also been found in Greenland, this suggests that the round and the foursided forms of houses have their own source of origin and that both must be due to ancient tradition. Having regard to the connection of the Ruin Islanders with the Punuk culture, it may be taken for granted that the foursided form of house in Greenland was the result of influence from Alaska.

The chronological arrangement of the culture elements from Thule has been made first and foremost on the basis of the stratification in Comer's Midden, which contains finds from the 14th century up to modern time, though the 17th—18th centuries are but weakly represented, if at all. The foundation of the chronology is the occurrence of Norse relics.

On the basis of the chronology of the Thule District it has been possible to conclude that the Canadian Thule culture, as known especially from Naujan, Mitimatalik and Qilalukan, must mainly date from the 14th century.

The presence of features in the culture of the Ruin Islanders which are referable direct to early Punuk, leads to the supposition that the Punuk culture was dominant in Alaska at any rate in the 11th—12th century, and the Old Bering Sea culture in the time up towards the year 1000 A. D. As thus the ancient Alaska cultures must roughly be contemporaneous with the Thule culture, it is out of the question that the Thule culture from the first was derived from the Punuk culture. The Thule culture is based upon a special tradition, characterized by round houses and harpoon heads with two opposite barbs (Thule 2 type), whereas foursided houses and other forms of harpoon heads are characteristic of the western cultures. The culture forms were only gradually mixed by contact between western and eastern coastal cultures, presumably in North Alaska.

As the earliest known Thule culture displays more of an inland character than the subsequent phases, and moreover is in fundamental agreement with the Dorset culture, in respect of both ice-hunting technique and a number of elements of a more general nature, there is reason for believing that both the Thule culture and the Dorset culture signify parallel developments from a common proto-Eskimo cultural foundation, one which must be assumed to have had at any rate some knowledge of a sea-coast existence.

There is such a great resemblance between so many elements of the Old Bering Sea, Thule and Dorset cultures respectively that these cultures may be supposed to rest upon a common foundation which, of the three, was nearest the Thule culture. In the event of its being possible to find round houses older than the Old Bering Sea culture, in Alaska or East Siberia, we must assume that a Thule-like culture (and the Dorset) from the very first came from the regions along the Bering Strait or the Old World; if not, then the Thule culture (and Dorset) arose independently within a more easterly region of development, and the western strain in the Thule culture is a secondary phenomenon.

LIST OF QUOTED LITERATURE

(I have included only those works which have a direct bearing on the subject. For more compendious lists of the literature I cannot do better than to refer to some of the works listed below, e. g. Mathiassen 1927, Birket-Smith 1929, Collins 1937, Thalbitzer 1941. Meddelelser om Grønland is abbreviated MoG.).

Bergsøe, Poul: Where did the Eskimo get their Copper? — Ethnographical Studies. Nationalmuseets Skrifter, Etnografisk Række, I. — København 1941.
Birket-Smith, K.: A Geographic study of the Early History of the Algonquian Indians. — Int. Archiv für Ethnographie Bd. XXIV. 1918.
— Ethnography of the Egedesminde District. MoG Bd. 66. — København 1924.
— Eskimoerne. — København 1927.
— The Caribou Eskimos. Rep. 5th Thule Exp. Vol. V. I—II. Copenhagen 1929.
— The Question of the Origin of Eskimo Culture: A Rejoinder. — American Anthropologist n. s. 32 No. 4. — 1930. (a).
— Contributions to Chipewyan Ethnology. — Rep. 5th Thule Exp. Vol. VI No. 3. Copenhagen 1930 (b).
— Moeurs et Coutumes des Esquimaux. Paris 1937.
— Anthropological Observations on the Central Eskimos. Rep. 5th Thule Exp. Vol. III. 2. — Copenhagen 1940.
— and Fr. de Laguna: The Eyak Indians of the Copper River Delta, Alaska. — København 1938.
Boas, Fr.: The Central Eskimo. 6th Ann. Rep. of the Bureau of Ethnology. — Washington 1888.
— The Eskimo of Baffin Land and Hudson Bay. Bull. American Museum of Natural History XV, I 1901, II 1907.
Collins, H. B.: Archæological Investigations at Point Barrow, Alaska. — Explorations and field-work, Smithsonian Inst. 1932. — 1933.
— Archeology of St. Lawrence Island, Alaska. — Smithsonian Misc. Coll. Vol. 96 No. 1 — Washington 1937.
Egede, Hans: Relationer fra Grønland 1721—36 og Det gamle Grønlands ny Perlustration 1741. Udgivne af Louis Bobé. — MoG. Bd. 54 — København 1925.
Geist, O. W. and Fr. G. Rainey: Archaeological Excavations at Kukulik. — Washington 1936.
Glob, P. V.: Eskimo Settlements in Kempe Fjord and King Oscar Fjord. — MoG. Bd. 102 Nr. 2. — København 1935.
Greely, A. W.: Three Years of Arctic Service, I—II. — London 1886.

GREELY, A. W.: Report on the Proceedings of the U. S. Expedition to Lady Franklin Bay, Grinnell Land. Vol. I. — Washington 1888.
HATT, G.: Kyst- og Indlandskultur i det arktiske. Geografisk Tidsskrift. — København 1916.
— North American and Eurasian culture connections. — Proc. 5th Pacific Sci. Congr. Canada 1933. Bd. 4 (1934).
HAWKES, E. W.: The Labrador Eskimo. — Canada Geological Survey. Memoir 91, Anthropol. Ser. No. 14. — Ottawa 1916.
HOLTVED, E.: Foreløbig beretning om den arkæologisk-etnografiske ekspedition til Thule Distriktet 1935—37. — Geografisk Tidsskrift Bd. 41. København 1938.
JOHS. IVERSEN: Moorgeologische Untersuchungen auf Grönland. — Medd. fra Dansk Geol. Forening. Bd. 8. København 1934.
JENNESS, D.: A New Eskimo Culture in Hudson Bay. — The Geographical Review, July 1925.
— Comparative Vocabulary of the Western Eskimo Dialects. Report of the Canadian Arctic Exp. 1913—18. Vol. VX, Part A. — Ottawa 1928 (a).
— Archæological Investigations in Bering Strait. — National Museum of Canada Bull. 50. Ann. Rep. for 1926. — Ottawa 1928 (b).
— Notes on the Beothuk Indians of Newfoundland. — National Museum of Canada Bull. 56. Ann. Rep. for 1927. — Ottawa 1929.
— The Indian Background of Canadian History. — National Museum of Canada Bull. 86, Anthropol. Ser. No. 21. — Ottawa 1937.
— Rapport du Musée National sur l'Année financiere 1936—37, Service d'Anthropologie. — Nat. Mus. Canada, Bull. 98. — Ottawa 1938.
— Prehistoric Culture Waves from Asia to America. — Congr. Int. des Sci. Anthropol. et Ethnol. Copenhague 1938. — (1939).
KNUTH, E.: Under det nordligste Dannebrog. — København 1940.
KOCH, L.: Resultaterne af Jubilæumsekspeditionen nord om Grønland i 1921. — Naturens Verden, Febr. 1923.
DE LAGUNA, FR.: The Archaeology of Cook Inlet, Alaska. — Philadelphia 1934.
— (see BIRKET-SMITH and DE LAGUNA).
LARSEN, HELGE: Dødemandsbugten. — MoG. Bd. 102 Nr. 1. — København 1934.
MASON, J. ALDEN: Excavations of Eskimo Thule Culture Sites at Point Barrow, Alaska. — 23rd Int. Congr. Amer. New York 1928 (1930).
MATHIASSEN TH.: Archæology of the Central Eskimos I—II. — Rep. 5th Thule Exp. Vol. IV. — Copenhagen 1927.
— Eskimo Relics from Washington Land and Hall Land. — MoG. Bd. LXXI. — København 1928 (a).
— Material Culture of the Iglulik Eskimos. — Rep. 5th Thule Exp. Vol. VI. — Copenhagen 1928 (b).
— Some Specimens from the Bering Sea Culture. — Indian Notes Vol. VI No. 1. New York 1929.
— Inugsuk. — MoG. Bd. 77. — København 1930 (a).
— Archaeological Collections from the Western Eskimos. Rep. 5th Thule Exp. Vol. X No. 1 — Copenhagen 1930 (b).
— Arkæologiske Undersøgelser i Uperniviks Distrikt i Sommeren 1929. — Geografisk Tidsskrift 1930 (c).
— The Question of the Origin of Eskimo culture. — American Anthropologist n. s. no. 32. — 1930 (d).
— Ancient Eskimo Settlements in the Kangâmiut Area. — MoG. Bd. 91 Nr. 1. — København 1931.

Mathiassen, Th.: Prehistory of the Angmagssalik Eskimos. — MoG. Bd. 92 Nr. 4. — København 1933.
— Contributions to the Archaeology of Disko Bay. — MoG. Bd. 93 Nr. 2. — København 1934.
— Skrælingerne i Grønland. — København 1935.
— The Former Eskimo Settlements on Frederik VI's Coast. MoG. Bd. 109 Nr. 2. — København 1936 (b).
— Grønland gennem Tusinde Aar. — København 1941.
— and E. Holtved: The Eskimo Archaeology of Julianehaab District. — MoG. Bd. 118 Nr. 1. — København 1936 (a).
Murdoch, John: Ethnological results of the Point Barrow Expedition. — 9th Ann. Rep. of the Bureau of Ethnology. Washington 1892.
Nansen, Fr.: Eskimoliv. — Kristiania 1891.
Nelson, E. W.: The Eskimo about Bering Strait. — 18th Ann. Rep. of the Bureau of Ethnology. — Washington 1899.
Nørlund, P.: Buried Norsemen at Herjolfsnes. — MoG. Bd. LXVII. — København 1924.
— Norse Ruins at Gardar. — MoG. LXXVI København 1930.
— De gamle Nordbobygder ved Verdens Ende. — København 1934.
— og M. Stenberger: Brattahlid. — MoG. 88 Nr. 1. København 1934.
Porsild, M. P.: Studies on the Material Culture of the Eskimo in West Greenland. — MoG. LI. København 1915.
Rainey, Fr. G.: see Geist and Rainey.
Rasmussen, Knud: Grønland langs Polhavet. — København og Kristiania 1919.
— Report of the II. Thule-Expedition. — MoG. Bd. LXV. — København 1927.
— Intellectual Culture of the Iglulik Eskimos. — Rep. 5th Thule Exp. Vol. VII No. 1. Copenhagen 1929.
— Observations on the Intellectual Culture of the Caribou Eskimos. — Rep. 5th Thule Exp. Vol. VII No. 2. — Copenhagen 1930.
— Intellectual Culture of the Copper Eskimos. — Rep. 5th Thule Exp. Vol. IX. — Copenhagen 1932.
Roussell, Aa.: Sandnes and the Neighbouring Farms. — MoG. 88 Nr. 2. København 1936.
— Farms and Churches in the Mediaeval Norse Settlements of Greenland. — MoG. 89. København 1941.
Simmons, H. G.: Eskimåernas forna och nutida utbredning samt deres vandringsväger. — Ymer 1905.
Smith, Harlan I. and W. J. Wintemberg: Some Shell-heaps in Nova Scotia. — National Mus. Can. Bull. 47, Anthrop. Ser. No. 9. — Ottawa 1929.
Solberg, O.: Beiträge zur Vorgeschichte der Osteskimo. — Christiania 1907.
Steensby, H. P.: Contributions to the Ethnology and Anthropogeography of the Polar Eskimos. MoG. Bd. 34. — København 1910.
— An Anthropogeographical Study of the Origin of the Eskimo Culture. — MoG. Bd. 53. — København 1916.
Stenberger, M. see Nørlund og Stenberger.
Thalbitzer, W.: Ethnological Description of the Amdrup Collection from East Greenland. — MoG. Bd. 28. — København 1909.
— The Ammassalik Eskimo, I. MoG. Bd. 39; 1914. II. MoG. Bd. 40; 1923 and 1941.
— Cultic Games and Festivals in Greenland. — XXI' Congr. internat. des Americanistes. Gøteborg 1924. — Gøteborg 1925.

THALBITZER, W.: Eskimoernes kultiske guddomme. — Studier fra Sprog- og Oldtidsforskning Nr. 143. — København 1926.
— Die kultischen Gottheiten der Eskimos. — Archiv für Religionswissenschaft XXVI. — Leipzig-Berlin 1928.
THOMSEN, TH.: Implements and Artefacts of the North East Greenlanders. — MoG. Bd. 44. — København 1917.
— Eskimo Archæology. Greenland Vol. II. — Copenhagen and London 1928.
THOSTRUP, C. B.: Ethnographic Description of the Eskimo Settlements and Stone Remains in North-East Greenland. — MoG. Bd. 44. — København 1911.
WINTEMBERG, W. J., see SMITH and WINTEMBERG.
WISSLER, CLARK: Archæology of the Polar Eskimo. 1918. — Anthropol. Pap. Am. Mus. Nat. Hist. Vol. XXII. — New York 1924.

Færdig fra Trykkeriet den 21. Juli 1944.

GRØNLANDS STYRELSE

MONOGRAPHS ON GREENLAND | MEDDELELSER OM GRØNLAND

ABOUT THE SERIES
Monographs on Greenland | Meddelelser om Grønland (ISSN 0025 6676) has published scientific results from all fields of research on Greenland since 1878. The series numbers more than 345 volumes comprising more than 1250 titles.

In 1979 Monographs on Greenland | Meddelelser om Grønland was developed into a tripartite series consisting of Bioscience (ISSN 0106-1054), Man & Society (ISSN 0106-1062), and Geoscience (ISSN 0106-1046).

Monographs on Greenland | Meddelelser om Grønland was renumbered in 1979 ending with volume no. 206 and continued with volume no. 1 for each subseries. As of 2008 the original Monographs on Greenland | Meddelelser om Grønland numbering is continued in addition to the subseries numbering.

Further information about the series, including addresses of the scientific editors of the subseries, can be found at www.mtp.dk/MoG.

MANUSCRIPTS SHOULD BE SENT TO
Museum Tusculanum Press
University of Copenhagen
126 Njalsgade, DK-2300 Copenhagen S
DENMARK
info@mtp.dk | www.mtp.dk
Tel. +45 353 29109 | Fax +45 353 29113
VAT no.: 8876 8418

ORDERS
Books can be purchased online at www.mtp.dk, via order@mtp.dk, through any of our distributors in the US, UK, and France or via online retailers and major booksellers. Museum Tusculanum Press bank details: Amagerbanken, DK-2300 Copenhagen S, BIC: AM BK DK KK, IBAN: DK10 5202 0001 5151 08.

DISTRIBUTORS
USA & Canada: ISBS International Specialized Book Services, 920 NE 58th Ave. Suite 300 - Portland, OR 97213, Phone: +1 800 944 6190 (toll-free), Fax: +1 503 280 8832, orders@isbs.com

United Kingdom: Gazelle Book Services Ltd., White Cross Mills, High Town, GB-Lancaster LA1 4XS, United Kingdom, Phone: +44 1524 68765, Fax: +44 1524 63232, sales@gazellebooks.co.uk

France: Editions Picard, 82, rue Bonaparte, F-75006 Paris, France, Phone: +33 (0) 1 4326 9778, Fax: +33 1 43 26 42 64, livres@librairie-picard.fr

www.ingramcontent.com/pod-product-compliance
Lightning Source LLC
Chambersburg PA
CBHW081157020426
42333CB00020B/2529